THE OFFI

SMALL BUSINESS

OWNERS MANUAL

A Comprehensive Blue Print for Building
A Profitable Small Business

Larry Brown

Copyright 2006 Larry Brown

All rights reserved. This book, or parts thereof, may not be reproduced in any form without permission from the publisher; exceptions are made for brief excerpts used in published reviews.

This publication is designed to provide accurate and authoritative information in regard to the subject matter covered. It is sold with the understanding that the author or publisher is not engaged in rendering legal, accounting or other professional services. If legal advice or other expert assistance is required, the services of a competent professional person should be sought. Recommendations presented are made without any guarantee on the part of the author or publisher, who also disclaims any liability incurred in connection with the use of data or specific details presented.

We recognize that some words, names and designations, for example, mentioned herein are the property of the trademark holder. We use them for identification purposes only. No compensation in any form was exchanged for the use or mentioning of names or designations of other businesses used in this publication.

ISBN: 978-1-4303-2660-1

TABLE OF CONTENTS

    Preface   vii

    Introduction   1

1   **It All Starts Here**   4
Hitting the Books, Business Mechanics 101, Your Most Valuable Resource, Perseverance

2   **Breaking Ground**   12
Getting Organized, Developing a Business Plan, Choosing a Business Structure, Choosing a Business Name, Your Business Bank Account, Locating your Business, 5 Vital Considerations of a Location, The Dreaded Lease Agreement, Build outs, Lease Improvements and Contractors, Your Store Front Five Features of Your Store Front, Developing a Strong Business Image, Neatness and Appearance, Partnerships, Start Up Costs,

3   **Capital and Operating Expenses**   42
Capital Expenses, Operating Expenses, Controlling Those Cost, The Different Colors of Money

4   **Business Hours**   50
Cost Analysis of Hours of Operation

5   **Advertising and Marketing**   55
Primary Methods of Advertising, Secondary Methods of Advertising, Advertising Effectiveness

6   **Pricing of Goods and Services**   62
Raising Prices

7   **Promotions, Sales and Discounts**   66
Effective Ways of Promoting Your Business, Sales and Discounts

8   **Customers and Quality of Service**   72
Customer Feedback, Customer Complaints, Consumer Reporting Websites

9	**The Competition**	79
	The 3 Hostile Zones of Competition, The 6 Battle Fronts of Competition	
10	**Setting Goals**	91
11	**Bookkeeping, Automation and Trend Analysis**	95
	Automation, Trend Analysis	
12	**Shrinkage, the Disappearing Act**	100
	Just How Much Are You Losing, Taking Action	
13	**Employees**	105
	Finding Employees, The Interview, The Job Offer Probationary Periods for New Employees, New Hire Training, Supervision Of New Employees, Employee Recognition, Departing Employees, Terminating or Discharging Employees	
14	**Federal Reporting Requirements When Hiring**	130
	Work Eligibility, Form I-9, W-4 Withholding Allowance Certificates, Questionable Form W-4, Verification of Employee's Name and SSN, State Reporting Requirements of New Employees, The American Payroll Association	
15	**The Department of Labor (DOL)**	136
	Consolidated Omnibus Budget Reconciliation Act (COBRA), Occupational Safety and Health Administration (OSHA)	
16	**Pay and Benefits**	144
	Forms of Direct Compensation, Commissions Plans Commissions with Guaranteed Salary Plans, Vacation and Holiday Pay, Medical Benefits, Games and Competition in the Workplace, Bonuses, Pay Raises, 6 Factors of Pay Raises	
17	**Work Schedules for Employees**	168
	Building a Typical Schedule, Weekend Scheduling Getting Your Manager to Build a Productive Schedule	

18	**Payroll**	176
	Payroll Workweeks and Pay Periods, Payroll Processing	

19	**State and Federal Deposits and Reports for Employers**	187
	Federal Tax Deposits, Who Must Make Deposits When to Make Payments, How to Make Deposits	

20	**Leadership, Managers and Owners**	195
	Leadership, Management, Responsibilities and Owner Manager Relationship, Initial Manager Training, Recurrent Training for Managers, Discharging Your Manager, Management by Walking Around	

21	**Delegating responsibilities and duties**	208

22	**Communications and Supervision**	210

23	**Policies, Rules and Operating Manual**	216
	Essential Policies, Employees Driving While On Duty The Operating and Employee Manual	

24	**Workers Compensation & Unemployment Insurance Benefits**	224
	Workers Compensation, Unemployment Benefits	

25	**Outsourcing and Consultants**	232

26	**Identity and sensitive Information theft**	236
	Types of Sensitive Information, Potential Thieves Protection of Sensitive Information	

27	**Rumors and Crisis Control**	241

28	**Growing Your Business**	246

29	**Turning Your Business Around**	249
	The Signs of Turbulence Ahead, Getting Out of Trouble	

30	**Exit Strategies**	257

31	**Summary**	261
	Web Sites for Business Owners	263
	Index	264

PREFACE

Congratulations! If you're planning on opening a small business then you are definitely taking the right step in that direction by educating yourself now. If you are already a business owner then you have found as I did that the learning process never stops, again congratulations. I read my first book on starting a business two years before opening my first business. And since then I have never stopped educating myself either through lessons learned from my own businesses or through experiences I found from books written by other successful business owners. Every book I read on small business ownership, whether it is on starting a business or how to improve your existing business, gave me new insights that helped me become a better business owner. This book, based on real life experiences, shows you the essentials of setting up and running a successful business from the inside. Many books, on running a business, are written from the "outside" based on an academic or theoretical perspective. One of the best approaches to learning a business from the inside is to shadow a business owner and learn the day-to-day operations from interviewing job applicants to marketing and advertising. This book provides the reader with that inside look of owning and operating a successful business. It is not intended to inspire or motivate someone to become a business owner but only to equip you with the tools needed to become a successful business owner.

If you are thinking about starting your own business then you have to ask yourself why is that a high percentage of businesses close their doors only after a few years while others become highly successful. Yes its true, about one half of small businesses fail within the first 4 years with only 1 in 10 surviving to 10 years! And yes, it is true that the top 3 reasons businesses fail is *financial, marketing* and *management*. Of course some would say what's left after these 3 areas! Of greater importance is the extent that these 3 areas are interrelated with each other with no one area unaffected by the other two. As you will find in the following chapters, every section of a business affects other areas with no one section immune to the others. The business owner must be able to see how decisions affecting one area will impact the other areas.   I encourage you to take your time in this book and don't merely read its contents – *study* it.   If your learning to be a surgeon you wouldn't just read the course subjects, you would study it with the intent of becoming proficient in the subject.   The same is true for the business owner - *YOU*.

INTRODUCTION

Many have made their fortunes with nothing more than a strong entrepreneurial spirit and a few bucks. Michael Dell began from his college dorm room building computers and eventually started Dell Computer Corporation with only $1000 at the age of 19! He didn't invent the computer; he just found a way to build them smarter and cheaper. John Schnatter started Papa Johns Pizza from a small pizza shop at an early age with barely enough money to buy his first oven. Again he didn't invent the pizza he just found a better way to market it at a cheaper price. The same is for Debbi Fields of Mrs. Fields Cookies. And the story is the same for many founders who started with only a strong desire to succeed. None of these founders started off with a marketing or human resources department or other layers of corporate departments. They didn't come up with some killer idea and then simply found a "top" manager to run the business. However, they all knew how to handle the challenges of running a small business with nothing more than what they could carry. If they didn't know how to handle the smallest detail of running a business then they learned how. And most of all, they were hands on people who knew what the customer wanted.

I wrote this book from my personal experiences of owning and running small businesses. Much of the material presented in this book are drawn from real life occurrences, many of which are common to today's business owner, some of which can be very unpleasant. The largest section of this book deals with employees and payroll processing for 3 main reasons. First, labor is usually the largest cost item of a business. Second, when you get down to it, success or failure of a business can usually be attributed to employee management. Third, management of employees is usually the most difficult to aspect of a small business.

Our most successful business was a chain of family hair salons located in high trafficked shopping centers. It is a service and retail business representative of many small businesses. Go to any major shopping center and you will usually find a dry cleaners, hair salon, fast food restaurants, a video store, a nail salon, a shipping and packaging store or a coffee shop among other types of businesses. These are the typical businesses that many first time owners find themselves running. They deal directly with the consumer public and generate cash every hour they are open. However, to me it is the battlefront of business competition. It deals directly with the consumer and competes fiercely with other competitors for customers as well as qualified employees. I favor small retail or service businesses operating in large anchored shopping centers for one reason, because they generate great cash flow. We selected the hair services business because it deals with small ticket items and is fairly immune to economic recessions. There is little inventory, no cold storage requirements for foodstuff and services are paid for on the spot. During our five year ownership, our businesses serviced nearly a half million customers, employed nearly 200 people all together, and best of all, made money! But the experiences and lessons learned did not come easy and sacrifices and mistakes were beyond our imagination.

Every successful business owner I talked with including myself, learned how to deal with challenges we never anticipated and all while maintaining a sharp focus on the customer. It's easy to lose sight of the customer when the challenges of running a business overwhelm the small business owner who is operating on a small budget. Even after I opened our fifth location, I still found many new unforeseen challenges. One of the biggest challenges common to many business owners is recruiting and management of employees. The second biggest challenge deals with the ability to effectively compete with other businesses. I can't tell you how many businesses owners I saw who lacked adequate planning when it came to their competition. Their common philosophy was that demand for their product or service will outweigh the effects of competition. In other words, demand will outstrip supply. How wrong they were. I'll never forget the business owner next door to us, loading up his truck one night. He was out of money and couldn't keep his business running any longer nor could he pay the rent. He was skipping out of town. This is the same individual who told me just 6 months earlier that he didn't have to worry about competition because of the strong demand potential for his product and services. Also the same individual who caught his manager stealing and pocketing sales money, after telling me that, "you simply have to trust your employees." And he had other problems such as not clearly defining his product, lack of a marketing plan and letting his employees dictate his operating hours.

On the positive side though, a successful business can be quite rewarding financially not to mention the independence enjoyed from being your own boss. There are many business owners who started with just one store or shop and became millionaires growing from one to a large chain. Many business owners adapt quite well to their new environment and become very resourceful in getting their business off the ground. While others find the change very difficult and become their worst enemy in trying to over come the types of challenges they never had to face before. And then there are those that do all the right things but just don't have the funds to get them through till they become profitable. I find it remarkable that many occupations not only require you to be trained by an approved institution, but also licensed by the state or federal government, yet no such requirement exist to run or own a business. For example, to be a real estate agent or broker you are required many course hours of approved classes and then pass an exam for your license as well as on-going classes. To be a real estate appraiser you are required to have about 2000 hours of apprentice time in addition to many hours of course work before your even eligible to take the state exam. As a business owner, you may be responsible for hundreds or thousands of employees and their future in you, yet no training or license is required of you. Survival of your business and your employee's jobs will rest with every decision as an owner. Remember, as the business owner you are ultimately responsible for the performance of that business, not your managers, bankers or friends. It's astounding to hear business owners say that their business failed because of bad management decisions or the lack of performance by their managers! Some have told me that they "lost" their business because their manager embezzled from them, as if there were nothing you could do to prevent it. Don't be one of them.

1   IT ALL STARTS HERE

People have asked me if having a college degree in business helps to become a better business owner. For most small start-ups, a college degree may help but it all depends on the type of business. I have a Bachelor's in Physics and a Masters in Public Administration with an emphasis on management. I was a fighter pilot in the Air Force and flew many aircraft including the SR 71. I also worked as a project manager for a research and development division of the military. Although my Masters course work involved many business courses, I found they had very little use in our business. In fact, I would say that my experiences as a military officer and pilot probably helped me more than my college education. However, I believe the greatest asset to the business owner is their ability to be analytical and organized with a knack of tackling problems in a methodical fashion. The ability to inspire others, handle conflicts, think clearly under pressure and above all to communicate effectively, are factors that usually give the small business owner a clear advantage. Whether you learn that from going to college or from having good street smarts is immaterial.

Hitting the Books

Before we started our business, I read many books on starting and running a small business. Many of the books available were written by individuals who were business consultants or who taught business at our colleges and universities having no experience as a business owner. After opening our business, I quickly found that the issues and challenges of running a business were far more complex than any book I read. I don't care if someone was the member of the board of directors, if they weren't down in the trenches running a business; they simply did not know first hand the problems and solutions of running a small business. They may know the laws and applicable state and federal regulatory requirements, but that's a very small part of running a business. To know how to run a small business you simply have had to run a small business *with employees*.

Without question, research and planning is the most important phase of any business development. Even if you already are a business owner, your business environment continuously changes requiring on going research and planning. Your library, bookstore or Internet are excellent places to get started. If your reading this book you've already taken a very important step to educate yourself. But I certainly would not tell you this should be the only book you should read. I would suggest to the business owner to read as many books and articles on starting and running a business. Learning different methods, approaches and techniques from different owners will improve your skills as a business owner. One important consideration when trying to educate yourself on small business ownership is limiting your subject to the size of your business. There are many books and articles on business ownership and management but most are geared for mid size to large businesses. Before we started our business, I recall reading several books on starting a business that talked about the resource manager, marketing officer or the advertising department. Well, for the small business owner, the resource manager is the same person as the advertising manager, the payroll officer or the facilities manager – you, the owner! You will most likely need to learn every aspect of running a business to include how to process payroll, how to recruit and interview employees, marketing, inventory management, managing employees and so on. The small business owner is required to wear many hats.

In addition to books and articles, another good source is your state and federal government. My wife and I attended a session offered by the Arizona Department of Revenue on sales taxes. This was an outstanding class and provided valuable free publications on businesses. It also provided every department and phone number that we might need to start and run a business relating to state and federal regulatory requirements.

There are three government departments that are essential for the business owner. These are the Internal Revenue Service (IRS), the Department of Labor (DOL) and the Social Security Department. These three agencies have great web sites set up to help the small business owner. In addition, the Small Business Administration (SBA) is another very informative agency providing a wealth of information for beginners and experienced business owners through their web site. These web sites as well as many others are listed at the back of this book and are referenced in the corresponding sections of this book. You'll find that every minute you spend now educating yourself will save you money and time in the long run.

Business Mechanics 101

Before we go any further, lets spend a few minutes reviewing some fundamentals. If you have a business then you have a service or product that is intended for the public consumer or other businesses. The amount of revenues generated from your product or services depends on three factors. First, there must be a need for that product or service, which we all know is *demand*. The second is your *competition* for both customers and employees. The third factor deals with the *price* of your product or service. These three factors will determine your revenues over the long run. Sure, there are other factors, but these three have the greatest impact on your ability to generate revenues.

Demand. You may have a great location with heavy traffic and no competition for miles, but if your product or service is not in the least demand, you have a loser! Your product or service must sell, period. You may think you have a great product or service, but the consumer is the one who will decide that for you. My point is that before you lay out the big bucks to get going, make sure you have a good idea of how the consumer will respond to your product or service. Nothing will be more discouraging then to open for business and find little demand for your product or services. Now, if your product or service is not new but a normal consumer item then you can sleep with a little more comfort, but beware. Take for example the hair industry. Prior to the mid sixties, short hair was in. However, a few years later, long hair was in which meant that the barbershop had a service that was out of date. Sure, the short hairstyle for men came back, but how many barbershops went out of business till that time came. In the mid nineties, bagels were the hot item, but then died out a few years later. Today's hot product or service may be tomorrow's loser.

Competition. You may have the hottest product since the cell phone, but if your area is crawling with competition, then you will have little pricing power and will struggle to break even. On the other hand, a good product or service with little or no competition means you have the opportunity to do well, at least until the competition moves in. We found competition to be the strongest factor in our ability to generate strong revenues. Just visit your local shopping mall and look at how many shops have closed and new ones come in over the last few years. Maybe you haven't noticed, and that was my case until we opened our business and began to take notice of the turn over of businesses where competition is strong. Many business owners will devote considerable effort and money into every little detail of their business but then underestimate the impact their competition will have on them. <u>Don't under estimate your competition</u>. Having a plan to deal with your competition is every bit as important as having a business plan. You do have a business plan, right? In fact, lenders will want you to address your competition as part of your business plan. But before you can compete effectively, you have to know and study your competition. Lets take Pappa Johns Pizza for example. As we know, the pizza has been around since the dinosaur, and there are plenty of big pizza businesses such as Pizza Hut that have been around well before Pappa Johns. Yet Pappa Johns penetrated the pizza market very successfully and now has a good chunk of the market share. They knew their competition and how to compete against them. The same can be said for many new businesses that penetrated the market and won market share away from their competitors. This brings us back to the customer. They knew what the consumer wanted and they knew how to precisely appeal to them. The passenger airline business is yet another example of new entrants taking market share away from larger more dominant carriers. Yes, your competition will be a major factor in your business, which will be discussed in more detail later in this book.

Pricing. If your product or service cost too much then it does not matter how terrific it is or how little competition you have. Your product or service must be priced so the consumer can afford it.

Brakes and tires for your auto are not luxury items that you can afford to go without. But if your tires cost $1000 each, then you might find a lot of people going out of town to get their tires or simply just drive a lot less. If you had the only barbershop in town, do you think you could charge $200 for a haircut? You could, but I don't think many people would use your services. I know I wouldn't. Your price has to be in line with what people can afford or else they wont buy it or at least change their use of it, no matter how good or superior it is. When theater tickets sold for $6.00, I didn't give it a second thought to take the family to see a movie. However, now that tickets sell for $9.00, I'll usually wait till the movie comes out in DVD. As you go through the following sections in this book keep in mind these three factors, demand, competition and price and how they affect revenues and profitability.

Money coming in the door is just one side of the equation. Business expense is the other side you will have to balance with your revenues. On the cost side of the house, there are certain things you can do to minimize your expenses. On some items you will have more control then others. When I first started my business, I asked myself, what are all the things that I could do my self to keep costs down. Such things as payroll processing, bookkeeping, cleaning, repairs, advertising, marketing, handling the reception and check out desk and other administrative jobs are things that I could do, or some part of, as oppose to paying someone else to do. If your business is losing money and you contract out for many things you could do yourself, then you need to revaluate if such services are justified. I knew that if I could learn from the start on how to do these functions, then if needed, I could do them instead of contracting out to someone else. My wife was great at controlling expenses, far better than I was at it. From how we scheduled our staff to what supply items we used, was a factor in keeping our expenses under control. As a business owner one of your main jobs will be in controlling cost. Large or small, businesses must know how to control costs. Businesses that have a difficult time controlling their costs will eventually fail. And usually the biggest expense is direct and indirect payroll costs. In the sections that follow, you will see how controlling cost is not confined to just one or two items, but is a process that involves many areas with each one interrelated to the others. For example, cost control will be one of your most effective means in dealing with your competition.

Your Most Valuable Resource

What do you think will be the most important resource of your business? If you said your employees, you're very close, but take a step back. If you said YOU are the most important resource of your business then step forward! No one will care for your business as much as you will. No one will attend to it as much as you will. And no one other then you will work endlessly in your business, at times without making a dime. Can you imagine if you walked in and said to your employees, including your manager, times are tough so you need them to work without pay for the next month. They would leave you on the spot and then file for unemployment benefits against your unemployment account, raising your tax rate. If your business fails you will lose your investment and most likely be liable for obligations such as leases and loans. No other factor alone will motivate a business owner to succeed then the fear of failure itself. Yes, you the business owner is the most important resource your business has.

The second most important resource is your employees. In our business, we could not have existed without our professional staff of employees. Some employees will be top performers while others will under perform. Each one of your employees will have varying needs and motivations. Some will see the value of hard work and its potential payoff while others will work hard at trying to get by with as little as possible and then wonder why they are left behind. And don't be fooled with the attitude that if the employees are paid well enough, then you wont have employee problems. I have seen people making over $200,000 with attitude problems that range from calling in sick, when they are not, to theft and falsifying. Just take a look at some of the CEO's of large businesses that have made the news and courtroom! And these guys make millions! I've also seen employees who are at $7.00 an hour with the highest ethics and work discipline around. When your employee's goals and objectives are the same as your business then you will have everyone on the same page and a strong employee group. <u>Aligning every one's goals with that of the business will be one of your biggest yet most rewarding challenges</u>.

You will find that running a successful business means being able to strike a balance between the customer, the employees and the ownership. Your business is similar to a triangle with the customer in one corner, the employees in another corner and the ownership in another. Your job will be to continuously evaluate the balance and make adjustments to the triangle to bring balance as much as possible. Sometimes you may have to lean more towards the employee corner while at other times you will have to lean more towards the customer corner. Too far in one corner for too long can spell trouble and eventually de-stabilize your business. For example, if you put too much emphasis on profitability, then you may eventually lose customers and employees. Or suppose that your employees don't want to be open on Sundays. So you agree and close on Sundays. Do you think you will lose some customers? Absolutely. Those customers will go somewhere else and be your competition's customers. We found this to be very true in the family salon business. Of course you can go too far with trying to please your customers. Staying open till 10 pm or being open on major holidays would be great for some of your customers but you may find it extremely difficult to retain employees if the labor market is tight. This all means that the current conditions of the economy and labor market are major factors in the business triangle of customer, employee and ownership.

Perseverance

Some people would have you think that all you have to do is open your doors and you're on your way to riches and a life of leisure. Many people find the challenges to tough and get out. The reasons span a wide range from overriding losses to just wanting out. I'll never forget an ad in the paper under the businesses for sale section that said it best, "I just want out." To be successful in business you have to have a deep desire to succeed. You have to be driven. Running a business is the toughest and most challenging thing I've done. You will definitely have bad days, but you will also have terrific days. You have to be prepared for it mentally and physically and that means knowing what the challenges are and how to handle them. Today's small business owners must equip themselves with all available tools to meet the challenges they will face. Being able to persevere is a lot more than just hard work. It also means having enough money to keep your business running during hard times. I've seen many businesses have to close their doors because they ran out of money before their business had a chance to "takeoff." Having the money available means reducing the cost of doing business as much as possible without reducing revenue growth. When we opened our first shop, we decided to learn and do every administrative task we could until such time we could afford to pay someone else. Being capable of doing much of the administrative tasks ourselves saved us a great deal of money allowing us to persevere the initial hard times.

When I was a young fighter pilot in my first operational fighter squadron in Germany, it became very apparent to me that in order for me to be a formable combat pilot I would need to focus on three areas. The three areas were physical fitness, knowledge and skill in my flying ability. I needed to be in peak physical and mental shape and I needed to know everything I could about my adversary (the soviet fighter pilot) and his weapon system. By doing so I knew that if the day came, I would have a better chance of beating my adversary. The same could be said for sports and other competitive arenas. And the same is certainly true for your business. When we started our business I found these three areas were just as vital in business ownership as when I was a young fighter pilot. The better shape and physical condition I was in, the more energy I had, the better I felt and the better I could deal with the business of the day. Knowledge of your business and every aspect of its administration are important. But it's also important to know your competition just as it was important to study my adversary as a fighter pilot. This is what I mean by perseverance. You are doing everything you can to run your business in the most efficient and effective manner. These are the core areas essential for any business owner. They also apply to managers or anyone else who is in a similar position. By continuously working on these areas, you will build a solid foundation from which to run your business on – a position of strength.

2   BREAKING GROUND

Fortunes have been made and lost as a result of the initial planning and development phase of a small business. A builder wouldn't build a house without a detailed set of plans and a schedule for subcontractors to follow. The same goes for starting a business, no matter how small or how big, you need to spend considerable effort on the planning and development phase. Many small business owners had great ideas with sufficient money for a business, but lacked adequate planning to get started in the right direction. Whether you are in business to make circuit chips or potato chips, your success could very well depend on getting off on the right foot. In the following sections, I briefly cover some important considerations for a new start-up business. The following should serve as a basic blue print to get your doors open for business since this will influence how you run your business.

Your type of business will dictate the specific business plan, but the following areas will apply to all small businesses and should serve as a checklist for the planning phase.

> Developing a business plan
> Choosing a business structure
> Deciding on a business name
> Opening a business bank account
> Choosing a location
> Leases
> Finding a contractor
> Stationary and business cards
> The office
> Partnerships

Getting Organized

If there was ever a time to get well organized this is definitely it. I don't care how messy your house is, how often you change the oil in your car or even if you live out of your laundry basket, getting this part wrong will haunt you. We will assume you know the business you want to start or purchase and have the money to get your business started.

The first thing you should do is acquire a large filing cabinet. A legal letter size cabinet with a minimum of four draws is advisable. Many documents such as rental or lease agreements will be in legal size making it difficult to file them in a normal letter size file. Don't mix personal files with business files. Have a separate file drawer or cabinet for each. Next, organize your filing system. This will be business specific but some files will be common to all such as bills due, operating expenses, capital expenses, start up cost, employee records and applications, business bank accounts, repairs and maintenance, contractor proposals, and so on. You will probably have many forms such as W-4's, I-9's and job applications so make sure you have separate files for each. As you progress through the start up phase, your filing system should be modified. A complete filing system will help you get organized and stay organized. I can't emphasize enough how important it is to be organized. Your filing cabinet should be the first step in getting your business organized.

Your second best tool is your computer. I found that a simple spreadsheet to keep track of expenses and projects was a great aid in being organized. In addition, there are many software programs for accounting, bookkeeping, payroll and business planning that are well suited for the small business planner. If you cant find what your looking for at your local computer store then try looking for it online such as on Google or Amazon. Not only will you find your computer a great aid in organization, but also as the following section shows, there is a wealth of information online to help you get started.

Developing a Business Plan

If you will be engaged in securing financing for your business then you will need a business plan. Banks and other lenders require it for a new business. If your applying for a small business guaranteed loan from the SBA, then you will need a comprehensive business plan. Even if you already have the funds to finance your business or expansion, its still a good idea to develop a business plan. There are many businesses that specialize in developing your business plan and there are also many software programs for such use. My recommendation is to search the web or visit your local computer store for a business plan program. The main body of a typical business plan has four sections: A description of the business, marketing, finances and management. Estimated expenses, revenues and growth are important elements of your business plan and you must show how you arrived at such figures. When developing your business plan, consider the following questions as an aid in helping you develop plan:

- What will be your main service or product and describe why it will sell?
- Describe your potential customers for your product or service and how will you market it?
- Define the area where you plan to locate your business and describe your competition?

You will also need to have a good understanding of how to construct a balance sheet, income statement and cash flow analysis for up to five years. Details of such requirements are usually laid out in a simple to understand format when using any of the business plan programs. A business plan may seem like a lot of estimating and educated guess work but it forces you to look well beyond the concept of your business. An outstanding web site that shows you how to develop your business plan is at www.sba.gov/starting_business/planning/basic.html.

Choosing a Business Structure

The IRS and Social Security have a complete web site with nearly every topic for the new business owner including the different types of business structures and how to register your business with the IRS. One of the best web sites I found for new small business owners is at www.irs.gov/businesses/. Once on this page, scroll down the left side and select "Staring A Business." This is a great place to start for new business owners. As a new business owner you will need to know your federal tax responsibilities and this site is just the place to get started. The first page provides links to basic federal tax information for people who are starting a business. It also provides information to assist in making basic business decisions. The list should not be construed as all-inclusive. Other steps may be appropriate for your specific type of business. Keep in mind that over time, some of the IRS web sites will have changed and may be slightly different than what is presented here. However, all the subjects will be the same although navigation to these pages may be different. Once on the home page, you will find navigation to the many different topics is quiet simple. Below is a list of subjects covered at this site.

What New Business Owners Need to Know About Federal Taxes

- Is it a Business or a Hobby?
- Selecting a Business Structure
- Employer Identification Number (EIN)
- Business Taxes
- Recordkeeping
- When Do I Start My Tax Year?
- Selecting an Accounting Method
- **Checklist for Starting a Business**
- Establishing a Retirement Plan
- Small Business Publications
- Tax Assistance

What Business Owners Need to Know

- Local and State Regulations
- Setting Goals for Your Business
- Writing a Business Plan
- Financing a Business
- Copyrights, Trademarks, and Patents
- DOL Regulatory Compliance

The second item on the list, "Selecting a Business Structure", provides you with the information to determine your business structure. It's a good place to start and get educated, but I would also advise consultation with your certified accountant before you make that final decision. Below is the list of available structures you must choose. Remember, you must select a business structure to get started.

- Sole Proprietorships
- Partnerships
- Corporations
- S Corporations
- Limited Liability Company (LLC)

An informative web site for the new business owners is at the Small Business Administration's (SBA) Selecting the Legal Structure for Your Business (PDF). A direct link to this web site is provided on the IRS web site mentioned above. This web site presents you with an easy to understand discussion of the differences, risks and requirements for the different business structures listed above. It is the best I've seen and it's free!

The third item on the list, "Employer Identification Number (EIN)" tells you how to apply for an EIN and has a link to the form, which is also shown on the next page. The form itself acts as a minimum checklist of things that you need to decide on before going forward. The rest of the items above provide the business owner with information about running a business. The 8th item, "Checklist for Starting a Business" consolidates much of the information into one handy page with links to all the needed sites. By the time you go through all the items, you should have a good understanding of what it takes to start and run your business in terms of the IRS and Social Security requirements. What's more is that it will provide the most current, up to date information. Its clear to me that not only do these web sites provide a comprehensive understanding of the IRS requirements for new business owners but it also tells me that there is NO excuse for not knowing my responsibilities and requirements, so be warned!

Form **SS-4**
(Rev. December 2001)
Department of the Treasury
Internal Revenue Service

Application for Employer Identification Number
(For use by employers, corporations, partnerships, trusts, estates, churches, government agencies, Indian tribal entities, certain individuals, and others.)
▶ See separate instructions for each line. ▶ Keep a copy for your records.

EIN

OMB No. 1545-0003

Type or print clearly.

1. Legal name of entity (or individual) for whom the EIN is being requested

2. Trade name of business (if different from name on line 1)

3. Executor, trustee, "care of" name

4a. Mailing address (room, apt., suite no. and street, or P.O. box)

5a. Street address (if different) (Do not enter a P.O. box.)

4b. City, state, and ZIP code

5b. City, state, and ZIP code

6. County and state where principal business is located

7a. Name of principal officer, general partner, grantor, owner, or trustor

7b. SSN, ITIN, or EIN

8a. Type of entity (check only one box)
- ☐ Sole proprietor (SSN) _____
- ☐ Partnership
- ☐ Corporation (enter form number to be filed) ▶ _____
- ☐ Personal service corp.
- ☐ Church or church-controlled organization
- ☐ Other nonprofit organization (specify) ▶ _____
- ☐ Other (specify) ▶

- ☐ Estate (SSN of decedent) _____
- ☐ Plan administrator (SSN) _____
- ☐ Trust (SSN of grantor) _____
- ☐ National Guard   ☐ State/local government
- ☐ Farmers' cooperative   ☐ Federal government/military
- ☐ REMIC   ☐ Indian tribal governments/enterprises
- Group Exemption Number (GEN) ▶ _____

8b. If a corporation, name the state or foreign country (if applicable) where incorporated

State

Foreign country

9. Reason for applying (check only one box)
- ☐ Started new business (specify type) ▶ _____
- ☐ Hired employees (Check the box and see line 12.)
- ☐ Compliance with IRS withholding regulations
- ☐ Other (specify) ▶

- ☐ Banking purpose (specify purpose) ▶ _____
- ☐ Changed type of organization (specify new type) ▶ _____
- ☐ Purchased going business
- ☐ Created a trust (specify type) ▶ _____
- ☐ Created a pension plan (specify type) ▶ _____

10. Date business started or acquired (month, day, year)

11. Closing month of accounting year

12. First date wages or annuities were paid or will be paid (month, day, year). Note: *if applicant is a withholding agent, enter date income will first be paid to nonresident alien. (month, day, year)* . . . . ▶

13. Highest number of employees expected in the next 12 months. Note: *if the applicant does not expect to have any employees during the period, enter "-0-."* . . . . ▶

Agricultural | Household | Other

14. Check one box that best describes the principal activity of your business.
- ☐ Construction ☐ Rental & leasing ☐ Transportation & warehousing
- ☐ Real estate ☐ Manufacturing ☐ Finance & insurance
- ☐ Health care & social assistance ☐ Wholesale-agent/broker
- ☐ Accommodation & food service ☐ Wholesale-other ☐ Retail
- ☐ Other (specify)

15. Indicate principal line of merchandise sold; specific construction work done; products produced; or services provided.

16a. Has the applicant ever applied for an employer identification number for this or any other business? . . . ☐ Yes ☐ No
Note: *If "Yes," please complete lines 16b and 16c.*

16b. If you checked "Yes" on line 16a, give applicant's legal name and trade name shown on prior application if different from line 1 or 2 above.
Legal name ▶   Trade name ▶

16c. Approximate date when, and city and state where, the application was filed. Enter previous employer identification number if known.
Approximate date when filed (mo., day, year) | City and state where filed | Previous EIN

Third Party Designee
Complete this section only if you want to authorize the named individual to receive the entity's EIN and answer questions about the completion of this form.

Designee's name | Designee's telephone number (include area code)
Address and ZIP code | Designee's fax number (include area code)

Under penalties of perjury, I declare that I have examined this application, and to the best of my knowledge and belief, it is true, correct, and complete.

Name and title (type or print clearly) ▶

Applicant's telephone number (include area code)

Signature ▶   Date ▶

Applicant's fax number (include area code)

For Privacy Act and Paperwork Reduction Act Notice, see separate instructions.   Cat. No. 16055N   Form **SS-4** (Rev. 12-2001)

Choosing a Business Name

There are 4 factors you need to consider when selecting a name for your business:
>Easy to Remember and Spell
>Keeping it Short
>Energizing your Name
>What your business does

Simple. A business name should be simple and easy to remember for your customers, especially first time customers. Such names as SuperCuts, Burger King, FedEx, American Airlines, Papa Johns, and Pizza Hut are all names that are easy to remember and spell. Don't get caught up in a fancy name that has some antique hidden meaning only you would know. It has to be simple enough that someone going through the yellow pages or doing an Internet search can easily locate. If people cannot find it on the first try then they are likely to skip it and go on to another name. The name should also have a certain ring to it such as Great Clips, Subway or JetBlue. The simpler and cleverer the better.

Keep it Short. If you have a business in a shopping mall, then the name should be short enough for your storefront signage. Those big neon signs in front of businesses are not cheap and if your name is too long then there may be a problem trying to fit the name in your allocated space. If you have too many letters then the size of each letter may have to be reduced in order for your sign to fit according to the dimensions required by the shopping center. Small letters will be hard to see by customers at a distance. So make sure your sign is clear and readable from the street. Short names are also easier to remember and easier to fit on banners, signs and business cards. As a rule of thumb, if you will be in a retail shopping center then try to keep your name below 13 letters.

Energize it. Names that contain words like Super, Great, Best, Ultimate, King, Champion or Peak deliver a positive and energetic message. They are also easier to remember. Putting an energetic face to your name obviously is not suited for all businesses, but many types of businesses can certainly benefit from it. Super Cuts or Great Clips not only carrier an energetic theme to their name but also deliver a positive visual image that is very appropriate to the beauty and salon business. If going with an energetic name is not possible then at least try to stay away from negative or weak connotations in the name.

What your business does. The name of your business should say something about what your business is all about. Such names as American Airlines, Burger King, Super Cuts, Pizza Hut or Just Brakes may be nationally recognized names but without ever have seeing their name, you would know what they do from the first time you heard their name. If you're getting into a franchise then the business name is not an issue. However, you will still need to choose a business name that the franchise will fall under. For example, you may choose the name BROWN ENTERPRISES, from which your "Subway" franchise shop will operate under. To the IRS, your business is known as BROWN ENTERPRISES, but to your customers, you are Subway. Your business bank account will be known as BROWN ENTERPRISES doing business as (DBA) Subway and any other names you choose to do business as.

Choosing the right name for your business is one the most important first steps of any business. It deserves careful consideration and may take weeks for you to come up with the right name and logo. However, don't feel that this will be your name for life. If at some point down the road your business has changed or another name would be more appropriate, then don't hesitate to change your name. Some businesses names have changed to not only reflect a more up to date image but the original name may carrier negative connotation that maybe wasn't so negative decades ago. KFC has a very successful tradition of making great fried chicken but not too long ago they changed their name from Kentucky Fried Chicken to KFC. KFC not only is easier to remember but also doesn't highlight the "fried" word in their name. On the other hand, it was the original name itself that carried the success of this company for so many years. Following the 4 factors mentioned above may not make your business successful but it sure is a great place to start.

Once you select a trade name, you must then register the name with the state. Check with your states register office for the exact procedures since applying for a name varies from state to state. Your state will let you know if the name you have applied for is available or if it has already been taken. Many states have simplified the process by allowing you to search online for the name you wish to use. Once the name is registered with the state, then you are ready to register your business structure with the IRS. The form on the next page is a sample trade name application from the state of Arizona.

Office Use _____

Please mail Registration to:
Secretary of State Jan Brewer / Trade Name Division
1700 West Washington 7th Fl. Phoenix, Arizona 85007
Walk-in service: 14 N. 18th Ave., Phoenix, Arizona
Tucson Office: 400 W. Congress, Ste. 252
(602) 542-6187
(800) 458-5842 (within Arizona)
Filing Fee: $10.00

APPLICATION FOR REGISTRATION OF TRADE NAME
(A.R.S. §44-1460)

The Registration of Trade Names and Trademarks is not legally required in Arizona, but is an accepted business practice. This is a registration for an Arizona Trade Name only in accordance with A.R.S. §44-1460. The registration of a trade name is a public record and does not constitute exclusive rights to the holder of the name. Names with a corporate ending (e.g., Inc., LLC or Ltd.) are not acceptable.
Please clearly print or type your application to avoid registration errors.

Name, title or designation to be registered: _____

Name of Applicant(s): _____
(If more than 1 applicant, an "or" designation is assumed unless otherwise indicated)

Your certificate and renewal notices are dependent on accurate address information including suite numbers. Remember to update your registration if you move.

Business Address: _____
              Street or Box Number   City   State   Zip
Phone (Optional): _____

Applicant must check one. Do not select "Corporation" or "LLC" if you are not currently incorporated, or your application will be returned to you.

☐ Individual   ☐ Foreign corporation licensed to do business in Arizona
☐ Partnership   ☐ Association   ☐ Organization
☐ Corporation   ☐ LLC   ☐ Other _____

The date in which the name, title or designation was first used by the applicant within this state. This date must be today's date or prior to today's date: _____
                                    Month   Day   Year

General nature of business conducted: _____

_____   _____
Applicant's Printed Name   Applicant's Signature

_____   _____
Applicant's Printed Name   Applicant's Signature

State of Arizona
County of _____

Acknowledged before me on this _____ day of _____, 20____

_____
Notary Public

Your Business Bank Account

Even though its not required, a business bank account should be opened after your business name has been selected and registered. Although your business may be far from generating revenues, your start up cost will begin soon if not already. Funds identified for start up expenses should be deposited into your business account from which you can draw from. This way, checks or cash used for start up expenses are separate from your personal account and provide a well documented paper trail for your records and financial books, not to mention the IRS. If you have a line of credit, then money you withdraw from the line of credit to deposit into your business account should be documented as such. Keep a simple spreadsheet of the amount, where and when funds were withdrawn and deposited into your business account, even if the money is from your personal saving account. If audited by the IRS, they may think that money deposited into your business account comes from revenues, not money barrowed. Keep an accurate log of where the money comes from.

Locating your Business

We've all heard that it's location, location, location, right? I wish I could tell you to just set up your business at a great location, flip the open sign on and watch the money just pour in. If it were that easy, you would not have to read this book. A lot of other things have to happen in order for you to capitalize on a so-called "great location".

We certainly found location to be a dominant factor in the success of some of our shops. But what makes a great location so great anyway. Some of the factors in a great location include the vicinity to a major intersection, a major store as an anchor for the center, vehicular traffic, the amount of residential homes or apartments, nearby schools, the local population age and of course the average household income. You can be at a great geographical location in terms of population density, ease of access, household income and so forth, but you may be in a poor spot that might be hidden and hard to see from the street. We opened our fifth shop in a new shopping center that was regarded as a great location within a large developing area. Our shop was situated to gives us maximum exposure to the main street with easy access and plenty of parking. As predicted, we had good volume after opening and we were profitable the second month. Not bad, I said! About a year later, to my surprise, a new strip of 5 retail spaces was being built between our shop and the street, making our shop impossible to see from the street, in addition we lost much of our parking due to the new shopping strip. Our growth began to taper off as a result of our poor visibility with many new customers having difficulty finding us. Although we were in a great location, we were in a poor position that affected our business.

Expect Fierce Competition for a Good Location

Finding that great location is one thing, but getting into that location is quite another. There is about a half million new businesses that open each year. You can bet that you will be competing with some of them for a place to set up shop. The degree of your competition will certainly be a function of the type of business you have such as a fast food business versus a manufacturing plant. Many other competitors just like you are doing everything they can to get into a great location. This is exactly what we discovered when we tried to get in at those "great locations". Those great locations, if not already taken by a competitor, had a waiting list. We found that even before construction began at many planned shopping centers, similar hair salons already had a signed lease. And it was the same story for every other type of business, from cleaners to video stores. A lot of this had to do with the area, interest rates and the economy. The Phoenix valley has enjoyed tremendous growth over the last decade. Competition is very strong with national companies as well as small independent investors. Usually at the first sign of a new shopping center going up, even though it maybe years away from completion, potential business owners will line up for a chance to grab a space.

One thing that will help you get a reasonable shot at a good location is to make your intentions known to property managers and developers. A simple letter explaining who you are, what your business does, the amount of space you need, and any other data that will help you should be included. You should request to be placed on their mailing list for any developments in the future or if a space become available at an existing center. Make sure your letter looks professional and positive. Don't layout negative criteria such as a limit to what you'll pay or that the lease better provide this or that. Doing so is sure to keep you *off* their list. Negotiating the terms of a lease comes after you receive the lease and they show clear intentions in dealing with you, not before. Remember, you can always turn down a space or site offered to you. More than likely, for every space available, there will be many letters sent out to prospective renters. Make sure you back up your initial letter with a phone call. They are more likely to keep you in mind the more you build a rapport with them. One agent told me that they preferred to go with local businesses or owners than a national company for the simple reason that is was much easier to deal on a personal basis than a large company with endless committees and layers of approval processes. Then again I found some property managers wanting to deal only with national companies since they had name recognition and were more likely to succeed then a small mom and pop business. You might be thinking to yourself that the roles seem to be reversed. After all, you're the customer or client and they are the vendor, right. Shouldn't they be the ones catering to you? That is certainly true, but this is a market of supply and demand. I' am sure that if economic conditions deteriated significantly, demand would become weak resulting in over capacity leading to a more willing landlord. But what I've seen in the last decade is almost a take it or leave attitude by many retail space owners. Occasionally, you might be able to negotiate significant concessions on their part but usually in exchange for something else. In all five of our leases, we were able to only gain small concessions but we were never able to get the base rent reduced. They were just not willing to budge on that one. On the other hand, strip centers or retail spaces at less desirable locations will not be in as much demand as a corner or high volume center and therefore more willing to negotiate with you. But don't expect the same volume of customers as a large shopping center located at a major intersection.

  Another method of trying to find a location is to contact an agent at a retail broker's office and specify your desires. Working with one agent who has many contacts is well suited for the beginning business owner and saves you valuable time. The phone book or Internet is a good place to start. When a location is found, the agent will notify you and present the details to you. You deal directly with the agent just as you would in a real estate transaction. If you decide to go with the site or space, the agent handles the contract and covers the details of the contract with you. The owner of the center pays any broker fees and commissions to your agent. This is what we did for two of our locations. Any concessions or changes to the terms of the lease are made through the broker. You are under no obligation to exclusively use your agent and I would certainly never agree to such a requirement.

Now, what about if your going to go with a franchise that has locations picked out for their potential new franchisees. You might ask what could be better. I would be very careful to how the agreement is worded with the franchise. Remember, you are the one liable for the lease, not the franchise! If the franchise says they have a site selected, which you find is unattractive, then I would certainly not want to be bound to have to accept it. Some franchises may require you to sign a contract along with the franchise fee before they present you with one of their selected sites. I saw this with a large national salon franchise when they moved into the Phoenix valley. At first, their franchisees were moving into unattractive small strip centers with poor exposure. Later, their locations improved with many getting into large centers with good exposure. I personally saw almost every one of their first shops go out of business within a few years. Their other shops located at larger, more visible centers however did well. Remember, a franchise is in the business of selling franchises and their royalty fees comes from your total sales regardless if you are profitable or losing money! Fortunately, it's only a few franchises that take advantage of the independent owner. By far, most franchises offer good service and look out for the best interest of the franchisee. But I would certainly be cautious and consult an attorney specializing in franchises before accepting a contract.

5 Considerations of a Location

After a site has been located, there are some things you need to do before you even look at the contract. **First**, go out and talk with the other merchants in the center. Try and get a feel about the property management and how they are to work with. Some property managers are very difficult to work with and always seem to be away from their phone when you are having problems. **Second**, if there is a major anchor at the center, call the corporate office and try to determine if there are any plans of the anchor leaving or closing. Nothing could be worse than you agreeing to pay top dollar at a center with a major anchor, only to see them close and move down the street a year later. The terms of your lease agreement will never specify that the major anchor will remain at the center. **Third**, ask the property manager or your agent if there are any major modifications, repairs or refurbishments planned at the center. Most if not all such costs are passed on to the tenants. If the roof is redone or the parking lot is resurfaced, guess who ends up paying for it? The tenants do through the end of year adjustments to the common area maintenance and repair fees. These adjustments are charges for extra maintenance or repairs in addition to your set common area maintenance fees or if routine items end up costing more than estimated. It was quite common to see those extra costs for maintenance or repair work. I wouldn't turn down a site because of scheduled modifications but at least I know that it's coming and will plan for it. **Fourth**, look around the area and try to determine the economic activity potential. This entails driving through the nearby residential areas and determining whether the area is progressing or declining. For example, a major employer may be scaling back and laying off employees or a major electronics firm is building a plant and will be employing many people. Along with this, determine whether a new shopping center is planned for the nearby area. This will bring in competition and certainly impact your business and your center. Next, call your highway maintenance department to see if there are any plans for major road reconstruction work along or near the frontage roads. Shutting down lanes or reducing access to your center because of major work lasting months will certainly reduce business. **Fifth**, make sure the space you intend to move into will be properly inspected. Plumbing or electrical problems are usually the responsibility of the tenant unless they are part of the original structure or shell and even that has limitations. If a door is not working properly or a window is cracked ask the property management if they will repair the items. If the property manager agrees to pay for it then make sure it is put in the lease. More often than not, the property manger will leave you with the responsibility of having the item repaired but will reimburse you after you open for business. If this is the case, then make sure the lease specifies when you will be reimbursed. Realize that location will play a major part on how successful you are if your business deals directly with the public. Most terms are for a minimum of five years so it's important that you know as much as you can before signing the lease.

The Dreaded Lease Agreement

This now brings us to that dreaded lease agreement. Leasing retail or office space is most likely one of the biggest transactions you will be involved with in setting up your business. My best advice is to take your time with the lease and consider having an attorney review it with you. If you don't have an attorney or wish not to use one then seek someone who has experience with commercial leases or visit your library and look for books on commercial leases. Another great source for understanding leases is of course the Internet. You can do a search on "commercial leases" or visit Nolo at www.nolo.com, which is a great guide for small businesses. There will be many terms and concepts in a lease that will be unfamiliar to you. The term of the lease can range from a year to over ten years, but the normal term is five years. In fact, we could not find a property with anything less than a five-year lease, so be prepared for at least a five-year commitment.

One of the biggest hurdles of a lease is an understanding of all the terms, conditions and requirements of the business owner. In most cases, your lease can be modified to fit your specific requirements. For example, under the rent section, rent is defined as *base rent* and *percentage rent*. In every lease, we requested that percentage rent be deleted along with any audit requirements that went along with percentage rent. Another area is rent increases. Annual increases to your rent will be defined in your lease. Don't assume that just because they have it in the lease that it can't be changed. We always negotiated with the property agent to reduce rent increases to be more in line with the inflation rate. However, one item that was particularly tough to change was the base rent. Property owners were not very willing to lower base rents in a booming economy. Not every aspect of a lease must be negotiated with the property agent before the lease is signed and delivered back to the agent. We always made changes to the lease and then submitted it for approval except for four items. The base rent, annual rent increases, build-out allowance and period of free rent were four items we discussed with the agent prior to signing the lease. Most property managers will approve a period where no rent will be charged to allow for the *build-out* or lease improvement of the rented space or office. The build-out is any construction improvements required of the leased space for the purpose of tailoring the space for the specific type of business. Counters, rooms, plumbing, lighting, cabinets, electrical outlets, etc are items that would fall under the build-out. The free rent period can be anywhere from 30 days to 6 months but is usually for 90 days. After the agent receives your lease then it is submitted to the owner for final approval. The term of the lease begins on the day you receive the lease. Most business owners will have a contractor ready to begin work shortly after the lease is approved. The one thing you want to avoid is having your free rent period expire without being able to open for business because of build-out delays. Make sure your contractor is ready to start shortly after the lease is signed!

Most leases come with an option to extend the lease to another term. This does not bind you to another five-year term but gives you that option with the same conditions as in your lease. Rent increases are included for the next term of the lease. If you decide to exercise this option then you must notify the property manager by a certain date defined in your lease. This is usually six months before your lease is due to expire. Don't assume that the property manager is going to contact you with a reminder that your lease is coming up for renewal. I have seen a business owner receive notice that they had to leave at the end of their term for a new business coming in. The owner never notified the property management about renewing their lease. The property manager found another business willing to pay more in rent than what was called for in the option. The property manager can't refuse to extend the lease option if you desire to extend it as long as you have abided by your lease during the first term and notify them in plenty of time. For example, not paying your rent on time could be justification for the landlord to deny extending the option for another term. The lease option benefits the business owner assuring them another term if so desired.

A build out allowance for improvements can and should be included with your lease. This means that you will be reimbursed up to a specified amount for certain construction costs associated with getting your space ready for business. This may be in the form of an allowance such as up to $3 a square foot of your space. If you have 1000 square feet of space and your build out cost you $10,000 then you would be reimbursed $3,000 after the construction is complete and you are open for business. In addition you must show proof that your contractor has been paid in full!

Build outs, Lease Improvements and Contractors

More than likely, the space or building you will be using for your business will need to be modified or improved to accommodate your type of business. For example, a restaurant will require a different build-out or lease improvement than a clothing store or cleaners. Many build-out requirements are governed by federal, state or city regulations. When selecting a contractor for your build-out, it's advisable to choose an experienced contractor in the type of build out for your business to avoid certification problems down the road. In most cases, the contractor's plans must have an architect or engineers stamp before the city will approve the plans. Once the plans have been approved, only then can the contractor begin construction work. During construction, a city inspector will inspect for code compliance of certain items such as plumbing and electrical work. After construction is complete, the city inspector makes a final inspection before issuance of a certificate of occupancy. In some cases, the electrical power company must have a certificate of occupancy before they are permitted to turn the power on. This means that the contractor must find or supply electrical power to run power tools and equipments during the build-out phase. In many cases, the tenant next door to you will allow you to use their power but may require some type of payment.

When signing a contract for the build out, make sure you specify a time when the project will be complete. As you can imagine, contractors will not want to agree to a time limit. But failing to get some type of time limit means the contractor could take years before completion. And don't forget, you'll be paying rent after your free rent period is over. In addition, your rental lease agreement may specify a time that you need to be open for business. Failing to meet that requirement could spell trouble down the road or could cause the property manager to terminate your lease and rent it out to someone else before you have a chance to complete the build out! The build out is usually the last phase before you are ready to open for business. The business owner has gone through a lot up to this point and will usually begin to relax before the build out is complete. My best advise is don't relax. Stay on top of your contractor until the walk through inspection is complete. Every day you are not open is lost revenues. You should be out to your site every day monitoring the progress. If a day goes by without work being done on your site then call your contractor and let him know that you didn't see anyone out working that day. One last item concerns any build out allowance you have with the property owner. As mentioned above, your lease may have a build out allowance that reimburses you a set amount for any build out cost. The build out allowance will be sent to you after the build out is complete and the property manager receives a copy of the statement from the contractor that says you have paid in full. Many property managers will also require that the statement be notarized. Getting your contractor to send you that notarized statement can take some time, especially if it must be notarized. As a requirement of final payment, tell your contractor that final payment will be made when a notarized statement can be furnished at time of payment. You hand him a check for the balance and he hands you the statement. Otherwise you will have to wait for that statement which could take some time. On one of our shops, it took several months before we received the notarized statement from our contractor! Along with this, don't pay off the balance until construction is complete and your build out or construction passes the city inspection.

Your Store Front

If you have a retail or service business located at a busy shopping center then your storefront can be a valuable tool to promote your business. I find many businesses spend a great deal of money and resources to open their business and then think very little about what to do with all that window and frontal space. Before you plan your storefront, take a day and walk by stores and note for each what is appealing about their storefront. I think you'll find some that are too busy, some are confusing, some say very little about the quality of their product and some have the right appeal. Have you ever walked by a store, then stopped and went back to take a second look at something that caught your eye? Sure, we've all been there. This is what you want to achieve for your storefront. You want people to take notice of something that will bring them in now or at least entice them to return later. When we first opened, we had stenciled in big letters, "Kids Cuts $5.95" on our windows. It was interesting to see people walk by and either stop or slow down observing the prices and then focus beyond the windows into our salon. If you have a retail or service business, then there are five features to consider of your storefront.

Five Features of Your Store Front

Who Are We. What is it about my business that I want to project? This may seem obvious to you, but it may not be so obvious to someone walking by. Suppose you have a small pizza restaurant that also offers other items on your menu such as burgers and sandwiches. Your window front should have something that clearly tells the public that your business specializes in pizza's, such as "Pizza Special..." or a picture of a pizza. I have seen hair salons that say nothing in the windows about the services it offers. The window would have hours of operations, some specials on retail products and something else that says, "Feel and Look Wonderful". As you look in you find shelves of retail product and in the very back there is a salon chair. At first glance you would think this place only sells retail hair products and not discover that it is also a hair salon. Suppose you see a sign that says health store. What does that mean to you? Does it mean they sell supplements and vitamins or does it mean they sell just organic fruits and veggies? Sure you could walk-in and determine what they sell but there are many who would not make the extra effort. Don't forget that you are not just appealing to those walking by but also to those driving by. In our business our bread and butter was haircuts, but we also did color and perms. Many people would come in and ask if we also did color and perms since we had no mention of these services on our windows. We finally began advertising those services on our windows, which made a big difference to our bottom line.

When Are We Open Second, say something about your operating hours. In our business, we were open 7 days a week and at nights. Posting your hours on the door or window would say it all. However, there were many salons that were closed on Sundays. People naturally assumed that we were closed on Sundays unless they walked up to the door and looked at the hours. On our door, we had "Open Sundays" in big letters so that someone driving by could see it. We also operated on a walk-in basis for most of our services. Many salons operated on an appointment basis only and we wanted to make sure that the public new we operated on a no appointment, walk-in basis so we had on our window, "No Appointed Needed". We also had one or two signs that promoted a special such as $5.00 off all perms and color or a special on retail product.

Our Prices. The third area to consider is the general range of your prices or specials and sales you might be running. This is especially effective when your prices are generally lower than your competition's prices. When we advertised on our windows, "Kids Cuts $5.95", that not only said a lot about what we did but also said a lot about our prices. It also tells the public that we cater to the entire family. If your prices are at the higher end of the scale then you should not post your prices. Only post your strong points that would appeal to the consumer passing by.

Image. The fourth area that deserves attention is the image your business projects to the public. We will discuss image in more detail later, but the thing to remember is that your storefront is a great place to promote your business image. It doesn't have to be separate from everything else. You can project your business image along with the other areas discussed above. We used a photo of a family with our mail out advertisement as well as in our storefront with the phrase, "We put family values back in styles". And on occasion we would also hang photos in our storefront of young adults wearing some of the latest styles in cuts, perms or colors with the phrase, "Get a great look at a great price".

Keeping It Simple. The last area ties it all together. Avoid cluttering up the windows and store front with so much information that the public is overwhelmed. Too much information can drown out the important things that might not get observed by the public. It's the same as trying to drink out of a fire hose. I am sure many of you are familiar with the term KISS, "keep it simple stupid". It's easy to convince yourself to keep adding things to your storefront until every inch of your window has something on it for the public to view. Limit the information so that the public can quickly identify your primary message. An effective way to keep it simple is with large prints or posters that displays what you want the public to know. A picture is worth many words and can transcend language barriers. Posters can also be made for special occasions such as the holidays, Mothers Day or Valentines Day, which also promotes a special. Posters are one way of keeping it simple; there are many forms that allow you to do the same depending on the type of business and available storefront space.

Developing a Strong Business Image

As business owners, we would like to be all things to all people, but the fact is that it becomes very difficult and costly. For example, you can't appeal to the price conscious customer when you have prices that are on the mid or upper end of the scale. Nor could you expect heavy volume if you only accept appointments. We can't appeal to the weekend shopper or customer if we are closed 50% of the weekend days such as Sundays. In our business we knew we could make up for low prices with strong volume and sales. That meant we had to be open nights, 7 days a week, on a walk in, no appointment needed basis. And most important, it also happened to be what the customer wanted. However, this also meant that we could not pamper and spend unlimited time with our customers as they might expect at a pricier, upscale appointment only salon. You probably have already narrowed down the scope of your business and have a good idea of the market your trying to go after. Now you have to decide how you want to project that image. As an example, take a look at Southwest Airlines. When you hear of Southwest Airlines, what comes mind? Lots of domestic destinations, good frequency, but most of all low fares! From their advertisements to check-in, to their famous peanuts, they project their image clearly. Of course they differ from other airlines that provide first and business class, larger more comfortable aircraft, more destinations including international, advanced seat selection, and baggage interline among other frills. The same goes for many large corporations. I am not saying you have to go out and hire a public relations firm but you should be taking good notes on businesses in your area and catalog those with clear and definitive images as opposed to those who have a cloudy or undefined image. Developing your image should be a natural extension of your business. If your business is unique with a select customer base then your image should project that tone.

Neatness and Appearance

Whatever type of business you have, the cleanliness and overall appearance of in and around your business affects it's performance. I remember I had a job interview with a large national company some years ago. The interview involved almost a full day and covered several offices and buildings. The carpets looked worn and unclean, some of the walls needed painting, and some of the staff members interviewing me looked unhappy and disorganized. I elected not to take their job offer and about twelve years later they ended up in bankruptcy. Did the appearance have anything to do with its failure?

Maybe not, but it certainly did have a lot to do with my decision to not work there. And I wonder how many other well qualified applicants made the same conclusion. The point is that appearance not only affects your customers but also your employees and could be a factor in why some decide not to work there.

If you and maybe one other employee work in your business, then appearance is not difficult to control. But with many employees, then it can be difficult to manage. Before any further discussion, lets define what we mean by appearance. Cleanliness is a major factor in appearance and includes everything from how clean your windows are to the cleanliness of your restrooms and floors. It not only involves daily cleaning but weekly and monthly maintenance such as the polishing of floors. Neatness is another element of appearance and involves how well everything is in place such as magazines, furnishings, and display items and general arrangement of furnishings. The third area is shop or facility condition involving more permanent items such as the walls, doors, pictures, carpeting or floors, restrooms, lighting etc. Not only is the condition of these items important, but how they coordinate with each other is also a factor. All three of these areas contribute to the business's overall appearance and of course image the public has of your business.

Have you ever walked into a restaurant only to find magazines and newspapers on the floor, doors and windows dirty with handprints, food on the floor underneath the tables and crumbs on the seats? If this is what it looks like in the customer area then think what it looks like in the kitchen and storerooms. Your immediate impression of this place is negative and it may get you wondering about the quality of the food and the overall sanitation. Would this be a place you would bring a business client or a date? First appearance shapes your opinion and can influence future decisions of whether to return again. If only 1 percent of new customers decide not to return because of appearance, then over a 1 year period that adds up to a lot of customers who did not return and could make the difference between a profitable or unprofitable business.

Most if not all would agree on the importance of a clean and neat place of business. However, the issue involves who and how much. Are you going to have a cleaning service come in every night to clean or are you going to assign your employees the job. And, what about the time from opening to closing. Our policy was that our employees had the responsibility of keeping our salons clean. This was spelled out in our operating manual and disclosed to our new hires so that there was no question about cleaning. Every night as part of our closing duties, our staff would each take an area to clean. For example, one would sweep the floors and arrange the magazines while another would empty the trash containers and clean the windows. Everyone would chip in including my wife and I if we were there. Granted, some employees would take a more active role in cleaning then others. If the cleaning became to one sided then a meeting would be called by either myself or the manager to discuss the issue. Usually a note or letter posted at the reception desk was sufficient to highlight my concern if I found that a salon was being lift unclean. When our customers walked in I wanted them to feel this was the cleanest salon they had ever been in. And on a number of occasions, we had customers tell us just that. This was our goal and it ranked high on my priorities and our staff new it. I remember a receptionist we had for a short time. She came well dressed and handled most receptionist duties fine. However, I noticed on one occasion when I walked in, there were magazines on the floor, dust on the display racks, and the windows and doors filthy with handprints and dirt. When I asked my manager about it, she told me that our receptionist "told" her that she was not there to clean. Needless to say, she was no longer on the payroll! Its important that as an owner you have a plan of how you are going to keep your place clean. Merely, telling your employees its up to them will not work. If needed, you or your manager should post cleaning responsibilities. We found most of the time our employees did a pretty good job of maintaining our shops clean.

If your business deals directly with the public consumer, such as in a salon, then the décor and interior design becomes as much of a factor as the cleanliness. If your ambition is to grow into several locations then consideration should be given to standardizing your interior with a well thought out design. During the design phase, you should consider three factors. First, consider a theme or a style that fits your business product. Many restaurants chains carry a theme as well as many other types of businesses. Second, your design should be functional to serve your customers as well as in the performance of your employees. Third, the overall interior décor should be appealing to your customers as well as your employees. In summary, your interior design should look good, be functional, and have a unique theme or style to remember your business by which again is part of your image.

The last area is the working order and condition of your business. Are some of the lights burned out or does the carpet look worn or the tiles cracked? Has the roof leaked leaving water stains on the ceiling tiles? These are all things that people notice immediately and form lasting impressions with customers. Job applicants coming in for an interview will also take notice and may give them reason to work somewhere else. Don't forget about the exterior condition including the landscaping. Does the landscaping looked groomed or is it overgrown and appears to be neglected. If you lease your space or building then contact the property manager and bring the issue to their attention.

Partnerships

While there are advantages in having a partnership, there are also many disadvantages to be aware of before you make that decision. A major advantage of having a partner is the financial aspect. Splitting the cost of starting or purchasing a business is quite appealing especially when you are limited in cash or borrowing ability. Another advantage is having someone else to help manage the business. This aspect is very beneficial in allowing you to take time off such as for vacations without worrying about the business. Expertise is another advantage that a partnership brings to the table. For example, you may have an expertise in certain areas of the business while your partner has expertise is other areas. There is also a negotiating advantage with a partnership. Having to "consult" with your partner can be an advantage when dealing with vendors, employees or customers. An unfavorable decision to your employees becomes less personal the more partners that are involved in the final decision. But this advantage is not a reason by itself to choose a partnership. The main reason most people go with a partnership is financial and expertise.

There are also a number of disadvantages associated with partnerships. Conflicts usually arise between styles of management or responsibilities. You may decide that a certain employee deserves a pay raise or promotion while your partner disagrees or your partner wants to limit advertising while you believe in the opposite. While no one can predict future areas of conflicts, the one thing that is for certain is that there will be conflicts between partners. How effective the partnership is in resolving the conflicts depends on several factors of which character and personality play a big part.

Start Up Costs

There are three main categories of expenditures that you will need to plan for as a business owner. These are your initial start up costs, capitals expenses and operating expenses. Obviously an accountant or tax attorney is the best source for understanding how these relate to income tax reporting. But it's safe to say that start up and capital costs are amortized overtime while operating expenses are expensed annually. Now as far as the IRS is concerned, your capital expenses include all start up cost, business assets and improvements. These types of expenses must be capitalized rather than deducted in whole. Operating expenses such as payroll, rents, insurance, loan interest, utilities etc, are deductible costs. A capital expense such as for office furniture or a lease improvement are depreciated or amortized over a certain number of years thereby allowing you to deduct these costs overtime instead all at once as you can for an operating expense. An outstanding web site that every new business should visit is www.irs.gov for a good discussion on business start-ups.

The amount of money it takes to get your business running up to the day you open for business is your start up cost. This can also be the amount needed to purchase an existing business. If there was ever an area deserving more meticulous planning it is here. For IRS purposes, the costs of getting your business started are capital expenses and may include advertising, travel, or wages for training employees. Before the first penny is spent you should have a pretty good estimate of what it's going to cost you to get your business started. Referring to the example below, I highly recommend laying out your estimated costs on a spreadsheet with 5 columns. The first column is for each item of expense, the second for estimated costs and the third column for actual cost with the 4th and 5th reflecting the difference. Your objective should be to carefully examine these areas and look for where you can save or use the money more wisely. For example, in our first two salons we used heavy-duty linoleum for the floors, which required routine polishing and buffeting with an occasional stripping and re-waxing. From then on we had our new salons with ceramic tile for the floors and thus avoid the monthly expense associated with the maintenance of the linoleum floors. Shopping around, we would find specials on tile, usually at Home Depot for just 89 cents a tile compared to the standard price of $2.00 a tile. This saved us over $1,500 on tile not to mention the amount we saved on maintenance cost over the years. What we found was that the floor not only saved us a bundle in the long run, but also was easier to keep clean, looked better and gave our salon a more upscale appearance. Some areas you may not have any leeway. For example, if you have a leased space in an indoor shopping center, then you may have to comply with certain build out requirements such as the type of flooring or wall covering, thereby increasing your start up cost. If your borrowing most of your start up cost, then the more you can reduce you're cost without sacrificing productivity, the more cash flow you will realize on a monthly basis when factoring in debt servicing of the loan.

Every item on your start up cost worksheet (see example below) should be thoroughly researched. Guessing will simply not do, especially if you are using your estimates as a basis for barrowing. Usually your highest cost will be for the build out phase which should include architect or engineering costs. Other cost in this area should include any permits required by the city, county or state when submitting your build out plans for approval. Remember, your start up cost will not only be a function of your type of business but also its location. The larger the space or building the more your start up cost will be. We had an average build out cost of about $14.00 a foot in 1999 and that was for a very simple no frills build out. A restaurant will have a much higher cost due to special requirements such as fire suppression and ventilation requirements. The other items on the list will require research and can be involved. For our business, every item no matter how small was itemized and recorded on a spreadsheet giving me a fairly accurate estimate of our start up costs for each of our shops.

Spreadsheets

For the business owner, the spreadsheet is simply priceless! If you don't know how to use a spreadsheet then you will be left in the dark. I can not emphasize how important the spreadsheet will be to you. I used Microsoft's Excel and found it simple and versatile but any spreadsheet is fine, just use one. If you don't know how to use one then buy the program and a book on it and go to work. Give yourself a few weeks to get the basics down. With spreadsheets, gone are the days of hand written ledgers. Tracking of expenses, sales or revenues, employee hours worked, employee schedules, assets, inventory, retail products, cost to produce and much more are easily entered, stored and tabulated on spreadsheets. For me, it was one of my most valuable tools and will be for you too.

SAMPLE SPREAD SHEET OF START-UP vs ACTUAL COSTS

ITEM		COST EST	ACTUAL	DIFF	% CHANGE
Build out	$	80,000	$ 83,000	$ (3,000)	3.75%
Furnishings	$	20,000	$ 22,000	$ (2,000)	10.00%
POS system	$	4,000	$ 3,800	$ 200	-5.00%
Advertising	$	2,000	$ 1,700	$ 300	-15.00%
Hiring expense	$	1,800	$ 1,900	$ (100)	5.56%
Supplies	$	15,000	$ 14,500	$ 500	-3.33%
Utilities	$	1,100	$ 900	$ 200	-18.18%
Insurance	$	1,700	$ 1,700	-	0.00%
Transportation	$	900	$ 1,100	$ (200)	22.22%
Legal and Professional	$	3,000	$ 3,100	$ (100)	3.33%
Phone system	$	500	$ 600	$ (100)	20.00%
MISC	$	1,000	$ 900	$ 100	-10.00%
TOTAL >>>>>>		**$ 131,000**	**$ 135,200**	**$ (4,200)**	**3.21%**

3   CAPITAL AND OPERATING EXPENSES

Business assets and improvements you make to your business are classified as capital expenses. Business assets are such things as land, buildings, machinery, furniture, trucks, patents, or franchise rights. Freight and installation costs associated with an asset are also capitalized. The costs of making improvements to a business asset are capital expenses if the improvements add to the value of the asset, appreciably lengthen the time you can use it, or adapt it to a different use. You can deduct repairs that keep your property in a normal efficient operating condition as a business expense. Improvements include new electric wiring, a new roof, a new floor, new plumbing, bricking up windows to strengthen a wall, or lighting improvements. If in doubt whether a certain expense is a capital or operating cost, refer to the IRS web site or contact your accountant.

As your business grows and becomes profitable you will at some point begin upgrading, adding or replacing certain assets or imrpoving your dewling. These capital expenses are not operating expenses that can be deducted at the end of the year but must be amortized over a number of years. Most of the time the money to pay for these capital expenses has to be borrowed or must come from retained earnings. Either way, its money that will cost you over time through interest you pay or interest and dividends you lose out on from investment. Lets assume that you have decided to borrow $10,000 to outfit your business with a new and more up to date point of sale system and chairs and tables. After the refurbishment, you hear one of the employees saying, "well, he has the money to buy a new computer system but doesn't seem to have the money to give us a raise or provide us with medical coverage". That may seem like a valid argument, but it never makes sense to pay for operating expenses, such as payroll or supplies, with borrowed money or any other type of funds set aside for capital improvements. The only exception is when you are a new start up business or run into a unprofitable period and need extra cash to pay the bills. Operating expenses should only come out of operating revenues. I can't say this enough! If you don't have enough for pay raises from you operating revenues then raise the price of your products or servcies, but do not borrow for it. Its important to understand the difference between a dollar for investment in the business for the sake of the customer or efficiency and a dollar to pay for the operations that runs the business.

Another capital expense that deserves mention here is one that improves the working conditions of your employees. Many companies have seen the value of such investments. Providing a work out center, a microwave oven, a refrigerator, cushioned floor mats or better chairs are all capital expenses that improve the working conditions of your employees. This in turn can certainly improve the productivity of your employees or reduce the rate of injuries. The trick is to balance capital dollars spent for the benefit of your customers to that of your employees. Too much for one side may hurt the other and be counter productive. The same can also be said for capital and operating expenses. Hopefully dollars invested for capital items such as expansions or improvements will result in more business and more revenues. More revenues in turn should mean better profits. This in turn should lead to better wages and so on. But if higher profits does not result in better wages then resentment by employees could form and lead to reduced productivity and thus be counter productive overall.

Operating Expenses

Keeping control of your operating cost will be one of your most importants responsibilites as a business owner, large or small. It is central to nearly every aspect of your business and is the biggest element to the success or failure of your business. Operating expense are all the costs that keep the business running on an on going basis. These include, rents, payroll, insurance, utilites, transportation, interest, supplies and other such related expenses. Keeping track of your operating expsenses is a simple task which can be done on a spread sheet or on an accounting program such as Quickbooks or Peachtree. Subtracting these expenses from your total revenues yeilds your profit or loss. We kept track of our operating expenses on a simple spread sheet for each of our shops on a monthly basis. Factoring in our revenues gave us a clear picture of our operating profits. Obvisouly, if your operating expenses are greater than your revenues, then your are lossing money – your business is not profiting. If at the end of the month, your expenses are more than your revenues than you must either dip into your cash reserves, borrow the money or make arrangements with people you owe money to. However, continued mounting losses is unsustainable and will result in business closure.

Controlling Those Costs

As a business owner, you will find that controlling your operating costs will be one of the most challenging aspects of business ownership. At the heart of managing your business is having a firm handle on where the money is going and the necessary measures to control costs. Believe me, no one in your business has more at stake than you when it comes to operating expenses. Sure, you can make your manager responsible for controlling expenses, but no one will be better at it than you! I have had people say to me, "your manager will be just as motivated as you since it will be their job if you go out of business". If you, as a reader believes this is true, then you are traveling down a dangers road. Your manager will be able to get another job, but you will lose everything you put into this business and still be liable for unpaid obligations such as leases and loans. I remember a business owner of a small shipping store in one of our business locations. They evenutally went out of business with several more years left on their lease. The property management took them to court for the unpaid balance of the their lease. Depending on how the business was set up, judgements made against you can be collected through garnishment of wages if you become employed by someone at a future time. Yes, you have a lot more to lose than your manager or anyone else.

The rest of this section deals with cost control for both operating and capital expenses. Hopefully, you will have a very profitable business and not have to worry about running out of cash. But, more than likely, you will have only a limited amount of cash to keep your business going until you become profitable. Its not uncommon to expect losses for the first year and as such, your business needs to have a source of money to tap from during its unprofitable period. In other words, don't get rid of your day job just yet. As a small business owner, you are the chief financial officer and need to keep one eye on the losses, and another eye on money set aside to make up for the losses. Even when you do become profitable, there are going to be months or periods where you will see losses, especially if your business is seasonal.

Before you open for business, you should have a pretty good idea of what your average operating expenses will be for each month and first year. After your first month of operation, you will be able to check your actual operating costs with those you estimated. List your operating costs in order with the highest cost item on the top. If the actual expense for any particular item is higher than estimated, then you, not your manager or someone else, needs to look carefully and find the reason. For example, labor costs which is usually the highest cost item, seems to be the one that has the greatest overrun. If your payroll is running 5 percent or more than what you have planned for the month than you need to look for the reason. The first place to look is the payroll hours. If you or someone else makes out the schedule, then you should have the total number of hours scheduled either for the month or week. This number should be compared to the actual number of hours worked to determine how much you have gone over or under. If you find that the actual hours worked is more than what was scheduled, then each employee's time sheet should be examined. Some reasons for excessive hours are justified such a fast approaching deadline for orders, or an unusually high volume of customers at closing. But at other times the reason is nothing more than an attempt to milk the clock for extra time each day by one or more employees. For example, we had an employee who would close down her styling station befor her shift ended, then not clock out until her ride showed up. Sometimes her ride would not show up for up to 45 minutes after her shift ended. In this case, we simply would not approve the extra time beyond the schedule shift period. This type of abuse can cost you dearly when it is widespread over several months.

Other cost areas such as utilities and supplies can begin to creep up unexpectantly. Unusually high electric bills can mean that the air conditioning or heating system is running excessively or that

45

there is a problem creating an inefficient system to run longer than needed. I'll never forget the time we drove up to one of our shops to find the front door open with the air conditioning set at 68 degrees while the temperature outside was 108 degrees! When questioned why, the employee said she wanted to be able to hear the phone while she smoked outside, so she opened the door. The phone happened to be cordless so she could have taken it outside and there was another employee in the salon. I explained that either the front door needed to be closed or the a/c turned off, one or the other. The phone can be another source attributable to excessive costs.   If your business requires long distance phone calls then I would encourage you to shop around for the service providing the best rates. If you have several locations or require several separate lines, then some long distance providers will work with you to reduce or illiminate the monthly service charge. One area to be aware of is use of the phone for personal long distance calls by employees.   Your long distance bill should be itemized with the date and time of the call giving you a good idea of who at work may have made the call. We had many occurances of employees using our phone to make long distance personal calls without telling us. Supplies is another area subject to overruns. Little things such as stationary, paper towels, cleaning supplies, etc can get out of control. Many business owners buy in bulk at large discounters where savings is achieved through bulk purchases. However, if you keep these supplies where access is unrestricted then you may discover your supplies beginning to dissappear. We have seen everything from laundry soap to toilet paper get consumed at an astonshing rate! Keeping extra supplies is not a bad idea and no one is saying not to do so. But, restricting access to many of these extra supplies can and should be achieved. A locked supply cabinet is something many businesses do and accessable by a few individuals and even under the watchful eye of a camera and time lapse recorder. By now, you may have summized that the thyme from the discussion above entails abuse and theft! That's not entirely true, but it is certainly more of a function of the business your in and how many employees you have. The real lesson here is that of keeping an eye on your cost and identifying areas where cost are going up more than you are comfortable with.

When we announced that we were going to open a new shop at a new location, some employees took a negative view of this. Their view was that we had the money to build a new shop but not for raises or employee benefits. The reality though was that almost 100% of the money to build a new shop was borrowed or on a payment plan with the vendor. In otherwords it was not coming out of our operating revenues and it was not an operating cost. This is a lot different than money available from revenues at one business location to be used for a new shop. But even if the money in the form of accumulated earnings is used to build an entirely new and separate business, so what! Everyone benefits from expansion in the form of more management job opportunities, greater consumer recognition and other advantages as discussed under the section titled "Expanding your business." And as an owner, you took the risk when you invested your own money into the business and as such are entiled to a return on your investment. The point is that if and when you decided to expand, realize that some employees may develop a negative attitude towards your ambition. How you deal with this is up to you just be aware that it will happen. My method was to simply explain to our employees the benefits of expansion and leave it at that.

The Different Colors of Money

One area that deserves special mention is the funding associated with the three main cost categories. When we talk about start up cost versus operating expenses, for example, we are really talking about different funding categories or as I call it, the different colors of money. Suppose you estimate that you will need the following amount for the first year of your business:

PHASE	ESTIMATED COST
START UP	$80,000
IMPROVEMENTS	$5,000
OPERATING COSTS	$120,000 – includes loan repayment

Your improvement costs are for equipment purchases or lease improvements that you have decided will come during your first year but after opening for business. For example, you have determined that you can get by with three copy machines the first month, but then you will need an additional copy machine afterwards. Your operating costs include payroll, loan interest, rent, insurance, supplies, utilities and advertising costs to run your business after you open. You have estimated that your revenues for the first year will be $110,000 leaving you short by $10,000 ($110,000 minus operating costs of $120,000). In other words, after paying all the bills including loan repayments for that first year, you will be short $10,000 when you factor in your estimated revenues. You have decided to set aside $15,000 to cover you in case your revenues fall short of your estimates the first year or about $1,250 a month. This is in addition to the amounts you have acquired for start up and capital improvements for your first year. Lets say that you have decided to purchase additional equipment in the amount of $10,000 making your total start up cost $90,000. This additional amount is for items that will not improve your revenues such as a computer server, upgraded floors and window treatment. Unless you have increased your credit line or amount borrowed by an additional $10,000 you will have to dip into the $15,000 budgeted for operations to pay for these added start up expenses. This leaves you with $5,000 to cover an estimated shortfall of $10,000 for operations. This mixing of funds can get you in trouble down the road. If after opening for business, you are not able to get additional funds and your revenues are not sufficient to make up for your shortfall, you will run out of money and not able to pay your bills! If you are short $1,200 a month, you're $5,000 will cover you for about 4 months. After that you will need additional money to cover your shortfall. This is exactly what happened to a business owner who opened a business in one of our shopping centers. He spent more on his start up phase without securing additional funds to cover his operating costs. His revenues fill short of estimates and after a little over one year was forced to close his doors loosing all his personal investment. Had he been able to last maybe another 6 months, he may have been too able to turn the corner. But we will never know if that would have occurred. The point is that it is easy to rationalize using funds you have budgeted for other requirements in hopes that the extra money will be acquired somehow. There is nothing wrong with having an optimistic view as long as you don't gamble on it!

4   BUSINESS HOURS

As many business owners find, the hours they are open for business is a driving factor for many elements of their business. The biggest factor will be the number of employees you will need to meet your schedule and total payroll hours. The type of business you operate will also be a major factor in determining the hours and days of your operation. A manufacturing business may have a different set of operating hours and days than a retail or service business. The location of your business is also a major factor determining your hours and days of operation. If you have a retail business located in an indoor shopping mall, then your operating hours will be dictated by the shopping center's hours. Failure to comply with operating hours specified in your lease agreement could result in fines and ultimately in loss of your lease. The other factor is the needs of your customers. If you have a coffee and bagel shop then your customers expect you to be open early. A restaurant that is closed on Sundays will obviously lose business. As we found, there will be customers that always come in during a certain range of hours or days. You may have customers that can only come in from 6 pm to 8 pm or Sundays for example. Not all businesses on the retail or service side need to be open nights and weekends either. We had our employee name tags engraved at a trophy and engraving shop. The husband and wife ran the business and seemed to do well enough to close on weekends and nights. In fact they were normally closed by 5 pm! And when they went on vacation, they closed their shop until they returned. They could do this because of the business they had. Yet other businesses will have be open nights and weekends just to make it.

Once you have established the hours of operations then the next concern is whether you will be able to meet the staffing requirements, especially if it entails evening hours. Being open till 5 pm is one thing, but staying open till 9 pm is quite another. I have seen cases where businesses had to begin closing early or not open on Sundays because of a lack of employees available to work the later hours. The other concern is the volume of business during certain hours and scheduling your staff to meet those demands. In our business, we remained open till 8 pm. From about 5 pm to 7 pm was our busiest time of the day thereby requiring us to adequately staff that period to meet the demand. One thing is certain, the later you are open the harder it will be to find employees who will work the shift and the same for weekends. Night and weekend shifts have typically the highest call out periods. As one might expect, weekends are the busiest days for many retail and service type businesses. Overall, keep in mind that your business hours are for the convenience of the customers.

Some businesses are greatly affected by the season. For example, in the East Phoenix area, winter visitors would add a significant volume to businesses from October to April and then slow dramatically during the warmer months after the visitors have left. Many of the hair salons around these winter visitor locations would open early. This was due to our winter visitors being early risers who tended to be out and about in the early mornings. The same could be said for other types of businesses that are located in and around these winter visitor hot spots. If you decide to modify your business hours due to the seasonal affect, then make sure your target customers are aware of these hours. As a minimum, post the change on your storefront window. I would also highlight your new hours in your advertisements. If you have an automated phone answering system, then include the change in your opening message. If you decide to open early to take advantage of seasonal visitors, then make sure you also keep your same closing hours. Closing earlier because you open early may drive away your later hour customers.

Cost Analysis of Hours of Operation

When determining or adjusting your business hours, you must look at whether your current staff can support an increase in hours and what will it cost. The following example illustrates the complexity of staffing your hours of operation as a function of your employees and their needs. In our business, we were open from 9 am to 8 pm on weekdays with slightly different hours on weekends. These hours were primarily dictated by our customer needs with some regard to our staffing levels. Closing earlier would cause us to lose customers while extending our hours would force us to hire one or two additional employees. Hiring two more employees didn't make sense for the additional 8 hours per week. Extending your hours may bring in more revenues but at what cost. Lets say you want to extend your operating hours so that your total hours increases by 25 per week and lets say you currently have four employees working 35 to 40 hours per week each. You have two options, the first is to ask your employees to work more hours so that the additional 25 hours are covered by your present employees. This may mean that some employees will have to work an additional day or work one or two 12-hour shifts. If your employees are close to 40 hours a week then they will not want to work more hours on a routine basis. In addition, closing later at night and weekends is not something they will be eager to do. I remember when we were going to extend our hours from 7 pm to 8 pm at one of our locations. As anticipated, two of our stylists told us that they would quit if we did so. We ended up doing so and of course having to recruit new employees, which took considerable time resulting in loss of sales.

      The other option is to hire a part time employee for the additional 25 payroll hours. This is easier said than done, as finding someone who is willing to work just 25 hours is not easy. Many times during an interview we found that other than pay, the amount of hours was a primary factor. Most wanted no less than 33 hours and if given anything less they would find employment somewhere else. In fact, many of those responding to are help wanted ads were leaving their employer because they weren't given enough hours and didn't want to work evenings and weekends. So lets say the best you can do is hire someone for no less than 30 hours per week. This means that you will have an overage of 5 payroll hours per week or about 260 hours per year. At, say $13 per hour (includes direct and indirect employee costs), your additional annual cost would be $3,380 for 260 hours of additional payroll hours. The question to ask yourself is whether that extra 260 hours per year is going to add to your revenues. In other words, would your revenues be the same with or without those extra 260 hours? In our business, we found that those extra 260 hours would not increase our revenues. To determine whether those extra non-productive 5 hours a week is going to be justified you must determine how much revenues you anticipate by extending your business hours by 25 a week. Lets say those extra 25 hours a week will produce an extra $500 a week to your revenues. The extra 25 payroll hours at $13 an hour will cost you $325 per week. So to make an extra $500 a week will cost you $325 plus those extra 5 hours for a total of $390 a week. OK, so your $110 a head per week. Is it worth it? That depends on several factors such as future pay increases, future price increases, the comfort of knowing you have an extra employee incase someone leaves you without notice or calls in sick. The other factor is how much will your business increase overtime. That $500 per week in additional revenues may be stable for your first 6 months but what about 1, 2 or 3 years down the road. Lets say 2 years later those additional 25 hours a week is adding an additional $1500 a week in revenues. In our business, we found that our revenues did increase over time due to a pick up in the number of customers. Increasing your payroll to accommodate an increase in operating hours may not always be cost justified but as a business owner you have to look at the long-term prospect, specifically 6 months to a year. It may not be cost justified in the short term but the benefit over the long term may certainly justify the initial "investment".

    Reducing your hours of operation can have a detrimental effect. Reducing your business hours usually means reducing payroll hours, which will not be well received by your employees. Some employees may actually look for work somewhere else while others will want more pay for the reduction in hours. At a minimum, moral will be affected and productivity to include customer service is going to suffer. Reducing your hours may save you an extra $300 a week in costs, but it may cause an erosion of productivity affecting revenues. The other impact will be on your customers. Closing on Sunday's or an hour earlier on weekdays will certainly cause you to lose some customers. As an example, in one of our locations we had been open 7 days a week and we were doing a fair amount of volume. When we got short handed, we found it very difficult to staff our Sundays with the remaining uncooperative employees. Unable to hire someone in the short term, we ended up having to close temporarily on Sunday's. Obviously we no longer had revenues on Sunday and we thought that

53

many of those customers who found us closed on Sunday would come in on Monday. To our surprise we discovered that our average volume of customers began to decrease on the other remaining days! This was simply because many of those customers who came to us on a particular Sunday and found us closed would go somewhere else and became regular customers at another salon. Overtime, your average volume will decrease to the point it will significantly impact your bottom line. To add insult to injury, these same stylists who wouldn't work on Sundays then wanted more hours to make up for the hours they lost by not working on Sundays. So not only would our revenues be going down but also our cost would be increasing. We didn't accommodate the extra hours unless they were willing to work Sundays, which they were not. We tried to recruit another stylist but the labor market was so tight we weren't able to find anyone for some time. We also didn't need just one extra person; we would need 2 extra people since our volume on Sundays required two stylists. But hiring employees to work just on Sundays for 8 hours was not very likely unless you could work them more hours on weekdays to bring their hours up around 30. Our current stylists were not willing to lose their weekday hours to new employees. Basically, we would have to replace our entire staff if we wanted to reopen on Sundays. We eventually replaced the entire staff with employees who were more customer focused. I know many would be saying at this point, I would have never let this gone this far. Believe me, its easy to say that now but looking back it was not that straight forward of a decision. I discovered that we weren't the only business having these problems. Other similar businesses were finding the same problems leading to inconsistent operating hours due to a lack of employees. Sure you can just schedule them but whether they show for work because of "illness" is another story. As you can see, your hours and days of operation have a great impact on your operating costs as well as on your revenues and can strain the owner – employee relationship.

5   ADVERTISING AND MARKETING

What does advertising do for your business? This may sound like a trick question but believe me you would be surprised on how many business owners don't have a clear objective of advertising. How you market and advertise your product or service is a crucial element of your business. Advertising is not cheap and could easily chew up a good percentage of you revenues. There are three objectives that advertising and marketing should accomplish. First, it should tell the consumer who you are and what market your business is intended for. Our business was for the cost conscience family who didn't want to spend a lot of money on hair care such as cuts, perms and color but who also wanted reasonable quality. We were open nights, 7 days a week on a no appointment basis and that is exactly who our advertising appealed to. It also appealed to male customers looking for that clean barber cut which was the majority of our customers and the style at the time. Along with identity and price range, your advertisements should project your business theme or values. Photos or artwork with a slogan that delivers an image of your values works well. We usually advertised with a photo of a young family with the caption reading, "We put family values back in style". That clearly identifies with young mainstream family values.

Second, your advertising should offer a discount or some other incentive for the customer. How much of a discount? Big enough to catch their attention and bring them in. Our haircuts were priced at $11 for adults, men or women and $9 for kids, so we would advertise a coupon that discounted the price of our services by several dollars. Some might say that's too much and opt for a dollar discount. Believe me, a $1 discount is not going to bring them in! You need to make an impact that the customer is not going to forget in a couple of minutes. Some might say that many of your regular customers coming in with coupons would have come in anyway. Giving them a discount might be regarded as unnecessary. It might be, but it's the price you have to pay to get new customers in the door and don't forget, your competitors will also be offering discounts in attempts to lure your regular customers away. But you can regard it as a reward to your customers for their continued loyalty. We found that the few days after our advertising hit the streets our shops were busy with people coming in with our coupons. It definitely brought new customers in and kept our regular customers coming back. On many occasions, first time customers coming in on a coupon would return either later that day or the next day with their spouse or family member. Advertising should not be regarded as the ultimate solution to generating new business. Its one part of many factors that go hand in hand with your business.

There is also an effect that advertising has on your competition. I remember when a local competitor would run a deep discount of $5.00 on their cuts. Seeing that much of a discount demoralizes you and your employees. It also will take customers away from you at least in the short term. After such an ad would come out, we would see a drop in our average daily volume for several weeks. Although many of our customers would eventually return, that type of an ad would hit us hard in our top line. This type of an ad was not just intended to gain customers, it was meant to impact its competition financially and force those that were already weak to shut down. Where it was particularly effective was during such events as back to school where volume was especially heavy. Advertising with deep discounts during those special occasions as the holidays can greatly impact your competition.

The third objective of advertising should highlight what distinguishes you from your competition. If your business offers a service or product that the competition does not offer then consider including this in your advertisement. For example, some of our competitors did not perform certain services as color or perms as we did. Our advertisement highlighted these services as well as the haircuts that we performed. If your open Sundays or nights and your competition is not, then highlight in your advertisements that your open nights and Sundays. Of course the item that will have the biggest impact as compared to your competition is price. A distinct price advantage over your competition is something you should highlight in your advertisement from day one. Knowing the differences between you and your competitor means you have to know your competition. If a person off the street came in and asked you why they should be your customer, as opposed to your competitor's, what would you tell them?

Knowing the answer to this means you have to know your competition, which in turn will help you design your advertising more effectively.

Primary Methods of Advertising

There are many forms of advertising that range from costly TV ads to less expensive door hangers and coupon mailers. Most small businesses find that direct mail is a cost effective form of advertising. There are many direct mailers such as Val Pac or Money Mailer that have distributions of 10,000 or more residences per area. And many of these direct mailers will list your ad on their Internet giving you even wider coverage. We used several direct mail venders depending on our location along with door hangers. We also printed our own direct mail using post card size advertisements that we mailed out ourselves. The cost was significantly more but we had a larger percentage return than a direct mail vender. The disadvantages of a direct mail vender is that your ad is among many other ads in the envelope and not as visible than a stand-alone post card. In addition, the distribution or mail out dates is set giving you no alternative but to accept their mail out schedule. The advantage with standalone direct mail is that you control the mail out date and your post card is not hidden among many other coupon advertisements enveloped together. A business directory such as the Yellow Pages gives the business owner the opportunity to buy large display ads. The advantage of the Yellow Pages of course is it's large distribution area.

For printed advertisements, careful consideration must be given to your layout. It's very easy to get carried away putting too much information on your advertisement. I found that in our mailbox we could find almost every type of ad from the very effective to the very poor. Almost every day, people receive many ads in their mailboxes. Over several weeks, gather all the ads whether direct mail or newspaper ads and look to see which ones appeal to you as a consumer. Try to see what makes a good layout from a poor one. I found that one characteristic of a poor ad was the amount of information presented. You may have a lot of information that you feel you need to present but this tends to detract from the ad. Keep your layout simple with a clear message. Many people will sort thru their mail giving no more than a few seconds glance at the ads. You want a layout that captures the attention of the reader after a few seconds in hopes the reader will put your ad in the save pile and not the throw out pile. Our most important message in our ads was the discounted coupon price of our haircuts, which was in large bright red print. It only took 1 second to see and it would be enough for the reader to read on or put it aside for further reading later. Consider using color especially for the prices. This tends to make the prices jump out of the ad. Price will not always be the dominant or key factor in your ads. Other factors such as store hours, free pick up and delivery, warrantees or response time can be dominant factors as well. For example if you have a plumbing business and you advertise that a plumber will be out within 30 minutes of your initial call, that will catch the attention of many people. Key words such as free, half off, no additional cost, same day service, no appointment needed, open Sundays or money back guarantee play a big role in advertising.

  Radio and TV advertisements is very effective if you are trying to reach a large or spread out area. TV offers the viewer the ability to hear your ad as well as to see it in action, while radio only offers the ability to hear it. Each has their advantages and disadvantages but the question is can you afford it and will it be affective for your type of business. If you have a chain of pizza shops or restaurants, then a TV ad will cover all your locations with one ad and provide the wide area coverage you would need. The form of advertisement you go with will depend on such factors as your advertising budget, type of business, area coverage, size of your business and possibly the time of year.

  Door hangers are also an effective form of advertisement that is stand alone and cost less than direct mail. There are blank door hanger forms you can purchase or order that allow you to print them from your computer. Or you can have them made and distributed from a number of businesses specializing in this type of advertising. Distribution can be done yourself, your kids or hiring someone to do it.

  Another form of advertising we found very effective was small printed flyers (3X8 inch sheets) distributed at other nearby businesses. We found that nearby nail shops were well suited for our type of business. Of course, permission to leave your advertisement must be obtained but is usually not a problem provided you reciprocate the favor.

Secondary Methods of Advertising

There are many other forms of advertisement that are limited to the name, phone number or web site for example. Below are examples:

> Business name on clothing
> Sponsorship of a youth sports team
> Pens and Magnets
> Your automobile
> Storefront banner
> Banners at high school sports events
> Bulletin boards

Although this type of advertisement plays a limited role, it is an effective way to reinforce your primary means of advertisement. Some of these types are limited to your business name while others allow more information such as phone number, web site and location. The Internet has also become more popular for advertisement. Many businesses have a web site that allows them to advertise their site as a link on another web site such as on Google or any of the other search engines. Price is usually a function of how many hits on your link. The more hits the higher the advertisement fee is. However, if you are a local business with little or no retail for shipment then advertising on the web may not be cost effective. But I would certainly consider a web site for your business.

Advertising Effectiveness

For every dollar you spend on advertising, how much sales will be generated? This is a fair question you should be able to ask yourself of your business but it is more difficult and complex then meets the eye. The first thing you would want to know is how many new customers came in due to your advertisement. There are two ways to find this out. One is to ask each customer who comes in on a coupon if they are new and did they come in based on the advertisement. The other is to have a database of customers and identify a new customer (one that wasn't in your database as a previous customer) with a coupon special. This means that you must enter into your point of sale system whether your customer came in with a coupon. If you sent out 10,000 direct mail coupons and 200 came back as new customers, then you have a return of 2 percent or 2 out of every 100 mail outs for new customers. If your cost was $500 for the advertisement and the revenues generated from the new customers was $2000, then you have a return of 300 percent ($2,000-$500)/$500 for your new customers. This type of analysis is straightforward and not difficult to determine. Another factor that becomes harder to analyze is the long-term effects of advertising. For example, lets say that a new customer comes in on one of your coupon flyers. This customer becomes a regular who over 3 years has brought in $1,000 in business to your store. It's hard to say whether this customer would have come in at some point without receiving any advertisements but that's something you will never know. The fact remains that money spent on advertising today contributes to revenues from return customers over many years. Furthermore, how many people have these regular customers referred your place of business to? The residual effects of your advertisements are hard to measure but it's safe to say there is a long lasting effect from it.

  Now lets say that 3 years after you have opened, new customers coming in on your advertisements has gone down to 50 out of 10,000 mail outs for a return of $500 or the same cost as your advertisements. Is your advertisement still effective? Well it may not be as effective as in the beginning in bringing in new customers but the more relevant question is how effective is your advertisement in *keeping* your regular customers as return customers? Now the effectiveness of your advertisement becomes more complex to analyze. Without ongoing advertising, it's difficult at best to say whether some of your regular customers might be pulled away by one of your competitors. One thing is certain; advertising will bring in new customers as well as keep your regular customers coming back. If you really wanted to determine the effectiveness of your advertising, you would have to stop advertising after several years of advertising and analyze the effect on the average volume of weekly and monthly customers. A simpler but less costly and accurate method is to see how many customers bring in coupons from your advertisement, assuming you offer a coupon discount in your advertisement. If after several days of the advertisement coming out, you are having many customers coming in with coupons, then it would be safe to say that the medium you are using for your advertisement is working well. In our shops, we would see a large pick up in volume right after our advertisements came out. Some shops showed better results than others, but the increase was indeed significant adding between 15 to 40 percent more volume in customers!

6 PRICING OF GOODS AND SERVICES

How much should you charge for your products and services? The price you get for your products or services can be a big factor affecting the success of your business. However, price is influenced by many factors some of which you will have less control than others. These factors include competition, direct cost to produce your product or service, general overhead, commissions, royalties and transportation expenses. It seems reasonable to ask yourself, why not charge enough to make a profit, period. The short answer is that it's not what you think the worth of your product should be but what the customer is willing to pay for it that counts. You can charge whatever you think is reasonable but your customers will decide whether the price is competitive for what they receive. Volume of sales is another factor that has a significant bearing on profitability. Generally, the more you charge, relative to your competition, the lower your volume will be. This combination of price to volume to achieve maximum revenues is difficult to predetermine and usually involves "trial" periods in order for the business owner to build a more conclusive database. In our business, we found that by offering specials of 10 to 20 percent off our regular price, we would see greater overall revenues than with no specials offered! Greater volume was the factor that made the difference producing greater revenues. In just about any business, what the competition charges for the same product or service will be the basis of your price structure. Your customers won't care that you have to pay higher rent, higher wages or other operating costs that's higher than your competition. The price they have to pay is the bottom line for them.

If you had no competition, then you could base your prices as a function of your cost of business. As a general rule of thumb, retail products have about an 80 to 100 percent mark up. We usually marked up our retail products by about 100 percent of what we paid for them. As an example, lets take a bottle of conditioner we sold for $10. Of that $10, $5 is our cost for the product, so we are left with $5. We paid our employees a 15 percent commission on retail they sold. So 15 percent of $10 is $1.50, leaving us with $3.50. General overhead, shrinkage and royalties are about another 10 percent, which leaves us with $2.50. So for a $10 item we sold, we were left with $2.50 for a margin of 25 percent. Other factors, which are more difficult to measure, could add another 5 percent chopping your profit down to $2.00. So you can see that a 100 percent mark up is not exactly gauging the customer.

If you have a service business then a general rule of thumb is to charge about 3 times what your labor costs are. For example if your paying an employee $10 an hour than your price to the customer should be a minimum of $30 an hour. We charged $11 for a haircut which on average took anywhere from 15 minutes to 30 minutes, depending if the customer was a male or female and length of hair. Our stylists on average made about $13 an hour not including benefits such as paid vacations, holidays and medical. Of course one has to remember that an employee is not always going to be busy with customers. You may have a period of a few hours where the employee is on the clock and not doing any customers. Sometimes we would have periods where the labor cost was more than what we did in business. And other times where our labor costs were one fifth of our revenues. Factor in various types of services and cost basis becomes much more complicated. Another factor is the volume of customers you have. If you have a new business then you can expect to have fairly weak volume as compared to a more mature business. Higher volume of course means more revenues per hour for about the same cost in labor. This translates to higher productivity. As a new business, your labor costs may be 60 or 70 percent of your revenues but over time that should come down to about 30 percent. So you can see that setting your prices of your service is not as straightforward as one might think.

Now, what about a business that manufactures products. Raw materials, labor costs and general overhead are the main factors in determining your cost basis. Having different products complicates the problem requiring you to assign certain values for overhead and other indirect costs. Once your cost basis is determined then your selling price becomes a factor above your cost basis such as 20 percent above cost, for example.

This type of analysis is used in determining the price of your products or services. But in reality, market forces such as demand and competition will have a larger role in what you charge for your goods than anything else. By going through the type of analysis described above, you are really determining what your profit margin would be for a specific line of products sold or services performed. Its not your actual profit margin you achieve but an estimate for the specific items involved. If your competitors are offering the same product or service for say $20 but it cost you $18 to produce the same product or service, then you can see that your margins will be limited to about 10 percent unless you charge more. Charging more than your competitor will most likely drive your business away. In our business, we set our prices at or below our competitors of similar businesses. However, we discounted our prices in our advertising specials more than our competitors, giving us a price advantage. If your operating costs are at a level that requires you to have a higher price than your competition in order to be profitable, then your investment in that business will certainly be at risk.

Raising Prices

On average, we raised the prices of some of our services about once every 18 months, as did many other businesses around us. The question always arose whether we should post a sign telling our customers that we had raised our prices. The concern was that a regular customer would walk in, get serviced and then find that they had to pay more than last month. I elected not to do so. Sure you had some customers that would complain about a price increase, but there were few who complained and many understood why the increases. Our customers usually paid the price without even questioning the increase. There is no right answer on whether to post changes to your prices. I can certainly see the benefit of letting your customers know before hand of price increases. But if you have many retail items, take for example a supermarket, do you think its reasonable to post price increases for every item you increase. Your store would be covered with posters not to mention the time involved in having the posters produced, which is not cheap. I am in favor of keeping it simple and not posting the fact that your prices have gone up.

Remember, as a new business, your objective is to get new customers in the door. Lower prices, promotions and sales will impact your bottom line but it's an investment you may need to make to establish you customer base. When we would open a new location, we offered a deep discount to our services of up to 50% for up to 2 months after opening. This obviously brought in new customers and allowed us to establish our presence.

7   PROMOTIONS SALES AND DISCOUNTS

Promoting is the process of making the public aware of your business and the services or products it offers. It includes all activities that have the ultimate objective of influencing the public in buying or using your services or products. Advertising is but just one of the many elements of promoting although it is usually the most effective as well as the most expensive. When we would open a new shop, my first goal of promoting was to get every person within 2 miles to know who we were and what we did within the first 30 days. And that meant using all available means, within reason, to accomplish this goal. We used direct mail advertising, banners, door hangers, flyers, handouts, freebies and any other form of "getting our name out". In addition, we found our new customers to be one of the best means of promoting our services and products. Of course that meant our services had to be exceptional. A bad experience can also travel at the speed of light gaining you a negative reputation. There are many tools or ways to promote your business. I've included 6 highly effective ways of promoting your business that don't cost much and that apply to almost every type of business:

6 Effectives Ways of Promoting Your Business

Business Cards and Stationery. Business cards should be readily available to all your customers. In each of our locations we would go through about 2000 cards every 3 months. Our cards were stocked at the counter, carried and distributed by each stylist and of course carried and passed out by my wife and I. I also distributed our cards to other merchants at our shopping centers for distribution to their customers. You can believe that I posted or distributed our business cards wherever I could. Any stationery that leaves your office should be a vehicle in promoting your business. Your letterhead and envelopes should not only have your business name but a catchy slogan and your web site.

Cross Promoting   There are probably a number of businesses that you could hook up with to help cross promote each other's business. We would always cross promote with a nail salon or other type business within our shopping center.   Having one of your flyers attached to each of their receipts with a discount is an effective form of cross promoting.   We would have green colored coupons the size of dollar bills with some type of discount that would be handed out to their customers.   And of course our business would do the same for their business.   Other ways include packaging your advertisements together, hosting a charity activity or contest together or even a "how to Class".   In addition, if you have a service business such as a salon or barbershop, consider offering the manager and owner of the other businesses a free or deep discounted price.   Nothing works better than to have these folks personally recommend your business to their customers.

Moving signposts   T-shirts printed with your business name as well as magnetic signs on your vehicles are inexpensive forms of promoting your business.   Think of how many people see your car on a daily basis.   Don't put too much information since people may not have long to look at your signs.   The main purpose with "moving" signs is simply to get your business name out where people can see it.

Sponsorships   Sponsoring youth organizations or sporting teams is an excellent form of promoting.   This provides money for organizations as well as advertises your business.   Both parties benefit from each dollar spent.   We would sponsor our sons little league baseball teams and thereby get our name on each of their shirts.   There are many youth organizations and teams that you could team up with.

Hosting a Chartable Event   Not only do you get to help people in need but you also get to promote your business, and some times the event will be covered by the media.   You could have a weekend where $5 dollars of each sale will go to a charity or help fund research.   You can even have the event to benefit the family of a fallen police officer or fireman killed in the line of duty.   However, you must contact the organization and get permission before you host the event. Using their name without their permission is not the right thing to do and can land you in some trouble. At a minimum, you should contact every media company and radio station to let them know about the event. This type of promotion can bring a lot of people so make sure you are well staffed to handle the load.

Special Events Every year there are holidays or events that are excellent opportunities to promote your business. For example, each July we would promote our back to school specials. The same was true for other annual special events such as the start of summer, the Christmas holidays, Easter and so on. In each of these annual events there is a theme from which our advertisements would capitalize on. For back to school, we promoted kids cuts as well as the latest hair color styles and trends for older high school and college bound students. For Valentines Day we would promote women's hair services such as a color, perm or style through gift certificates. In addition to hair services we would also promote our hair products for these occasions. Failing to take advantage of these events is a missed opportunity to generate sales. For each of these events we had unique pictures with wording (slicks) to highlight the event with our services and products. And we also ran promotions that wouldn't necessarily follow an annual event. For example we would sometimes promote family values (we put family values back in style) or some other theme that resonated with the public. How you promote these events in combination with your products or services is unique to your business but it certainly deserves consideration. If you sell retail products, then some of your suppliers or manufactures have promotional material for your displays. Some of our retail hair product companies had slicks or posters we could use in our advertisements or display on our windows. These slicks were very professional and included many variations to fit the occasion. In addition, if we used their slicks in our advertisement and we had bought a certain amount of product, then they would reimburse half the cost of our advertising in retail products. This is a great way to reduce your advertising cost while using a professionally produced slick at no cost to you. However, not many suppliers will offer this deal. I would certainly approach them and ask them if they would consider it. Both parties benefit from such an arrangement.

There are many other forms of promoting your business that are also very effective. Just like any other expensive item though, you must set a budget and stick to it. It's very easy to get carried away and spend a fortune. Keep in mind the goal, which is to get the public aware of your business and what you offer. Promoting can be limited to just having magnetic signs on your car or passing out flyers. A grand opening promotion is an excellent opportunity to get the public aware of your business. Also don't forget about the Internet. The Internet can be a great place to promote and advertise specials depending on the type of business.

Sales and Discounts

There can be no doubt that offering a sale will increase your customer volume, at least for the short term. A sale can be a part of your advertising efforts or in conjunction with a promotion. As part of our grand opening promotion for a new shop, we would always advertise a deep discount of our hair services to get new customers in the door. In addition, we also offered discounts through cut out coupons in our regular on going advertisements. But sales or discounts can also be associated with efforts to clear your old inventory of retail products. We have all seen the "end of year" clearance sale offered by the auto industry and many other businesses. Sales and discounts can also be used to generate cash. If you are lacking enough cash to get your business through the next few months, then having a sale is one way to bring the cash in, at least temporarily. It certainly is not the most profitable way to run a business, but it can be an effective way to survive for the short term. But in a more conventional sense, the objective of having sales is to get new customers who will become regular customers or to bring back customers who were regulars at one time.

Sales and discounts should also be one of your tools as it relates to dealing with your competition. If you had little or no competition and had strong demand for your product or service, then it's reasonable to say that you probably would not see the need to having a sale or discounts. However, with today's competitive environment, the use of discounts and sales is a must if you hope to increase market share. When one of our competitors opened a new shop, they would promote $5 haircuts as compared to the regular $10 price. As you can imagine, this type of deep discount indeed brought in the customers. Not only does it bring new customers in, at the same time it takes customers away from their competition. When we would open a new shop every new customer that walked in for the first time is one less customer for our competition. And the most effective way to get new customers is through deep discounts. If for example you offer a $15 service and advertise a discount of one or two dollars, then you are wasting your advertising money. If you're going to discount your product or service then make it worthwhile. Remember, your discount has to be strong enough to take customers away from your competition. A weak discount is usually not going to pull customers away from their usual place.

Advertising a deep sale or discount also has a psychological effect on your competition's employees and owners. Imagine you have an oil and lube shop, which charges $22 for oil and lube service. You notice one day a door hanger on every other house in the area with a competitor's special of $10 for the same service you offer. How do you think you would feel about that? You would feel discouraged and for good reason since some if not many of your customers will probably take advantage of this special. Ok, so you say, well I can endure this for now with the optimism that you will see those fleeing customers during the next cycle of their oil change. The following month, the same door hanger again reappears with the same special! Believe me, if you didn't feel discouraged the first time the special went public, you certainly will now. To make matters worse, you decide to drive by this competitor only to find their shop packed with customers. The point that I am trying to make here is the effect that a deep discount will have on competition. Not only would I feel discouraged but our employees would also feel the same whenever our competitors advertised a deep discount and I am sure the same was true whenever we advertised a deep discount.

You may not want or feel the need to advertise with discounted prices and that is certainly your option as a business owner. But at least keep it as an option, especially when you first open your doors for business. The important thing to remember is that those customers your trying to bring in when you first open are usually someone else's customers and will require a significant incentive to switch them to your business.

One more issue that can be a problem deals with employees who are on commission. If you have employees who are entirely or even partially on commission, then having a sale or discounting your services or products will obviously affect their commission amount. From the opening of our first shop, stylists would "tell" us that they wanted to be credited for the full amount of a service for pay purposes. Our stylists could earn an extra pay, dependant on the amount in revenues from the services they perform. This of course was in addition to their regular wages they earned. So by discounting the services such as haircuts, the stylist would earn a smaller amount in extra commissions. We found this to be a much bigger problem in other businesses that had their staff entirely on commission. The question is, do you hold their commission to the discounted or sales price, or do you pay them the same commission amount of the regular price. It was our policy; that any commissions or bonuses would reflect the price the product or services were sold at, regardless of the regular price. The reasoning for this, and this was backed by conclusive data of our own revenues, that our over all sales would increase when we ran a sale as compared when we did not have a sale. In addition, having a sale would usually add to our regular customers thereby increasing our business. And our stylist knew this; it was nothing knew to them. Sure they had to work harder, but the end result was a bigger paycheck and the opportunity to gain more regular customers. My recommendation is to keep the commissions or bonuses tied to the actual amount of the sale not the regular price.

8   CUSTOMERS AND QUALITY OF SERVICE

I would always tell our new employees that we spend a great deal of money to get new customers in the doors. Then added that they had about 30 minutes to convince that new customer to come back. One of the challenges you will face, as an owner is to get your employees to see how vital customer service is in the same way you do. Many employees will not value the quality of service as much as you do. You know that your bottom line has a direct correlation with how your customers perceives the service they receive. If the service is lousy or better somewhere else, they will not keep coming back. When we look at quality of service we are talking about a wide range of factors affecting the impression a customer has on your business. Factors such as how they are greeted, the cleanliness of your business, how long they have to wait, how problems or questions are handled, the attitude and appearance of your employees and many other factors that affect how your customer rates your quality of service. One of the most important factors is how your employees handle customers. You may have a product that is defective after a customer takes it home, but what makes the difference with the customer is how they are handled when they return with that product. In a online electronics retail business that I owned, we occasionally had returned items for defective reasons. The customer would receive a refund or a replacement in a timely manner. Many of these customers appreciated our quick response and became regular customers for other products we offered.

How many times have you heard the statement that the customer comes first or the customer is always right? Now, what does that really mean to you? You can have the top employees in the world, but without customers you have no business. Have you ever walked into a store and saw one person at the cashier with a long line of customers waiting to check out. Then you look around to find several employees walking around, one or two stocking products, a couple doing inventory, another writing some report, one on the phone and the manager in his office doing paper work. That is not putting the customer first! Sure, they all may be doing work but the priorities are not in line with the customers. In our business, we had a strict policy that when a customer walked in, we would stop what ever we were doing and attend to the customer. My employees knew that this was a critical issue with me. If a customer came in, I didn't want to see our employees to continue folding towels, sweeping, taking inventory, rearranging product or doing the schedule. I wanted them to drop what they were doing and attend to the customer, period. That is what I mean by putting the customer first! The other day I was at one of those national home supply hardware companies looking for a particular water valve. I walked up to an employee stocking items, and I asked if he had time to answer some questions. His reply was, "well, I don't have much time, I have to get these items stocked, what's your question?" I almost said, "Well, with that attitude, eventually you won't need to stock the shelves".

In the salon business as with many service businesses, the quality of the service performed on customers is certainly a big factor. A bad haircut assured us we would never see that customer back no matter how good everything else was. But a good haircut doesn't guarantee a return customer if the customer is treated poorly by the employees either. When we first opened our business, we would on a rare occasion have a customer tell us that they would never return. Reasons varied and sometimes-included factors not associated with the quality of their haircut such having to wait too long or the stylist not thanking them for the tip. In fact, most of these people who decided not to come back, where for reasons other than the quality of the hair service. Take the passenger airline business for example. I have seen where the aircraft arrived at the destination 30 minutes early only to find that we had to hold off the gate for 20 minutes waiting for the gate to open up. Even though the passengers deplaned about 10 minutes earlier than scheduled, some were very furious for having to wait on the ground for those extra 20 minutes. Another example is the automotive repair business. Have you ever received your car back only to find that the same problem was still there after driving away from the shop? What's even more troubling is when you bring the car back and they tell you that what they fixed needed to be fixed anyway and the problem is due to something else, meaning you will have another repair bill. Its important to understand that there will be an occasional problem as in the examples above. But if the problem keeps recurring then it will affect your business and impact revenues.

Having good quality service whether it's in the products you make or the service you provide does not happen by accident. It happens through a dedicated effort that includes training, standardization and evaluating. As a new business owner you will quickly know what factors determine good quality. In our business, we looked at every detail from the way we answered the phone to how we thanked them as they left. We then incorporated a policy on customer service in our operating manual that explained how we would do the things necessary to achieve good quality service. With every new employee, we would go over these items and evaluate them on an on going basis. Such things as how we greeted the customer, how we would take them back to the styling station, what we would do and say during and after the service and how we thanked them when they checked out were all important elements to quality service. Managers had the responsibility to ensure their staff members handled customers with the quality we set forth. We found that little things could make a big difference in some customers while in others nothing would make them happy.

Customer Feedback

I was at home one evening when I got a call from an irate customer who had just left one of our salons. As she explained, neither of our two stylists on duty greeted her or told her the approximate waiting time when she came in. She really became annoyed when a customer who came in after her was taken before her; again no one took the time to explain the circumstances. However, our two stylists were very busy as it approached closing time. Her service was a just a trim and she had no problems with the haircut which was done by one of our more competent stylists. The customer left a tip with the stylist at which time the stylist rang her up for the service. After the customer paid, the stylist turned around and went back to her station for the next customer. So what made our customer angry? Not only did no one say anything to her when she came in, but her stylist didn't thank her for the tip or for her business! After she explained the situation, I assured her that I would see to it that this wouldn't happen again. She told me that this was not the first time our stylists didn't show any appreciation and that she would never return to one of our salons again. No matter what I said, this customer was not coming back. Even though the stylist who performed the service lacked customer appreciation, the manager who was on duty should have thanked the customer before she walked out. Never let your customers walk out without thanking them even if they didn't buy anything. As an owner, you need to make sure that your staff realizes that their paycheck comes from those customers. Many employees lose sight of that reality or worse, have never gained that appreciation. This is something that continuously needs to be brought to their attention. Bringing it to their attention once is not going to last long. They have to understand just as you do as an owner, if these customers don't come back you will be out of business. One-way to drive the point home is with the words "This paycheck is provided by our customers" printed on every payroll check.

After the incident above, I started a customer feedback program allowing customers to rate their service with reply cards available at the checkout desk. This is nothing novel and requires very little effort and cost. If you have a word processor you can make them up on a standard post card size form. I asked 7 questions with room for comments including the name of the stylist who serviced them. On each question we would ask the customer to rate the particular item on a scale of 1 to 5. For postage we used post card rates and affixed a stamp on each one. This way the customer could take the cards with them to fill out at their convenience. As an incentive, the cards stated that a coupon would be mailed to them in appreciation for their time in filling out the card. We had a great response from all our salons with many of the customers expressing their satisfaction and continued loyalty. I would post each card in the break room for all our stylists to view. This was not only good feedback for us as owners but also for the employees. What is also very valuable were the comments on the cards. For example, some would tell us that the service was outstanding with the exception of "………". A few had disappointing ratings with some of those commenting that they would never come back again. What was most interesting was that the few customers who stated they would not return, none were because of their hair service such as the haircut or color. They were for other problems such as waiting too long or lack of appreciation by their stylist.

Another customer feedback method is via online. If you have a web site for your business, then encourage your customers to visit your site to fill out a customer feedback form. This can easily be accomplished by printing at the bottom of their receipt "Visit us at (your web site) and tell us how you liked your service". To encourage your customers to reply, offer them a discount coupon, which could be made available after completing the form or, you can mail the coupon to them provided they give you a return address. The other option is to contract with a company specializing in online customer feedback programs. There are many such companies and can be found through an online search engine such as Google, just type in "customer feedback programs".

Customer Complaints

When we first opened our business, our stylists were instructed to give out our phone number to any customer who couldn't resolve their dissatisfaction at the salon. And to my surprise, there were few customer complaints, especially for a young business. As we grew to 3 salons and eventually to five, our customer complaints increased with some valid and others not, and it became apparent that we could no longer try and resolve every complaint a customer had. What I also realized was that I was not the person in the best position to resolve the problem. That may sound funny coming from the owner but I was not a licensed cosmetologist either. Usually in the process of trying to resolve a complaint, I would have to go back to the manager and get her input, then refer the customer to the manager, again. In nearly all the cases, the customer wanted their money back. When the manager would review the complaint, they could tell if the service was performed correctly or not. In this business, you could not simply undo the color or haircut! However, if the service was not performed correctly, then the customer would be refunded the money or have the service redone. Basically, our managers had the technical expertise to make the proper judgment. As a result, I changed our policy making it the manager's responsibility for customer complaints. If you as the owner also act as the manager and work at the location, then you are the best person to handle complaints. I remember a particular case involving a customer who did not like her hair color. She came back a week later and complained to the manager but it was clear to our manager that the customer's color was performed correctly. The customer had simply decided that she did not like the color she had chosen. The manager refused to refund her money which was our policy given the circumstances. The customer then demanded to talk to the owner. The manager called me with the details and asked me if I would talk to the customer. I said no, and told the manager that she needed to be firm with the customer. Well, after a few minutes, the manager called me back telling me that our customer has called the police demanding her money back! The police actually did show up at the salon but informed the customer that they could not do anything for her and that she would have to find a solution with our salon. Our manager then approached the customer and offered again, to schedule an appointment for her to come back and have another color performed at our discounted price, which was five dollars off the regular price. The customer accepted the offer and to our amazement became a regular customer of our manager! How about that! So I ask the question again, who is in the best position to resolve a customer complaint? Sometimes it may not be you or even your manager but someone else who has either better customer skills or who has better technical expertise. Since I was not a cosmetologist, I did not have the expertise to judge whether a color or other service was performed correctly. If our manager could not appease a customer with a complaint, then our managers would tell the customer that she would get back with her or him. The manager would then discuss the problem with my wife or me from which a solution would be worked out. In my electronics business, I handled all complaints since I was the best person to handle them. In nearly all of these complaints the problems were a result of the unfamiliarity by the customer and were resolved quickly without an exchange or refund. Remember, this is not going to be something that goes on every day, hopefully. This will occur occasionally no matter how well you run your business. The point is that you should have a plan on how you want to resolve customer complaints.

Consumer Reporting Websites

This category of consumer reporting deserves a section all to it self. The internet has provided a whole new way to do business as well as to advertise and gain information. And this trend will continue to increase for both consumers and businesses. But a new field has popped up that businesses need to pay attention to. This is the field of websites devoted to consumer reporting of bad (or good) experiences they have had with businesses. One such websites is www.ripoffreport.com. As they state, this is a website for consumers to file and document complaints about businesses and individuals who rip-off the consumer. You may argue the merits of this type of mentality or even the legality of the website, but the fact remains that it is out there and growing with interest. I found out about it when it was mentioned in the news that seemed to be pitching the site. There are many documented complaints listed by consumers for the world to see as well as rebuttals by both businesses and individuals. And this is not the only website devoted for such uses, there are many others. My point is that as a business owner, you may want to include an occasional scan of such a website just to make sure your business name doesn't pop up. If you do find a consumer complaint, then you will have the opportunity to file a rebuttal.

9   THE COMPETITION

Would you help out or work for your competition? Some may be thinking, what kind of stupid question is that? Most would agree that competition is one of the biggest factors in the pricing of your products or services. If your prices are generally running about 20 percent higher than your competition, then you will lose business. For example, strong competitors offering deep discounts have largely affected the hair cut and dry cleaning business. For many years, I was a devoted customer to a dry cleaner business a few blocks from us. After some time we noticed a number of $1.50 cleaners opening. In our business locations, we saw more of these deep discount cleaners opening. We finally began taking our dry cleaning to a $1.50 cleaners; saving us over $2.00 per item which over a one-year period saved us about $175! We saw it in the hair salon business as well, where prices have remained low due to strong competition. The commercial airline business is another excellent example of strong competition. Customers are simply not going to pay more than they must. Face it, if there was no competition you could almost charge what ever price you wanted within reason. But the reality is that competition is here to stay and you will have to take the necessary measures to maintain or increase your market share or suffer the outcome.

The 3 Hostile Zones of Competition

Before we go any further lets define what we mean by "our competition". The first order of business is to categorize your competition as same, similar or dissimilar to your business. A business that offers the same products or services as you do can be classified as the same. A bagel and coffee shop across the street from your bagel and coffee shop would be categorized as the same. On the other hand, a bagel and coffee shop compared to a sandwich shop are similar but not the same, although both are in the fast food or snack category. Finally, a full menu restaurant is dissimilar to the bagel shop. A do it yourself car wash is similar to a drive through automatic car wash but not the same. The other significant area involves what I call the 3 hostile zones of competition. As a rule of thumb, anything less than a half mile was considered in the **target area**. Anything from 1/2 to 1.5 miles was in the **threat area** and over 1.5 miles was considered in the **neutral area**. Obviously, a competitor across the street categorized as "same" deserved primary consideration. Not only is this competitor an immediate threat for your customers but also for your employees! You should have a prioritized list of your competitors in terms of similarities and distances from you with the type of media they use for advertising. The higher the priority the bigger the threat and the more you should know them. This means that the closer and more similar your competition is to you, the more detailed information you should have on them concerning, hours of operation, prices, advertising and employee pay. Remember, this classification only applies to small businesses offering services or products in a local area such as you would find with merchants in a shopping center or strip center.

The 6 Battle Fronts of Competition

The question now is how do we effectively compete with our competitors? What are the things that you, as a business owner need to do to be a strong competitor. Remember, your competition is a business also trying to compete against you for customers and employees. There are 6 elements that you will need to understand in order for you to compete effectively. These are, customers, pricing, quality of service, advertisement, location and cost of doing business. These elements are interrelated in the long run, but each can be gauged on its own merits. There are other elements that could set you apart from your competition but these are more business specific and will be obvious to the owner.

Customers. Lets start with the customer since this is a driving factor for most everything else. With respect to your competitors, it's not only what you offer in terms of products or services but the means of how you make them available to the customer. A dry cleaning business may offer their service for $1.50, but if they are not open the hours and days convenient to the customer then they are not taking full advantage of their competitive price. They have to be competitive on both fronts of price and availability. Small things that may seem insignificant can mean a great deal with some customers. Such things as greeting customers, thanking them, asking them if they need help, listening to them and saying good bye are little things that will improve your rapport with customers. As mentioned earlier, we had comment cards for our customers that among other things would ask the customer how we could improve our service. This lets them know that we are interested in what they have to say. And it gives you the perspective from the customer. We are not saying you must act all the comments, but if the same comment keeps coming up then you have a trend, which you should act on. There are many other things you can do to show your appreciation to your customers. One of the things we would do was to have a monthly raffle for a free haircut. Customers would fill out a raffle slip with their name, address (for mail out coupon specials) and phone and placed it in our customer raffle box. The lucky customer would then be notified of their free haircut at the end of the month. Of course the more times they or a family member came in that month, the more chances they would have to win. The point is that anything you can think of to show your appreciation to your customers will most likely pay big dividends in the long run. A customer who leaves your competition for your business has a double effect of making your business strong while making your competition weaker. Remember, winning over a customer is the best way to effectively compete with your competitor.

Pricing. Given a choice, the public will usually opt for the less expensive product or service. There are other factors involved, but its safe to say that low price, compared to your competition will bring people in. Wal-Mart is an excellent example of this. When you run a two-day special of say 50% off, you can be assured your going to pull customers away from your competition. When one of our nearby competitors ran a $5.00 haircut special, our volume of customers was noticeably down. In fact, if on a particular day our volume was quiet down the first thing we would usually ask is if there was a special going on. Although this was temporary, it decreased our revenues, and it impacted our stylists since they would be making less money because of reduced tips, less retail commissions and less service bonuses. Deep discounts like this can also hurt your advertising effectiveness. Lets say you have an ad coming out on April 15th, and your competitor comes out with ad just days before yours with 50% off. How effective do you think your ad will be? Not only will it take business away from you, but your ad will probably be a waste of money and can send a message to your customers that your products or services are overpriced.

There are certain things you can do to be price competitive. First, if your main competitor runs a monthly ad with the same coupon special, then make sure your ad is comparatively priced if not lower. Running an ad that has a higher coupon price is a waste of advertising money. Some may argue that the slightly higher price is justified because there are some extra frills that are not offered by the competitor. Believe me, the customer in general is not interested in those extra frills, they are interested in the price. Take the airlines for example. I don't care how many extra frills come with an airline seat. The customer will almost always opt for the cheaper ticket. Second, honor your competitor's coupons and make sure your customers are aware that you will meet their price. In most cases, your customer will walk out the door if they bring in a competitor's coupon and you deny them the same price or similar price. In our advertisement, we would state that we would honor our competitor's coupons for the same service. We didn't do that when we first opened for business and in every case when we would not honor a competitor's discounted price, the customer would walk out the door. If you feel you can't honor their price then at least consider giving the customer your discounted coupon price. Third, offer your customers a discount for their continued loyalty. Airlines do this with their frequent flyer or rewards program. For example, customers may get a free sandwich or coffee after their 8th visit at a sandwich or coffee shop. Some grocery stores give customers a large discount after they have accumulated a certain amount in purchases. Be cognitive of what your competition is doing in terms of price specials. For example, one of your competitors may routinely run a deep discount the first week of December. Consider running an ad so that it comes out just before or at the same time as their ad with a significant discount. Your prices will undoubtedly determine your volume of customers. If your business plan relies on high volume then you must be price competitive, plain and simple.

Quality of Service. This is one area that shouldn't even have to be discussed but unfortunately it seems to be one major reason customers turn away. For starters, jot down the type of service you received on the next ten stores or businesses you visit. Ask yourself what you liked and didn't like about the service you received. This can be anything from how you were greeted to the quality of workmanship to the attitude of the employees. I cant tell you how many times we have had customers come in for the first time and tell us about how dissatisfied they were with the quality of service they received from our competition. I have also been on the other end of a customer complaint telling me that they would never come back to us because of the poor service they received from us. By the way, no matter what kind of business you have, you will eventually have a customer that will tell you that they will never return again for some reason. Nearly every business I polled, had customers so dissatisfied that they made it a point to let the management know that they would not return. In the salon business, quality of service is more than just how satisfied the customer is with the haircut or style. Complaints ranged from how long they had to wait to the type of music we played. I did learn that you just could not satisfy everyone all the time. For example, we might not be able to do much about an unusually long waiting period due to an unexpected surge in walk-in customers. However, a stylist making a customer wait while she is on a personal phone call is certainly something you can and should correct.

If you are going to be present at your place of business from open to close then you will have a pretty good handle on the quality of service your business provides. But, if other obligations preclude you from being at your business on a regular basis then you will need to gage the quality of service your staff provides. One technique we used was a customer feedback card. This identified problem areas that could be corrected before getting out of hand. It also sent a message to our staff that we were listening to our customers and what they thought about our service. It also told our customers that we were interested in what they had to say. Having a phone number for your customers to call with a comment on their service can also be effective. However, If you have more than one location then I would guard against handing out your business or personal number unless someone other than you will be receiving the call. A general manager's or area supervisor's business phone number would be more appropriate. If you maintain a database of customers with their addresses or email, then another technique available is to send a feedback card with return postage or email. Not only do these techniques provide you with the level of service provided in your absence, but it also lets the customer know that your aim is to improve the service they get.

A business that offers superior service to that of their competitor's will certainly enjoy a more satisfied customer and a distinct advantage over their competition. Our employees knew how important quality of service was to our business and I made sure they realized it was a priority with me. How you communicate your emphasis on customer service to your employees is up to you, but a complete or partial lack of it can certainly affect your ability to remain competitive. Remember, your employees can boost the quality of service giving your business a clear advantage over your competition.

Advertising. We found advertising to be one of the best tools in a competitive environment for a new business. If nothing else, it lets the consumer know that they have another option other than the main competitor on the block. Your competitor's advertisement also allows you to gain a great deal of information about them. If they run regular ads then you know when their ads come out as well as other things such as how much of a discount they offer, their operating hours and what kind of things they will be promoting depending on the time of year and son on. A change in the frequency of their advertisement can also be of interest to you. I remember in one occasion, a hair salon around the corner from us stopped advertising. I later found out that the salon was losing money and had limited their advertising budget significantly. They later went out of business. On another occasion, a very similar family haircutter across the street from one of our locations was no longer open on Sundays. We later found that they could no longer support Sundays due to a lack of employees available to work Sundays. On our next ad, we highlighted in large print, "Open Sundays". And as expected, our Sundays improved by a whopping 45 percent at that location.

When a person views your ad as compared to your competitor's, what will stand out in your favor? This is the question you need to ask yourself. I would always look at my competitor's advertisement and compared them with our own advertisements, looking for those areas that we could capitalize on. Prices, hours of operation, or the product you offer can give you a distinct advantage. Even the theme or image you portray on your advertisement can be an advantage. For example, all our ads had a picture of a family with the statement, "We Put Family Values Back in Style", with some words describing our services for the family. Within a few seconds of viewing our ad you could clearly see who our ads were meant for – everyone from granddad to his little granddaughter. This type of ad was clearly meant to go after customers of nearby family hair salons. Our prices were always in the low range that usually met or beat that of our competitors. If you see that you have a clear advantage in some area over that of your competitor, whether its price, product, services, or availability, you should highlight it in your advertisement. To gain a better understanding of how to effectively compete through the use of advertising, take a close look at advertisements in your mailbox. Your mailbox is full of examples on how to design your advertisement with your competition in mind.

As discussed earlier in the advertisement section, direct mail ads can easily be accomplished from your computer. Most publishing programs such as Microsoft Publisher, will allow you to design and print your own advertisements. There are also several inexpensive programs that have a database of residential addresses for direct mail purposes. If we had a competitor across the street, I would print out addresses within a half-mile radius of the competitor and then direct mail those residences with post cards offering deep discounts. This is a very effective way of targeting a particular competitor with selective advertisement. Even if the customer doesn't respond immediately, chances are that they will carry that post card around with them and use it on some occasion. The advantage is that you can pin point your area and mail out on the day of your choosing. Another similar means is using door hanger ads in the residential areas near your competitor. This is a much cheaper way to accomplish the same thing of selecting the place and time to advertise.

Location. The significance of location as it relates to your main competitor deals more with how visible and accessible your business is to the public. You may have a great business in a great location but poor exposure to the main street or center. If your competitor across the street has great exposure while yours is poor then consider moving to a space with better visibility, obviously easier said than done.

The significance of a great location implies strong customer volume and thus strong revenues. However, a great location in itself doesn't pay the bills or guarantee terrific profits. Suppose for example, you came across a great location for your sandwich shop in a new shopping center and it happens to be the only center at that intersection. It is surrounded by residential homes of primarily young families with a high school and junior high within one mile. The rent is high but based on your estimated revenues; you'll be in great shape. As expected, after opening you're doing a killer business and profitable on day one. Sometime later though, because of the outstanding area, other fast food businesses decide they want to be part of the action. Within a year, the area has developed with more strip centers with many new fast food restaurants. Your revenues have declined and your profits have nearly vanished. So, is this still a great location? To some extent, this is still a great location, but your competition has now soaked up much of the business that was once all yours. In this scenario, you have to face that you are going to lose business to your competition. How much of that business you lose depends on your coarse of action to retain your customers as well as your employees. We went through a similar scenario with our fourth shop. We got the opportunity to go in at a busy major shopping center when a space became vacant. The shopping center was at a major intersection with 16 spaces anchored by a major nationally known store. There was one shopping center across the intersection with a hair salon of a national chain. The other two corners were not developed yet. A high school was just a half-mile away and the area was surrounded with medium to higher income homes. Within two years of opening, the other two corners across from us were developed with shopping centers each containing salons that included another national chain salon. Our great location had now turned into a battleground of competition. Two years afterwards, one of our competitors who was first on the scene, which had enjoyed tremendous business before the competition showed up, finally closed its doors! We remained as a strong competitor.

If you move into a new area then you will most likely be getting some of your competitor's customers. Having said that, you can expect your competition to advertise in attempts to keep from losing their customers to you. When we would move into a new location, we would advertise aggressively with deep discounts along with a grand opening banner to bring in first time customers. Aggressive advertising means, newspaper ads, direct mail, door hangers, banners etc. In a similar fashion, when a competitor moves in, you can expect aggressive advertising to pull customers away from you, so be ready for it. If for example, a new shopping center is being built close by, then be prepared for a competitor moving in. Be ready with advertising and even consider handing out coupons or some other incentive to ensure your regular customers will come back. When a new competitor was getting ready to open nearby, we would give our customers a dollar or more off coupon (depending on the service) on their next visit. In addition, we would hit the area with aggressive advertising and further discounts.

Earlier we discussed the importance of the hours and days of operation as compared to your competition. You can have great visibility in a busy center, but if your closed on Sundays while your competition is open then you will loose customers. One of the biggest mistakes a business owner can make is to assume that their product or services are so superior that it doesn't matter if they are closed while their competition is open. I remember a particular Sunday when at one of our locations, our competitor across the street could not open that Sunday. Of course, we had a surge in customers requiring us to immediately call in other stylists from our other locations to help us out. I manned the desk, swept hair, got change, folded towels and so on, while our stylists continuously serviced our customers non stop all day.

This was a golden opportunity for us to shine for our competitor's customers of which we did. Many of those new customers said they would definitely return. Being a strong competitor means that your business will come through on those rare occasions when your competition has failed to deliver for whatever reason. In the above example, do you think that our competitor's customers said, "gee, that's too bad their stylist didn't show for work, I'll just go home and wait till tomorrow". Of course not, they were not willing to wait for tomorrow. When a customer goes from your place of business to your competitor's it is a customer you may never get back.

Cost of Business. Lets take a look at the airline industry in regards to how cost of doing business is an effective tool in competition. Many of us have heard about low cost airlines. These are airlines that have lower operating expenses which means their average cost per seat mile is lower than say a legacy airline such as one of the big three airlines. This lower cost allows an airline to be able to charge less for any given destination as compared to that of a larger legacy airline that has a higher operating cost. If the legacy airline doesn't match the same fare as the discount airline, then they will most likely lose flyers and in turn lose revenues. If they match the cheaper fares then they will have less revenues and possibly become unprofitable. Either way, the higher operating cost airline has more to lose than the lower cost airline. Overtime, this erosion of revenues can very likely put a business into bankruptcy and eventually out of business for good! That's the advantage of a lower cost operation. If you have a lower cost than your competition, then you can offer your product for less than your competitor and still be profitable while your competitor may not be profitable. This is one reason why we have seen so many jobs go over seas to a country where the operating cost is so much less. Consumers are just not willing to pay more for the same product or service. If you don't believe me than just walk into one of our super discount stores such as a Wal-Mart. The first thing you will notice is a packed parking lot.

Lets take two competing gas stations at an intersection across from each other. If gas station A is charging less than gas station B, who would you go to for your gas? Sure you have those that would choose B maybe for convenience (same side of the road), but overall, gas station A should have more customers. Lets say that gas station B has lost 30 percent of their daily average customers since A reduced their price and now has decided to match A's price to keep from loosing more customers. Both gas stations are paying the same whole sale price for their gas on average, but B is now loosing money on a monthly basis and is forecast to be in the red for the year, while A will have a small profit. If both are paying the same price for their gas, then why may one be profitable while the other is not? To answer this question you would have to look deeper into gas station B's cost structure, but a likely culprit is the difference in development cost between the two. Station A may have acquired the property year's prior and paid much less for the property and development. If station B barrowed the money for their higher development cost then the higher debt payments alone may be just enough to preclude them from making a profit unless they could charge more to the public. We experienced this in our own business. Our total cost to put up a salon averaged $38,000 per shop fully equipped with 6 styling stations. That was cheap compared to our competitor's cost of about $100,000 for a similar franchised salon. If you factor in the cost to barrow 75 percent of the development cost for say a period of 30 years at 7.125 percent interest, then the difference in interest cost alone amounts to $4,362 over a one-year period and a whopping $12,949 over a 3-year period! And that's just the interest alone. This amount of savings gave us an edge over our competitor allowing us more options. With a $4,000 a year cost advantage, you have many options such as additional advertising, higher pay for your staff, employee benefits, equipment improvements and many other options that can chip away at your competitor's ability to compete with you on a customer and employee basis. There is no doubt that a cost structure advantage can be a very powerful tool against your competition. This was just one example of a cost advantage. There are a number of areas where the business owner might be able to attain a cost advantage over their competition such rent, payroll, advertising, utilities and insurance.

Its safe to say that your business will dominate in some areas while you competitor will have the lead in other areas. One thing that I was always aware of at any particular location was our strengths over that of our main competitor. Whether your strength is in your prices, hours of operation, quality of service, location or products, you need to make sure the consumer is aware of them. Being open on Sundays while your competitor across the street is closed can be a big plus for some customers. Extending your hours to just one hour later on say Saturdays can be a big advantage. One of the things we would always advertise was the higher quality products we used in our color services compared to our competitor across the street that used a lesser quality product. Not only did we advertise the type of superior products we used, but included a $5 off coupon for all color or chemical services. A full service competing salon would charge $60 for the same service while our net price including the coupon was just $35! Although our profit margin per color service was less than our competitor, we more than made up for it in volume. Over time, our volume in color services picked up significantly allowing us to dominate in this area. As a business owner, the advantages or strengths you have over your competition will be apparent as well as your weaknesses. Take advantage of your strengths and advertise the areas you know you have a clear advantage over your competitor.

10   SETTING GOALS

One of the most overlooked elements of a small business is setting business goals or targets. Many small business owners will say that they don't need goals or that goals are for large corporations with many levels of managers. Believe me, setting goals for your business is important and can certainly be a big factor in your success. As a military officer we used goals to achieve many of our objectives that contributed to our combat readiness of our fighter squadrons. In our business, we set goals every year and monitored our progress in achieving those goals. After the first year in business we applied this to our businesses and found a distinct improvement.

There are five elements of goals. First, your business goals must be reasonable or achievable. Reasonable and achievable means that your goals can be met with the resources of your business and with your employees being able to support those goals. For example, in our business, a goal that met our reasonable test was to achieve $20,000 in retail sales for a certain year, such as year 3 of our business. An unreasonable goal would be to expect to achieve a goal of $40,000 in sales. Another reasonable goal was to reduce our shrinkage or unaccounted products to 3 percent per year. An unreasonable goal would be to expect to achieve no shrinkage per year. You have to determine what goals are reasonable and achievable which are specific to your type of business. If your pet grooming business is only open 5 days a week and closes at 3 pm, then it may be unreasonable to think you could attain revenues or sales that would be more in line if you were open say 7 days a week and open evenings. The number of customers we serviced in a year, month and week was another goal we set to achieve. Of course this was dependant on the location of our shop and how long that shop had been open. Setting unrealistic goals may seem like no arm can come from it but there is a psychological negative effect. Continuously under achieving your goals can put a dent in your moral as well as on your employees. This is similar as going to the gym and beginning an aggressive workout right off the bat. The next few days you are too sore to workout and may put off further workouts for sometime. Begin with small realistic goals that challenge your business, not make it impossible to attain.

The second element is a time factor defined for your goals. It was our goal to service 13,000 customers our *first year* of a new shop. It was our goal to redo a service no more than 2 out of every 100 customers our first year. A time limit for achieving a goal also allows you to set your next time period based on the results of the prior time period. If our goal was to service 13,000 customers our first year, but we actually serviced 15,000 then 15,000 would be the basis for my second year. I would then set a goal of say 16,000 for the second year and so on.

The third element of setting a goal is your method of measuring in quantifiable terms the performance of your goals. For example, I came up with the 13,000 figure based on the expected volume for each month of the year. Some months like November and December of course had more volume than others. Our customer volume was measured and tracked on a daily, weekly and monthly manner. This allowed us to see at any given time how we were doing against our set goals. Some goals like total sales are not difficult to measure on an ongoing manner, but others such as customer volume may require added mechanisms. Many point-of-sales (POS) systems allow you to measure your various goals with much ease.

Getting your employees or sales staff to work towards those goals is the forth and most difficult element of goal setting. You have to convince your staff in trying to achieve your business goals. They have to identify with your goals or else they will not work towards them. When they look at those goals they are not saying, gee I must work hard to achieve those goals so my boss will be happy or more profitable. They have to see what's in it for them. You may not agree with this but it's a reality you can accept now, or at a later time but at a higher price! This is where leadership and the ability to inspire others tie in and that's why I cover it in detail in this book. There are many different ways in getting your staff to go along. One way is with total performance incentives or TPI. TPI means that when certain goals are achieved, then you staff receives an incentive, which can be in the form of money, products or any other thing appropriate. For example, lets say your goal is $100,000 in retails sales your first year. And lets say you have broken that down to smaller goals for each month of the year with some months more or less than others. Your staff exceeds your June goals by 20 percent, which then entitles them to a $50 bonus in their check. Another method may involve "points" which can be cashed in for days off, money, products or other things. In our first shop during its first year, I told our employees that if they achieve a certain amount in shop revenues for a single month by the 6th month, than they would all receive a raise. They achieved it in the 4th month!

The fifth element deals with goals themselves. First, start off with few goals. Don't overwhelm yourself with too many goals. Keep it simple and straightforward. For example, list all goals no matter how many and then rank order them in importance. Now, pick the top three to five goals. These are your primary goals usually for your first year. Then break each of those goals down into a subset of smaller chunks. For example, you may set a sales goal of $100,000 your first year with a goal of $9,000 for the month of June. The level you break it down to can be as small as on a weekly or monthly level. Monthly is probably more appropriate for most businesses. Next, determine how you are going to achieve these goals. It means nothing if you set a goal and then leave out the specifics in achieving this goal. This translates into a plan of action. For example, in order to achieve a certain customer volume for the month of April we would increase our advertising level to cover 40,000 residences with deep discounted coupons. Remember, you are going to be on a steep learning curve your first two years. Be open to new ideas on how to achieve your goals. You'll learn quickly what works and what doesn't in achieving your goals.

If you have employees then its vital they are aware of your goals. I bet you that if you walked into 10 different retail or service businesses and asked the employees what their goals are, you would get a blank look. But if you asked the owner if they have goals, you would get a yes from everyone, hopefully. In the same token, if you asked the owners what actions they are taking to achieve their goals, you probably would find that they don't have any. I recommend that you post specific goals where all your employees can see them and the actions necessary to achieve these goals. Next, either distribute a letter or cover it in a meeting on how they are doing in achieving these goals. If they achieve a specific goal then let everyone know. The same if they don't achieve a goal, let them know. Achieving a goal can be celebrated with say lunch being brought in or some other type of celebration. This is in addition to any incentive program you may have of rewarding your employees. Last, reward yourself for achieving goals. Put it down in paper that if you achieve a specific goal then your going to treat yourself to a special event, whatever you decide. Other wise, goals become less meaningful to you.

11   BOOK KEEPING, AUTOMATION AND TREND ANALYSIS

With all the software out there, book keeping for the small business is simple and efficient. Programs such as QuickBooks and Peachtree offer user-friendly accounting programs well suited for the small business owner. We used a combination of Microsoft's Excel spreadsheets and Peachtree accounting to help keep track of expense items, daily revenues, employee payroll and inventory control as well as many other tracking items. At the end of the year, we printed out our operating and capital expenses and revenues, and then forwarded it to our accountant for tax preparation. The alternative is to pay someone to keep the books, which still requires some amount of work by you. Many of the current point of sale systems not only keep updated records but also allow you to process payroll to include check printing. These software systems allow you to maintain accurate records with options that allow you to determine productivity and sales trends.

One of the very useful outcomes of managing your business records is that it makes you well aware of what is going on behind the scenes. You become well aware of your operating costs and whether actual costs are inline with revenue or customer activity. I would encourage any small business owner to learn how to manage the business books and keep accurate records. If after some time you decide to outsource the job, then at least you will have the knowledge to correctly analyze the numbers for future planning. One of the elements we tracked on a daily basis was the number of customers we serviced. Our customers would initially sign in with the time they arrived. We would then enter the number of people who signed in for each hour into our tracking program. This program would show the volume of customers for any specific day or hour. Such information is very useful when estimating future volume especially for periods near the holidays. This then allowed us to properly schedule the right number of stylist to meet the anticipated demand as well as to make sure we had enough retail products on our shelves. Keeping track of the average daily volume also allowed us to gage the effectiveness of certain activities such as our advertising or when a competitor opened for business nearby. We found this trend analysis to be very useful for future planning purposes. The versatility of a spreadsheet allows you to customize it to maintain a database of any factors you want to track and gives you a simple format of entering and categorizing expenses. Many point of sales programs will not only keep track of how many customers came in hour to hour but also how much time they had to wait before being serviced.

Automation

I think most business owners would agree that automation of routine tasks is cost effective, eliminates the possibility of errors and allows you to focus on other business activities. For example, a computerized point-of-sale (POS) system is far more efficient than the old style cash register systems and integrates other elements such as payroll, schedules, inventory, expenses, customer data and sales into one central program. There are other elements that can be automated and integrated with a central computer that even include video monitoring, environmental control, employee sign-in/out and payroll tax reports. You can even have your doors modified with an entrance security monitor (entry key pad or card swipe) that allows you know which employees came in after hours and at what time. You can even have your point-of-sales system call in automatically after closing time to your office computer and download the day's sales numbers. However, one of the pit falls of automation is not having a plan when the automation no longer works. For example, the other day I walked in a coffee shop of a large nationally known company only to be told that they could not serve anyone because their computer (point-of-sales) system was "down". And that is not the only time I have seen a business close because their computer was down. As a business owner you need to have a back up to your automation systems, especially those systems such as your point-of-sales that handle sales transactions. For example, if your computer goes down, then you should have a procedure to handle sales the old fashion way. Having a calculator or inexpensive cash register with a price list is a good back up in case your point-of-sales system goes down. If your merchant credit card system goes down or the phone service is interrupted, then you should have a back up using a manual imprinter with charge slips. Your back up procedures should be posted in a separate binder covering in detail the steps in using the back up system. Clear guidance should also be established covering conditions requiring your cash register clerks to change to your back-up procedures. In other words, what set of conditions would require your employees to switch to the manual or back-up system. A manager of one business (not mine) told me that when their computer went down, they sat around waiting for it to come back up. I asked him how long their office told him it would be before the problem was resolved. He said he hadn't talked to anyone so he didn't know. Apparently there was no procedure or instruction to call the office if the computer went down, so there they sat, on the clock! Automation is a wonderful tool but reliance on it as the sole system of operation can be very costly. I would encourage you to develop a back up plan just incase your automation goes down.

Trend Analysis

If you have a business, ask yourself, how are my sales last month compared to 6 months ago, last year or two years ago, or how many customers did we have last month versus the same month last year. Trend analysis is a very useful tool to help you gage the direction of your business and should become a regular routine of how close you are monitoring your business. For example, if you keep track of your customer volume on an hourly basis then over time you would have an accurate database that would allow you to forecast customer volume as a function of the time of day for any particular day of the week. Analyzing this data for a given period will show a trend or pattern. This trend may show that customer volume is increasing or decreasing at a certain rate from month to month. In addition, this information can be compared to data you have from a year earlier. For example, you may discover that customer volume has increased in the month of October at a rate of 10 percent each year over the last five years. However, if volume shows a decline from the previous year, then this may be indicative of a problem. Analyzing customer volume or sales can help you determine manning requirements in anticipation of future demands. For example, based on previous years of customer volume data for the holidays, we were able to forecast the number of customers and the number of stylists needed. Similar analysis was used to forecast other special events allowing us to optimize our schedule to meet the anticipated demand.

Almost any quantifiable data can be tracked and analyzed for use in managing your business. A spreadsheet is ideal for entering your data and allows you to tailor it to your particular needs. You can even combine different sets of data such as customer volume and average sales per customer. Productivity can also be measured and compared over time. We would measure the productivity of our stylists and compare it over time allowing us to gage whether our productivity levels were in line with our forecasts. Such data can also be compared with another event such as advertising. Another useful product is comparing customer complaints overtime. For example, lets say you keep track of the number of customer complaints for each month. Comparing this data to previous months, you discover that the number of customer complaints has been increasing on average every month over the last 6 months. This clearly shows a trend but the data is more meaningful when compared to the number of customers per month. For example, if the number of customers per month has also been increasing along with the number of complaints then a more accurate analysis would be the number of complaints per 100 customers. You can see that a particular direction or pattern can be misleading without a comparison to other data.

Keeping track of expenses over time is probably one of the best uses of data analysis. We would keep track of every expense item such as supplies, utilities, payroll, rent, etc for each month and compare it with the same month from the previous year as well as from month to month. In itself, this analysis is useful but it becomes much more relevant when compared to total sales for the same period. For example, lets say that the cost of supplies has been increasing on average over the last two years. But when it is compared to sales, we find that the cost of supplies as a percentage of sales has actually decreased. On the other hand, if the cost of supplies as a percentage of sales has increased, then this would certainly warrant further investigation and further close monitoring. As one can see, good analysis of data overtime involves collection, processing and comparison and is a major factor in the health of your business.

12   SHRINKAGE, THE DISAPPEARING ACT

If you carry retail products then undoubtedly you will discover that you have missing products at some point. We usually inventoried our retail product about once every three months finding that we were usually short of what we should have in stock. Sometimes we were missing just a few items and other times we were missing a lot more. Of course this begs the question of where did it go? Over time, missing product can add up to a substantial amount impacting your bottom line. Of the five shopping centers that we were located at, encompassing over 70 merchants, I found not a single exception to missing product whether it was retail, supplies or other items such as hand soap dispensers or paper towels. Of these, missing retail product can be the most damaging to your business. This is because a missing $5 product at your cost is a lost sale of $10 to a customer. On occasion, we would get a call at our office from a stylist telling us that we lost several sales to customers because we were out of a certain product. This was product that our computer showed we still had in stock. Yet we were out of that product on our shelves, losing revenue due to lost sales. More on this subject later. The reality is that you will likely have missing product in the course of your business.

When we talk about shrinkage we also can include missing supplies and other items used in a business and even money out of the nightly deposit or cash register. We've all heard of stories where a trusted employee made off with thousands over time. There are many elaborate schemes employed by trusted ones and even family members that can completely devastate a business. It's reported that employee theft has surpassed theft by shoplifters. Nearly every business I polled, there was reported employee theft. In our business, I found it to be more of a problem than first imagined but it was a manageable problem and one that I made a high priority. There are a number of things you can do to minimize stealing or missing products, but first I will discuss means of tracking what you should have versus what's on hand.

Just How Much Are You Losing

One of the first things you need to do is have a system to account for your retail and supply products. I suggest a point-of-sale system that keeps track of products in and products out. There are many point-of-sale programs on the market that do this and a lot more. These programs will print out a current inventory list that you can use to compare with actual products on hand. For example, bar coding allows you to enter the quantity of products coming in, thereby updating your inventory of what is on hand. When an item is sold or used as a supply item, then it is "swiped" or entered as used for supply or sold, thereby updating your inventory automatically. Once you have such a system in place then you have an accurate means of determining the extent of your missing products and whether you are above or below what you should have. If you don't have a point-of-sale system, then there are other methods to keep track of your products and supplies. Programs such as QuickBooks and Peachtree let you maintain an inventory, which allows you to keep accurate records. Products that are sold or used as supplies can be easily entered with a few keys strokes, allowing the program to adjust your inventory levels and even alert you to when its necessary to restock a particular item. A cost of sales report can be generated at the end of the year for tax purposes or any time that you desire a profit or loss analysis. These programs will also generate reports that give you detailed information on products that are selling or being consumed the most. Another method, although it is more work, is to simply keep track of your products on a spreadsheet. Let me add that there is no single best method that will do the job all the time. Several methods may be required to accurately account for your products and supplies. You'll find that an accurate means of tracking your goods will also be one of your best defenses in deterring theft by your employees or anyone with access to your business.

Taking Action

Once you have a reliable and accurate inventory system in place then you can put a plan into action to minimize your loss rate. Be aware that the amount of money you spend to reduce your loss rate can get to a point which just doesn't make sense. For example, lets say you spend $5000 on a system that reduces your loss rate from 8 percent to 4 percent. But lets say you want to get that down to a max of 2 percent. To get your loss rate down to 2 percent may require a system expenditure of $10,000 above what you already have in place. You may be saying that over time the extra $10,000 system will pay for it self. It may but remember the system will most likely need maintenance and repair and eventually will become obsolete. In addition, that $10,000 may involve interest payments. A more accurate question to ask your self is whether that $10,000 can be spent somewhere else which will deliver you a greater return than the extra 2 percent you gain from your lost product. However, if you have a large operation with sales in the 100 thousands or millions, then a slight percentage reduction in missing product can amount to a large savings.

As we found in our business, some of the missing retail product was due to our employees not accounting for it when they removed it from the retail shelf to use as a supply item. If stylists ran out of hair spray from the back bar area, then it was necessary to take a bottle of hair spray from the retail shelf for customer use only. In this case our procedure required the stylist to fill out a retail ticket showing that the product was used as a back bar item. This way we could make an adjustment in our inventory program to account for the item. The problem arose when an item was removed without documenting it. The item would then show as missing when a count of our retail was accomplished.

One method we used to identify individuals engaged in theft was the use of surveillance cameras. In one instance we were able to identify that one of our stylist was servicing customers and then pocketing the money. The tapes of her activities gave the police conclusive evidence to arrest her. Our surveillance system also allowed us to detect if any of our employees were coming in after hours, engaging in any illegal activity, or if we had a break-in during the night. Our surveillance system also allowed us to monitor how our customers were being serviced. It's important that any surveillance system you set up be secure so as to reduce the chance of tampering. Our cameras were linked to a time-lapse recorder stored in a locked cabinet in our back room. The cabinet was secured to the wall over an electrical outlet. The cable was routed through the wall and then up through the ceiling so that there was no access unless someone wanted to rip the wall apart. This was all done to restrict any access to the recorder, electrical plug and cable unless you had a key to the cabinet. I might add that the cabinet was very sturdy and unlikely to be broken into without considerable effort. The time-lapse recorder is designed to allow you to recorder for longer periods over 24 hours with a single VHS tape. There is also technology that will allow you to monitor in real time from any where you have access to the internet. The camera is linked to your computer that records onto the hard drive as well as provides access through a phone line. This gives you the ability to monitor your business from anywhere you have access to the Internet or modem. One of the other benefits of the camera was the role it played in deterring theft. When you have that camera out there for everyone to see, people are usually going to respect it. They know that if something becomes missing, then someone is going to review the tapes. Occasionally I would take one of the tapes and play it on the monitor in front of some employees just reassure them that it is indeed a real surveillance system. The benefit of deterrence was my real objective for the cameras of which we found worked very well.

Another method of identifying an employ stealing requires a bit more undercover work and is not 100 percent conclusive but there it does provide some deterrence. Whenever we could identify missing money or items and were able to narrow it down to a certain time period, then over time you could narrow the list of suspects.

What ever the reason for the missing or unaccounted product, you should stress to your employees the cost and impact to your business. We would post the loss in dollar amounts of our missing products in each shop as well as discuss the issue at our meetings. Keeping an eye on the product to guard against theft as well as following the proper procedures when using the product as a back bar item was highly stressed. I would also stress to our employees that missing products not only takes away sales and reduces commissions, but also reduces profits, which is less money for other things such as pay raises! If you have a camera with a time-lapse recorder, then make sure you position the camera to cover your retail product shelves. This may require you to have several cameras with corresponding recorders.

13   EMPLOYEES

There can be no doubt that your employee group is essential to the success of your business. But it will also be the one area that presents the most problems and the most difficult to control and manage. From dental to hair salon businesses, the story from owners is the same. Trying to balance between the needs of employees with that of the business has become an enormous challenge to business owners. Trying to cover your schedule with employees that all have limitations to their work availability is like trying to wrestle with an alligator. Some won't work at night or can only work certain hours, some want a certain amount of weekly hours, some won't work certain days, some won't work alone, some want overtime and so forth. Factor in the rising cost of doing business with rising health care insurance premiums and you can see why business owners opt out for something less stress full. One thing is for certain, the more prepared and knowledgeable you are with employees, the more successful you will be in managing your employees.

Finding Employees

I used to tell our employees that one of our most important resources is our people and our customers will never let us forget it! Finding dependable and talented employees is probably one of the most challenging aspects of a business. What may even be more challenging is retaining good employees once you have found them. It's not as simple as just running a help wanted ad in the local newspaper and picking the best candidate from hundreds of applicants. Typically we would receive maybe 4 or 5 responses to a help wanted ad as with many other businesses seeking employees. And many of them would want to conduct a phone interview when inquiring about the job. Some people would call and immediately begin laying down restriction such as no nights or weekends, wanting overtime and willing to only work from 9 to 5 pm. Granted the pool of individuals we were seeking had a specialty, which involved about one year of cosmetology school, state board exams and tools of the trade. There are several avenues to take when it comes to recruiting and although it may seem like a lot of work, the right people can make the difference between a successful or unsuccessful business.

Recruiting should usually begin with your local newspaper help wanted section. Ask yourself, if you started looking for a job where would you begin looking. Most employees I interviewed said the help wanted ads of the local paper was the first place they would look for a job. Your local newspaper will have more guidance on how to place a help wanted ad, but usually the help wanted section is divided into categories depending on the type of position. Your first task is to look at the Sunday's edition of the paper and specifically the help wanted section you will be advertising in. Once you have found the section, look at the ads of other employers looking for employees, this is your competition. Not only do you compete with them for customers but also for employees! From these ads you should get a good idea of how to compose your ad so as to be competitive with other similar businesses. For example, other businesses in your category may be offering employee benefits such as medical/dental coverage, 401k retirement contributions, bonuses and so forth. If you don't have such benefits to offer, then you need to make up for it in other areas. Before we had medical insurance, many people calling on our ads would ask if we offered medical coverage. Of course we had to tell them no, but to make up for it we offered a slightly higher salary then our competitors and a generous incentive bonus plan.

One of the first items of your ad is describing the job and the qualifications of the individual you are looking for. For example, "need licensed electrician for full time position with homebuilder, must have 5 years experience," and then the rest of your ad to include resume requirements, if any. There are a variety of ways to state the job and qualifications requirements just remember to keep it brief. You can list further requirements and particulars when they call or apply for the job.

One of the most important decisions you will have to make when it comes to help wanted ads is whether to state your starting salary or wage. This can be a positive or negative based on what your competition is advertising or what the prevailing starting pay is. Remember, your advertising space will be limited and very costly. You cannot afford to describe all your benefits plus talk about what a terrific work environment you have without it costing a fortune. Always start off with your best item. If you know that you have one of the best starting salaries or wages, then put it down first. If however, your starting pay is slightly below the average but you offer greater incentives and benefits then word your ad accordingly such as, "great pay package with top benefits: medical, bonus pay, paid vacations, paid holidays and much more". Or if pay is your greatest asset then start with, "$15 an hour starting pay plus benefits, call for an appointment..." Putting down intangibles such as, "a fun place to work" or "this is the place you have been looking for" are a complete waste of money. Be specific with concrete items that appeal to the applicant.

When an applicant calls on your add, it's usually advantageous to limit the amount of information for several reasons. When someone responds to your ad you don't know if the person over the phone is one of you competitors trying to get detailed information from you. Yes, its been done and more often then you might think. The most important reason though is that it's very difficult to describe the entire pay package and benefits over the phone. You don't know if that other person is listening to what you're saying and may tune out at the wrong time or might not fully understand what you are describing. For example, as part of our pay package we offered a bonus incentive plan based on total service revenues. It was much easier to grasp it by looking at our bonus chart then by listening to someone trying to describe it over the phone. What happens is that people get information overload and will not be able to fully understand or retain what you are telling them. I remember on one occasion, a job seeker called on one of our ads and wanted to know in detail about our bonus pay. I could tell she was getting confused and was getting a negative impression of our pay. I explained it would be much easier to understand it if she could come in where she could take home our handouts on our entire pay and benefits package. Some people will call and immediately "inform" you of what they are not willing to work such as no weekends or nights. You might think this is good that these type of restrictions to work come out now rather then at the interview. However, we have had applicants who stated they were not able to work nights and then changed their minds after seeing the pay and benefits package, realizing that a couple of nights a week was worth the pay and benefits package. The other problem with giving too much information over the phone is that you cannot read their expression. By reading the reactions you get a good idea if the applicant understands you or if you have brought up something they didn't like. Remember, your objective of a help wanted ad is to get applicants to come in and fill out the employment application and conduct an interview.

Another source of advertising for employees is bulletin boards. We would post help wanted ads at beauty schools where we could recruit trainees as receptionist and then as stylist once they were licensed. Trade publications are another good source or other such publications that target the type of business you have. One other area that we found very useful was a mailing list of cosmetologist maintained by the state cosmetology board. The price of the mailing list was a function of the criteria we requested such as how many cities and so forth. Any type of licensed or registered trade group such as barbers or cosmetologist will usually have a mailing list maintained by the state or county or possibly by private firms specializing in mailing lists.

A mailing list will usually be the most expensive option in your recruiting efforts, however it can also be the most productive in many ways. When you advertise in a newspaper your ad becomes less personalized and confined in the amount of information you can present in the space provided. The advantage of the direct mail approach is that you can include much more information including more detail on your pay and benefits package. The other advantage is that although direct mail will be received by a majority of people not looking for work, it will allow some to compare between what you have to offer and what they are currently getting. Some of our most productive and talented employees were the result of our mail outs, who left their employer to work for us. In addition, the recipient for future consideration will likely keep your letter or card, whereas a newspaper ad will usually be tossed out. We had people call us inquiring about a job three years after receiving one of our mail outs!

Direct mail is expensive but there are several measures you can take to reduce your costs. We always printed our mail outs from our office using either a word processing program or another program such as Microsoft's Publisher for post cards. With a good black and white original you can make mass copies at a copy center. We created our post cards to fit 4 per an 8 x 10 inch sheet of heavy stock paper. You can then either have the copy center cut the sheets or cut them yourself with a slide cutter. Postage for postcards is minimal and even less if you have a bulk rate account with the postal office. A more expensive but appealing option is the letter mail out. Each letter is on a standard 8 x 10 sheet with envelope. The cost is significantly more, up to twice the amount as the post card option but you have a far more professional appearing product and a lot more room to add things. Be careful not to overload your main body of your mail out. If there is too much information, then your audience may set it aside until they have more time to read it. Bring up your power hitters to the top so they are read first. If your biggest item is pay then list that as number one. Always start off with your strong points. My rule of thumb was that people were not going to spend more than 15 seconds on it or read more than 5 lines. So I wanted to make sure that I could entice the reader enough in those first 5 lines to capture their attention and want to read more. I also used a bullet format making it easy to read and retain the information.

Another area that is very effective but many times overlooked is your own employees, especially a new employee. On several occasions, a new hire would bring in one or two applicants from their previous job. We had a cash incentive program to our employees for every person we hired that our employees recommended. Of course we had conditions such as the individual must remain with us for a minimum of 6 months and be available on a full time status. Your incentive plan should be generous enough to motivate them and should spell out the conditions to avoid misunderstandings in the future. Our incentive bonus would be paid after the six-month qualifying period.

Another option is through employment agencies or online web sites such as Monster.com. If your business has a web site then consider having an "Employment Opportunities" page for prospective applicants.

The quality of your employees is a direct result of your recruiting and screening efforts. The more people you have applying for your positions, the higher the quality you have to choose from plain and simple. The recruiting process should also be a continuum of your business operations. Failing to do this could very well get you in trouble later on. Probably our biggest mistake after we opened our first business location was to discontinue our recruiting and hiring efforts after we had our staff.

The Interview

I recall from several books, that hiring quality people requires you to sort through all your applications or resumes and after a thorough background check, select the best applicant. I guarantee you that these folks have never had a small business. It just doesn't work like that. In most cases, an applicant for a low skill job, typical of a small business, is not going to wait around for you to do all that stuff. You will find as we found that you better be able to ascertain at the interview the hiring status of the applicant. Your typical job applicant will go from business to business applying for a job and may take a job offer that looks good on the spot. And we are not just talking about low skill individuals either. I bring this up now before we discuss the interview process because in many cases, you may decide to hire someone during the interview as we had done.

After spending considerable time, money and effort to get a qualified applicant in the door, then comes the real work of conducting an interview and job offer. Before you show up for the interview, make sure you are organized with handouts so that they can reference the information at home. If an applicant has several interviews that day, which is the most likely case, then they are just simply not going to remember everything you told them. Below is a list of items that you should have in writing and serve as a checklist of things to cover at the interview. This way, you have eliminated a future misunderstanding that could be costly to you and your employee. Our biggest problem concerning the interview and hiring of employees when we first got started was the misunderstandings between the employee and employer.

Pay
Overtime, the rate, how its calculated
Benefits

                Eligibility
                How they are calculated
        Business hours of operation
        What days and times the employee is expected to work?
        Dress code
        Description of duties you expect from employees
        Services or products you offer to customers and price ranges

        To remedy the problem, we found that a questioner as part of the application package served to clarify gray areas that had haunted us in the past after we hired the applicant. It also served as a reference guide for me while conducting an interview. This allowed me to prescreen each applicant with the information they provided on the questioner to determine if this individual was suited to our operation. Examples of questions on the questioner were: How many Sundays a month can you work, are you able to work at least 3 evenings a week till 9 pm, what is the minimum hours per week you need, are you willing to travel to another one of our locations for a day if it means more hours and more money, do you have your own transportation to work, do you have your own equipment, are there any restriction we need to know about, do your feel comfortable with a hair color service, about how many men's haircuts can you do an hour and other questions that pertain to the applicants availability and desires. There are many other questions that will be job specific. We had questions that dealt with their experience and knowledge of cosmetology. When you have it in writing then there is little chance of an employee coming to you after you have hired them complaining that they didn't agree to this or that. For example, lets say, the applicant says they are willing to work every other weekend and work no more than 2 evenings a week. That looks good to you and you hire them. Now, after the schedule comes out, that new employee comes to you and says, "hey, I don't work Friday evenings and you scheduled me for the entire weekend, I was under the impression it would only be one weekend *day* every other weekend." If you think this example stretches it let me tell you it happened to us as well as to other employers. Misunderstandings do occur at job interviews. When we came out with our new job application and questioner, there was no "misunderstandings" keeping us out of trouble down the road. I just wished I had come out with the questioner when we first opened for business, it would have saved us time, effort and money.   For businesses that are open 5 or 6 days a week and from 8 to 5, then availability of employees to work the schedule is usually not an issue. But for those businesses that are open 7 days a week from mornings to the late evenings, then employee availability becomes a central issue to your operation, especially in a retail or service business. We found it extremely difficult to find employees who could or would work every weekend and evenings. Most will work some evenings and Sundays but not all. Applicants who would not work any Sundays or evenings, no matter what the reason, were simply not offered employment. A word of caution though when turning down an applicant because they cannot work your schedule. Be nice to that individual and explain the circumstances of why you need people available on weekends and nights. That person may be well qualified except for their availability. And that person may know someone they could recommend or they themselves may become available to work your weekends and nights down the road. We had many instances where an employee was not hired because of restrictions to their work availability but who later came to work for us when their situation changed.

What about that good old job resume, shouldn't that be a primary factor in evaluating their suitability. Job resumes are fine and I certainly recommend including them in the application phase, but we found the application along with the questioner was more than adequate to move forward without a resume. However, for advanced supervisory or management positions, then resumes play a more vital role. In general, one of the first things I would look at in a job resume or application is the total number of jobs the applicants had in the last few years. Too many jobs can spell trouble. In almost every case where the applicant had many jobs over a short time span, that individual did not stay with us very long. Next, if you decide to hold off on hiring them until you have more information, then call their last one or two employers, depending on how long they were at their last few jobs. A recommendation by a previous supervisor, no matter how positive it is, should not be the only factor to determine whether to hire someone.   Other factors to include job history, experience and availability should be considered. Once you have all the information, then you can determine the suitability of the applicant for your operation. As said, in most cases you can determine their suitability during the job interview.

There are many factors to consider when determining whether to offer employment to an applicant. We found the following six factors the most essential in determining whether we made a job offer to an applicant:

- Availability to support our work schedule
- Competence
- Appearance
- Customer skills
- Ethicalness
- Attitude

Ethicalness is a factor we found difficult to gage accurately at an interview but can be assessed by looking at several other factors. There is no single question or indicator that gave us a true measure of the ethicalness of a job applicant. However, I found that after 45 minutes to an hour interviewing an applicant I could form a reasonable opinion on the applicant's ethicalness by looking at such things as job history and prior convictions. If I suspected a problem, then I would dig deeper through interviews from prior jobs, especially if the applicant had not been at a job very long. The remaining factors are easier to judge by the end of the interview. I have had applicants begin to criticize previous employers almost as a warning to me that I had better watch my step. I even had one applicant tell me that he was going to sue his last employer concerning pay issues. I obviously did not offer jobs to these individuals.

Preparation on your part is essential prior to any interview. Remember, they are also going to be evaluating you, your business and your staff to determine if they want to work for you. On more than one occasion, an applicant would come back after the interview and talk with our current employees asking how they liked working for us! Rarely will an applicant have just one job interview scheduled. You may be saying why should your business have to go to such lengths to appeal to a job applicant, let them go work somewhere else. In a loose labor market that may be a temporary luxury, but when the labor market is tight as it was from 1996 to 2001, you will be fiercely competing for quality employees with other businesses. The key word of course is "quality". As the employer, you must be able to recognize quality applicants, which are very rare in a tight labor market. Keep in mind that the applicant your interviewing could be your next star employee, your future manager, your most loyal employee or that person who saves your business one day. On several occasions, that person who seemed to be just another person interviewing for a job turned out to be an invaluable employee. One question you should ask of every applicant is, "why are you interested in applying with us". Many applicants are there because of something they liked in a help wanted ad or mailer they received from you. However, some are just driving by and simply came in to apply on the spot. Some of these applicants will say its just one of many jobs they are applying for while others will tell you that they live very close by or that they know someone who worked for you. Sure many will say that they are leaving their present employer for this and that reason, but the question remains what brought them in to you in the first place. In our case, what I was looking for was the individual who said they wanted to work where it was busy. Many with this response had been in at one time, and some had even had their haircut or styled there. We found that applicants who came in on a referral or based on some knowledge of our shop performed better and were more reliable overall. Your reputation as an employer travels quick and far. If you've develop a good reputation then you can expect to see applicants coming in for no other reason than your reputation. And that has far better results than running help wanted ads in your local newspaper. You will undoubtedly develop your own techniques to determine the best applicants for your specific needs as we did with our business. Getting quality applicants in your door is one of the first crucial tasks in developing a successful business. Once that applicant understands what you have to offer along with the responsibilities of the position, then you are ready to move forward to the next step.

The Job Offer

You will find as we found that some applicants will accept what you have to offer flat out. But many will have conditions or restrictions that they will lay out on the table during the interview. Now comes the bargaining. Its easy to say, here is the package, here are the conditions, take it or leave with no discussions. I always felt that in many of our applicants there was some wiggle room and it was my job to determine just how much. Availability and pay were the primary issues of concern. My approach was always to test any conditions or restriction and try and negotiate more flexibility. You will have to determine your bottom line that you would not be able to live with. Lets take pay for example. Some interviewees will come in and agree to everything but then add something like this, "I can work all the weekends and nights with all the other conditions but I really need more pay". You may say, well maybe the higher pay is worth it if they will provide you with the coverage you desperately need. If this will be your only employee, then the higher pay may not be a critical issue. But if you have several employees, then you must consider what the effect will be on the other employees. You may think that your present employees will understand. Most likely, your other employees will not understand and some may even quit over the fact that your going to pay a new hire more than they are receiving. You may even be saying, they wont find out. They will find out! In this example, you simply cannot offer greater pay to this applicant, but you may be able to approach the pay issue from a different direction. For example, our pay system was composed of a base wage, a productivity bonus plan, which was a percentage of their service revenues and a 15 percent retail product commission. We also offered extra weekend pay if the employee worked a full weekend as well as other incentives. So when someone wanted a higher wage, we would point out that if they were willing to work the higher volume periods such as weekends and nights then they could add substantially to their gross pay with their bonus, weekend pay and retail commissions, which could easily add 20 to 30 percent more to their hourly pay. We would also point out that if they were willing to travel to one of our other nearby locations, when on occasion we became short handed, then they would have more hours and thus more income. All together they would have the potential to earn more than what they were asking. In addition, we offered medical insurance, paid vacation, holiday pay and more. The bottom line is that pay must be looked at in its entirety to include benefits, and not just simply the hourly rate or salary.

Anther example is one who wants a higher starting pay and when they realize they are not going to get it will then come back and say, "Well, if I am going to be at this pay rate then I want a minimum of 40 hours and no weekends or nights". At this point it would become apparent that the interviewee is someone that's just not going to workout and time has come to tell that person the offer you have presented them is the best. In a tight labor market, many will go on to the next interview and at the end of the day will take the best offer or try again the next day. How far you are willing to bargain must always be weighed with the condition of the labor market and your particular situations.

Some will tell you that they need a minimum of so many hours and will want you to guarantee it. Do not ever guarantee minimum weekly hours. Guaranteeing them so many hours a week means that you are guaranteeing their weekly pay no matter how little they are on the schedule. If for example you must close your shop for a day then your employee still gets paid the guarantee! When we would hear this we would tell them that its our business policy that we can not guarantee hours or pay but most likely they would be working so many hours a week. We would also let them know that the more weekends and nights they were willing to work, the more hours they would get. We would further tell them that they could get extra hours if they were willing to travel to another one of our salons to fill in, provided there was a need. Or, if they were willing to come in for someone who called in sick or couldn't come to work for some reason, then they would be getting more hours. Of the greatest challenges were applicants who were well qualified but who didn't want to work Sundays or evenings. Our condition of employment was that everyone had to work Saturdays and a minimum of two Sundays a month along with 3 evenings. However, some would be willing to work say every Sunday and Saturday but no evenings. This exception can be very beneficial if some of your employees are willing to work every evening provided they only have work one Sunday a month. This arrangement allows you to cover your schedule and please your employees. The only condition I would layout is that everyone must hold up his or her end or else we would go back to the original work schedule.

Lets say your applicant has agreed to everything and you are completely satisfied as the right person for the job, now what. Do you hire them on the spot or tell them you will call them soon to let them know? If you've decided to hire them, then let them know on the spot and give them a day to begin work. On the other hand, if you tell them that you will call them back in a couple of days to let them know if they are hired then you risk they will accept a job somewhere else. You will only make this mistake once or twice before you rethink when to offer the job. If we found someone right for the job we would hire him or her on the spot. We would also get them on the schedule as soon as possible. We found that the longer we waited to put a new hire on the schedule the more likely it was that person would not show for their first day of work. Even if you don't need them right away, have them come in and start work. If you need to checkout one of their references from say a previous employer, then try to contact them immediately before the applicant leaves so you can make a final determination. Another approach in the case you need to checkout a reference is to let the applicant know that everything looks good and hiring is assured as soon as their reference gets back to you. We had cases where we hired someone to replace an employee who was leaving but ended up losing the new hire because we waited too long to bring them in. How long should you wait? If you can, bring them in the next day after you hire them, or as soon as that person is ready to start. If at the interview you tell the applicant you will call them on their hiring status, they will most likely press on to their next scheduled interview. Why risk loosing a well qualified applicant to your competitor if you know your going to hire them!

There is a red flag you need to watch out for when you have hired someone. If you have offered a job to someone but cant get a firm date from them on when they would like to start work, then you might want to continue interviewing more applicants. On several occasions, we found that those individuals who told us that they would get back to us on a start date never called us back. Every time we would call them they would either tell us that they would let us know soon or would not return our calls. Its difficult to pin point the reasons why people become illusive but we found a few. It could be that an individual has accepted and started a job somewhere else and they want to see how things are going to work out with the other job. This way if things don't work out with their first choice then they can quit and work for you as a back up. Don't be so naive to think that people don't back up their jobs, they most definitely do. The other reason is that a new hire wants to lock in the job with you but still want some more time to look and interview at other places. Another reason is that the applicant has taken your offer to their present employer with the threat of quitting if they are not given at least the same offer you gave them. Then there are those that have agreed to all your conditions including working all weekends and nights to assure themselves that you will not hire someone else over them while they continue to look for a better offer. But when their other options have not materialized and their faced with working for you, they will call you up with a firm start date but then tell you that because of new "circumstances" they are just not able to work the nights and the weekends as originally agreed upon.

    You might be asking how can you hire someone on the spot without doing a background check or at least calling their last employer, if that is your procedure. It has happened to us where we hired someone at the interview and gave them a start date only to find out later that day the applicant had either lied on their application or had deceived us in one way or another such as telling us they quit there last job when in reality they were fired! In those cases we either called the applicant back and told them we have rescinded our job offer or told them when they came in for work, if we were not able to contact them prior. By signing and agreeing to the terms of the application, they are assuring the accuracy and truth fullness of what they put on the job application. And it should state that falsification of any sort is grounds for denial of employment at *any time*. That means that if we found that the applicant has lied or mislead us on any part of the application, then we could let them go even after they started work. But make sure you have such a statement on your application right above where they sign it.

It's not totally out of the realm that the person who you just interviewed, works for your competition. When we opened our first shop, we had an individual call and come in for a job interview. When the person showed up, she was very well dressed with a brief case and began taking notes as I described our pay package. She agreed to all the conditions and stated she would call us with a firm start date. Well, she never called us back. We later discovered that she was the person in charge of recruiting for a major salon chain in the valley! Her job was to find out what the competition was offering so that they were more prepared to compete with our pay package. This was not the only time our competitors would be visiting or calling us. On several occasions the manager of a nearby salon would walk in to our salon and try to recruit our staff on the spot. On one occasion to their job offer, a stylist replied to their manager and said why would we leave here to work for you making less money and working later evenings? To which the competitor's manager said, "because were the biggest chain in the valley". I wrote to their local corporate office and told them how unethical that type of action was, among other things. I found this situation at many other types businesses where a competitor would actively engage in recruiting efforts that went as far as entering the place of business to handout job applications!

Probationary Periods for New Employees

A probationary period puts your new hire on notice that a final decision on their job status is dependant on their performance. This allows the employer an opportunity to evaluate the employee's performance and determine if the employee is suitable for a permanent employment position. If the employer determines that the new employee is not performing to set standards then the employer can terminate the employee. As such, the employee is not able to claim an unfair termination or dismissal, provided that the employer has met certain conditions. We instituted a probationary period for our new hires after a couple of years in business and found it did actually make a difference. We had all new hires sign a statement acknowledging the three-month probationary period. As a business owner, if at the end of the probationary period you have decided that the new hire is not working out then by all means let them go. Don't keep them around another month to see if things improve. In most cases, things will not get better and in fact will probably just get worse. Another reason to let them go sooner than later is due to the unemployment benefits eligibility requirements. The longer you wait before terminating them the greater the chance that they will qualify for unemployment. If you wait a long period before you let them go for problems or performance (such as showing for work late), the unemployment office will question your motives as why you waited so long. They may grant unemployment benefits to which you will have a tough time fighting to get reversed. Remember, unemployment benefits are not free, you end up paying for unemployment claims against your business through higher unemployment insurance premiums, typically referred to as SUTA or State Unemployment Taxes. High unemployment rates can devastate your bottom line and certainly put you out of business! That's not only a de-service to you and your business but also to your employees since higher operating costs from higher unemployment taxes reduces your ability to grant pay raises!

A probationary period should not usually be longer than 3 months but in some jobs a longer or shorter period may be warranted. For example in many unskilled jobs where close supervision is maintained, a shorter probationary period is justified. Positions where close supervision is not maintained may justify a longer probationary period to evaluate the employee's performance. If you're not sure how long to make it, then go with 3 months to be on the safe side. Anything over 3 months may appear as if you are trying to escape from future unfair termination suits. There are certain steps that you should follow when instituting a probationary program. First, always put it in writing and have the employee sign it with the employee getting a copy, before they begin work. Don't wait days before giving them a copy. Second, tell the employee when the period starts and when it ends. Third, let the employee know what the probation period means and what criteria you are going to use to determine if you are going to offer a permanent job at the end of the probationary period. These three actions will keep you out of trouble down the road if you happen to terminate the employee. In some cases, courts have determine that an unfair dismissal or termination occurred because the employee either did not know they were on probation or were not informed of the performance requirements. If you decide not keep the employee, then give the employee notice of termination and make sure you have documentation to support your decision. A history of arriving late for work is an example and one that should be documented. You should also show that you gave the employee ample notices of any problem areas and discussed it with the employee. Finally, consult with your state employment agency or labor office for their policy on probation and unfair termination laws.

New Hire Training

Initial training or orientation for your new employees is essential for you, the customers and employees. We would usually set aside about two hours on the first day of work as orientation training for any new employees no matter how experienced they were. This type of training is designed to familiarize the employee with those procedures that are particular to your operations. It is your time to say to your new employee, this is how we operate and do business here. It is also a time to cover your rules and policies. We found that a checklist was very useful, but you could also use a lesson plan to cover your objectives. As each item is covered then I would initial the item and date it. If you prefer you can have the employee sign the completed checklist and place it in their folder. I would usually take the operating manual and go through it briefly but emphasize certain areas. This is not only a good review of the business operating manual but it also serves to familiarize the employee with the manual and how to reference it. Every phase of your operation should be covered from opening to closing procedures. I want to emphasize that this is not training as related to their primary trade skill but relates to how your particular business operates. In our business, the stylists came to us trained and licensed so there was no need to train them in their particular trade. But, no matter how many years they were experienced as a stylists, they still needed to be trained in those things particular to our business. As an example, our hours were from 9 am to 8 pm. Our policy was to accept customers up until closing time, which on a weekday was 8 pm. This meant that in our operations, an employee may not be leaving until well after 8 pm or at least until the last customer's service was complete and closing duties were accomplished. Some of our new stylists had worked at places where they would stop taking customers so that the stylists would be out at closing time. One may argue the merits of what closing time means, but in our business it was not left up to interpretation. Our customers expected us to take them up until closing time and that's exactly what we wanted our stylists to do. That's focusing on the customer!

Don't make the mistake of waiting too long to accomplish this training. In our business, a new stylist could come in the first day and immediately begin performing services to our customers with absolutely no training. She may not know how to operate the cash register or write a sales receipt but at least they could service the customer and with some help from other stylists there, be able to pick up the transaction procedures over time. The question is whether they are picking up bad habits from the other employees. If this is allowed to progress then problems will magnify over time as they are passed from one employee to another. The longer you wait to train your new employee, the less receptive this employee is going to be to what you have to tell them. They are going to feel as if they are doing something wrong and now someone has to come in and tell them otherwise. Don't wait; train them during the first few hours of being on the job, its well worth the time and money.

If you offer benefits that entail an eligibility period, then this would be a good time to cover those details now along with their initial training. For example, we had different eligibility periods depending on the benefit such as medical versus holiday pay. They would learn about these benefits during the interview and again during their initial training. Then, after they began work, we would include a letter with their first pay statement, establishing when they would become eligible for their benefits such as vacation. This way there would be no doubt in their mind when they would meet eligibility. If you offer medical insurance then its important to make sure they are informed about the medical plan and the necessary forms to be filled out and the cost to them. We usually had the forms filled out at least two months before the medical coverage would begin to insure the provider had everything they needed to begin coverage.

Supervision Of New Employees

After your new employee gets settled in, it's a good idea to have someone supervise your employee. Your new employee will have questions or concerns and may feel awkward calling you up for question they have. Another employee that works with them is usually the best person for this task. Your manager is a good source but again, your new employee may feel a bit awkward coming to her supervisor with questions.

Employee Recognition

Some of your employees are going to perform well and above the call of duty. As a rough figure, about 10 percent of your employees will consistently perform below your desired standards and about 10 percent will consistently perform above desired standards. Of those top 10 percent, you will have some that on more than one occasion have gone well above what you ever expected. It's the type of person who after working 6 days comes in on Sunday to fill in for someone who didn't show for work and does so with a positive and respectful attitude towards you and your customers. It's the type of person who will work alone when another employee didn't show for work and does so in a very busy climate and maintains a very positive attitude. We're not talking about a person who comes up with a smart idea on occasion. We are referring to that person who has taken the lead and kept your business open during a critical situation that would have otherwise been closed. I remember receiving a call from one of our stylist early one Sunday morning, which was one of our busiest days. She informed me that one of the other scheduled stylists, Amelia had not shown for work and that the salon was getting very busy. I immediately called Amelia's house and was told she had left for work. I went straight to the salon to do what I could to help our stylist which meant taking phone calls, writing out tickets, operating the register, sweeping hair, folding towels and so forth. Shortly after arriving at the salon, I got a call from Amelia, telling me that she had been in an accident and apologized that she would be late. She refused to follow my advice and take the day off. She kept insisting that she needed to come to work to help out the other stylist since it would be to busy for one. By the way, no one else I called to ask if they would come in to help, including the manager, returned my call. Amelia made it in about 11/2 hours later after getting her husband to pick her up from the accident and drive her to work. I later found that her car was totaled in the accident, yet she insisted on coming to work. How many people do you know that would come straight to work after being in an accident, after totaling their car? Not many! Amelia was one of those exceptional employees every business owner would love to have.

Ways to Recognize Employees

There are several ways to recognize outstanding performance other than handing out large sums of cash. The problem with cash bonuses and awards is that it becomes meaningless or counterproductive unless the award is substantial. Sure some employees will truly be appreciative over a small cash bonus, but many would resent anything other than a hefty amount. Three words can sum it up by an employee who receives anything but a large amount, "is that it"! Other means of recognizing that special employee include but are not limited to the following list:

> Birthdays off with pay
> Special mention in newsletter
> Special mention or plaque at annual dinner or meeting
> Picture and name in advertisements
> Personal letter of appreciation
> Designated parking slot
> Gift certificates
> Flowers and card (at location)
> Additional vacation day
> Pay raise for consistent performance

Any one or combination of the above would be appropriate in recognition of an employee. A pay raise would be considered but only if that employee continues with such outstanding performance. Certainly other factors would have to be considered as well to justify a pay raise but I would definitely not award a pay raise for a single noteworthy act. Placing an employees picture or name in your advertising is an effective way to recognize that employee's outstanding performance. Not only is it an effective way to recognize an employee, but it's also a great incentive for all your employees especially if they are involved with sales. Employee of the year or quarter is another effective way to recognize outstanding performance especially when awarded during an annual dinner or large group meeting.

Departing Employees

A time comes when either you must let an employee go or the employee has decided its time to move on for whatever reason. In either case it's never pleasant when an employee must leave your business but in this day and age employee turn over tends to be a frequent event. Long gone are the days of opening your doors for business and having many qualified job seekers. Today we live in a very competitive business environment where the competition is not only for customers but also for qualified employees. As such, our work force is constantly being bombarded with attractive offers to switch jobs for a more lucrative position somewhere else. Or, we find ourselves with employees that simply have decided that the work schedule means nothing and will show for work when it's convenient for them. Its no wonder that today's work place is suffering from the effects of a high employee turn over. But whatever the reasons, it's a factor that today's employer must deal with effectively or find a way to get the job done without employees.

Terminating or Discharging Employees

My attitude was that we were going to make sure that every employee was given more than a fair chance when problems arose.

Employees are not objects to be discarded and thrown away at the first sign of trouble. However, there comes a time when you feel that there is nothing more to do but terminate employment. When that time has arrived, there are certain things you need to consider. First and always, never fire anyone on the spot in a hastily manner. It could come back to haunt you later. When we had decided to let someone go, it would be at an appropriate time. One concern was the schedule and whether we had someone to cover the immediate shift of the departing employee. Further more, did we have documentation to support our position and did we have documentation showing we confronted the employee with these issues. The paper trail is very important so that if at a later time, the employee files a wrongful termination suit or tries to collect unemployment benefits, you will be able to support your actions. Even when you have a paper trail to justify your decision, it's a good idea to have a witness such as another employee or business associate that can substantiate your claim. The harsh reality is that an outside agency such as the office of unemployment benefits or a jury is going to look at the employee as a victim of a greedy business owner. I remember a case told to me by the owner of a large firm involving an employee they fired for stealing. The employer didn't fire the individual specifically for stealing since they did not have indisputable evidence as such. They terminated the employee without reason. The employee filed suit on the grounds of race discrimination against the employer. The employer's attorney recommended an out of court settlement for the reason that even though there was evidence to *suggest* the employee was stealing, it was not 100 percent clear and thus the jury would probably rule in favor of the employee! The reality was that it was cheaper to settle out of court then to pursue it in court. We had an occasion where one of our employees was stealing and we had her on video with indisputable evidence to fire her. This was a clear case for termination without worry of a wrongful termination claim. However, in another case involving theft, we did not have conclusive proof but we still went ahead and fired her for other reasons that we had documented over time. We later discovered conclusive proof that she stole from us.

    When you have decided to let your employee go, you can verbally give notice to the employee through your manager or yourself or hand the employee a letter stating your actions and reasons along with a verbal statement. Some people might argue the position that a lead-time would be the right thing to do. But if your letting the employee go for stealing or falsification or not showing for work, then I would not give any lead-time. We would always include a letter to the employee along with our verbal notification. Your letter should spell out the actions and date it takes effect, even if it's immediate. It should also spell out what things are required by the employee and the actions if your requirements are not complied with. For example, we would require the employee to turn in any keys or other items that were ours before leaving the premises. Also, we would require them to clean out their styling station after packing their equipment. The letter would state a certain monetary amount that would be deducted from their final paycheck if these required actions were not complied with. Remember these actions must be reasonable and should be spelled out in your employee manual as policy. When the employee complied with the actions such as returning a key, then we would give them a signed receipt showing they had complied. As always, consult with your state labor office to make sure any action you decide on is legal.

I would also place a note in the employee's file describing the circumstances of the termination along with the date of notification and last day of work. Terminating someone can be a very stressful matter for you and the employee and should be handled carefully to avoid problems later on. On one occasion, we had been having problems with one of our employees when we finally decided to let her go. One day as she was walking out the door after closing, she turned back and said to the other stylists, "I really had a good day", meaning she had done well with tips. After counting the cash drawer, we discovered we were missing $75 from what we should have had based on the receipts and register tape. We suspected this employee and for good reason when you considered all the other problems we had with her. But we did not have conclusive proof and would not unless she confessed. I had decided to fire her when she came in the next day of work for a host of other problems we had with her. I prepared a letter explaining that she was being terminated for a host of reason to include her lack of performance, not showing for work, tardiness and other problems, but I did not mention the missing money. When she came in for work I greeted her and told her I needed a word with her in the back room. I handed her the letter and told her that I was letting her go in which she replied, "for what reason". I told her that I did not owe her an explanation, but I was letting her go for a number of reasons as mentioned in the letter. She replied, "and what other reasons". I told her the reasons listed on the letter were enough to warrant her termination. To my surprise she replied, "You don't have the guts to tell me the other reason". I replied, "look, we are both very busy, I have a business to run and you have a job to look for, I want you to clean out your station and you are never to set foot in any of our salons again, good day". Later on, I found out from one of the other stylists that this employee, while on duty some time prior, had been contacting attorneys trying to determine what were good reasons to sue an employer. Apparently, she believed she could file a wrongful termination suit against us if we had terminated her for stealing without sufficient proof. That's why she wanted me to say that I was letting her go for the missing money. That's why she made the statement of "having a very good day" in front of me when leaving on the day of the missing money. She knew exactly what she was doing and had I not kept my cool, she may have ended up with a lot more than $75 from us! How you handle a termination is up to you, but this is one area that can have a devastating impact later on.

    Make sure that if you are terminating someone for improper behavior that you have proof that you have given the employee warnings, preferably written notices or a witness, if there were verbal warnings. There are things that would not warrant any warning before you let an employee go such as proof of stealing or coming to work intoxicated or hostile or threatening behavior. But try to have a witness when you let someone go for such onetime offenses. Consider that if you let someone go without sufficient proof then that individual could be awarded unemployment benefits against you. You will be given a chance to contest a claim for unemployment but if you are claiming you fired a person for problems at work then the unemployment office may ask for a list of incidences with dates and actions taken with proof of such incidences. If you don't have proof of the incidences then they may award unemployment benefits against your account, which will raise your unemployment insurance tax rate!

Remember, the tax rate is applied to your total payroll so if you have many employees, a small increase in your tax rate could have a large impact overall.

As an employer you need to contact your local labor board and make sure you know all the laws affecting termination of employees. What may apply in one state may not apply in another. Above all, don't rely on what another employer did or what you read about, have the current facts in front of you before you act!

14   FEDERAL REPORTING REQUIREMENTS WHEN HIRING

After you have decided to hire an applicant, there are certain state and federal requirements you must meet.   Not fulfilling these requirements can mean trouble for you that could involve penalties and fines.   I will cover all the latest requirements but it is the business owner's responsibility to ensure they are in compliance with up to date hiring requirements.

Work Eligibility, Form I-9

You must verify that the employee is legally eligible to work in the United States.   The employer and employee must each complete their parts of Form I-9, *Employment Eligibility Verification*, and the employee must show original documents that prove identity and work authorization.   We would always ask the employee to photo copy their social security card and drivers license and attach it to the I-9, thereby fulfilling the identification verification requirements of the I-9. Remember, it's not the employee's responsibility to complete the paper work; it's the employer's responsibility.   If you hand your employee the I-9 to fill out and the employee never returns it, then its up to you to get the form back for your records.   If you get inspected by Immigration Services of the Department of Home Land Security and get violated for a missing I-9, they are not going to accept the excuse that your new hire failed to return it to you!   If I had an employee who failed to return it on their first day of work, then they would not be allowed to begin work until the I-9 is turned in and all requirements are fulfilled.   You can download the I-9 form and a list of acceptable documents at http://uscis.gov/graphics/formsfee/forms/I-9.htm.

W-4 Withholding Allowance Certificates

This is the employee's entry into the U.S. tax system.   The employee should complete a federal Form W-4, *Employee's*

Withholding Allowance Certificate, and any applicable state or local withholding form so that you know how much income tax to withhold. If the employee does not complete a Form W-4, then you are <u>required</u> to withhold federal income tax based on a martial status of "single" and zero withholding allowances. You can download a W-4 and information on withholding at www.irs.gov/pub/irs-pdf/fwr.pdf.

U.S. Department of Justice
Immigration and Naturalization Service

OMB No. 1115-0136

Employment Eligibility Verification

Please read instructions carefully before completing this form. The instructions must be available during completion of this form. ANTI-DISCRIMINATION NOTICE: It is illegal to discriminate against work eligible individuals. Employers CANNOT specify which document(s) they will accept from an employee. The refusal to hire an individual because of a future expiration date may also constitute illegal discrimination.

Section 1. Employee Information and Verification. To be completed and signed by employee at the time employment begins.

Print Name: Last	First	Middle Initial	Maiden Name

Address (Street Name and Number)	Apt. #	Date of Birth (month/day/year)

City	State	Zip Code	Social Security #

I am aware that federal law provides for imprisonment and/or fines for false statements or use of false documents in connection with the completion of this form.

I attest, under penalty of perjury, that I am (check one of the following):
☐ A citizen or national of the United States
☐ A Lawful Permanent Resident (Alien # A_____)
☐ An alien authorized to work until ___/___/___
(Alien # or Admission #) _____

Employee's Signature   Date (month/day/year)

Preparer and/or Translator Certification.
(To be completed and signed if Section 1 is prepared by a person other than the employee.) I attest, under penalty of perjury, that I have assisted in the completion of this form and that to the best of my knowledge the information is true and correct.

Preparer's/Translator's Signature	Print Name

Address (Street Name and Number, City, State, Zip Code)	Date (month/day/year)

Section 2. Employer Review and Verification. To be completed and signed by employer. Examine one document from List A OR examine one document from List B and one from List C, as listed on the reverse of this form, and record the title, number and expiration date, if any, of the document(s)

List A	OR	List B	AND	List C
Document title: _____		_____		_____
Issuing authority: _____		_____		_____
Document #: _____		_____		_____
Expiration Date (if any): ___/___/___		___/___/___		___/___/___
Document #: _____				
Expiration Date (if any): ___/___/___				

CERTIFICATION - I attest, under penalty of perjury, that I have examined the document(s) presented by the above-named employee, that the above-listed document(s) appear to be genuine and to relate to the employee named, that the employee began employment on (month/day/year) ___/___/___ and that to the best of my knowledge the employee is eligible to work in the United States. (State employment agencies may omit the date the employee began employment.)

Signature of Employer or Authorized Representative	Print Name	Title

Business or Organization Name	Address (Street Name and Number, City, State, Zip Code)	Date (month/day/year)

Section 3. Updating and Reverification. To be completed and signed by employer.

A. New Name (if applicable)	B. Date of rehire (month/day/year) (if applicable)

C. If employee's previous grant of work authorization has expired, provide the information below for the document that establishes current employment eligibility.

Document Title: _____   Document #: _____   Expiration Date (if any): ___/___/___

I attest, under penalty of perjury, that to the best of my knowledge, this employee is eligible to work in the United States, and if the employee presented document(s), the document(s) I have examined appear to be genuine and to relate to the individual.

Signature of Employer or Authorized Representative	Date (month/day/year)

Form I-9 (Rev. 11-21-91)N Page 2

Questionable Form W-4

When an employee submits the withholding Form W-4, you are not required to send it to the IRS. Obviously, you should retain the original for your records and give a copy to the employee. However, if the employee submits a W-4 that looks questionable, such as claiming 10 dependants, then you should include a copy of the W-4 when you file your *Employer's Quarterly Federal Tax Return* (Form 941). This allows the IRS to review the employee's tax filing history to see that the employee has generally paid the proper tax amount without any delinquency. If the employee claims an exemption from withholding tax then I would submit a copy of the W-4 with your next 941 report.

Verification of Employee's Name and Social Security Number

It's a good idea to verify the match of the name and SSN, in case of a name change or fraud. I have on several occasions received notice from the Social Security Department after submission of the W-2's, that one of my employee's SSN did not match the name on the W-2. The reason can be a simple mistake or that the employee's name had changed from the original Social Security card. Asking to see their Social Security card is allowed as well as making a photocopy of it so that you can verify the correctness of the name and Social Security number (SSN) that you enter in your payroll records as well as any payroll processing software (QuickBooks, Peachtree etc) and to check the correctness of the W-4. Accuracy ensures that the employee can get all the benefits to which he or she is entitled, such as unemployment insurance and eventual federal retirement payments, and it ensures that you wont receive notices of errors and potential penalties from the IRS. You can call the Social Security Administration at 800-772-6270 to verify the information of up to five employees at a time. Be prepared with your name (employer's name or business name), and federal tax ID number and employee's name, SSN, sex, and date of birth. More information, including ways to check on more than five employees, how to correctly format complex names, and what to do if the employee never gives you a SSN, are available at www.socialsecurity.gov/employer/critical.htm.   As always it is your responsibility to make sure you are following the correct procedures and a good way to do that is to refer to the IRS web site listed above. The IRS will send you a quarterly pamphlet describing any changes for employers as well.

State Reporting Requirements of New Employees

The employer is required to report all new employees to the state shortly after the employee begins work.   This information is matched against child support records at the state and national levels to locate parents who owe child support.   In addition, this information is used to combat fraud by cross checking with other departments such as unemployment insurance, disability insurance and workers compensation benefits.   The method of reporting to the state varies from state to state but can usually be accomplished by faxing a copy of the W-4 to the state new hire department.   Other methods include Internet online reporting, interactive phone reporting or the good old fashion mail in report!   More information, including links to each state's requirements is found at:
www.acf.hhs.gov/programs/cse/newhire/employer/private/nh/newhire.htm.

This is a great web site that allows the employer to see what their state requirements are for reporting; including the time limit you have for reporting, which is usually 20 days.   Phone numbers are listed along with what documents are needed.

The American Payroll Association

The American Payroll Association works closely with the IRS and SSA and offers classes and publications with accurate information to educate employers.   IRS and SSA experts speak at many APA conferences and one-day seminars.   Information about the APA is available at www.americanpayroll.org.

The above requirements are for the reporting of *new* employees to state and federal agencies.   After these employees are hired and become part of your payroll, then there are other federal and state requirements that pertain to incomes taxes, social security, Medicare taxes, and unemployment taxes that must be deposited and reported. These requirements are discussed under a separate section entitled "STATE AND FEDERAL DEPOSIT AND REPORTS FOR EMPLOYERS".

15   THE DEPARTMENT OF LABOR (DOL)

As a small business owner, the Department of Labor (DOL) can be your best friend or your enemy. As an employee, DOL is certainly a best friend in the work place. I will say though that many small business owners view DOL as too anti-business, impeding progress and productivity. However, I view DOL as an agency that levels the playing field for all businesses, large or small. Otherwise, some businesses, especially larger businesses, could exploit workers making it more difficult for other smaller businesses to compete effectively for any given state. There is no doubt that conforming to the laws and policies under the DOL increases the cost of doing business. For example, without it, some businesses would not be required to pay overtime or comply with minimum wage requirements. Businesses that can comply with the DOL laws and policies in an efficient manner will certainly enjoy a more competitive advantage than businesses that cannot comply with the same level of efficiency.

As a small business owner, I found that knowing the federal and state labor laws was essential to our operation. This means sitting down and studying the federal and state labor laws. The U.S. DOL has an excellent web site at www.dol.gov that provides the business owner with volumes of material to study and reference. For example, the DOL web site offers you a section just for employers and covers the following areas:

Wage and Hour Division
Wage and Hour Division Compliance Assistance Materials
The Minimum Wage
FairPay Overtime Rules
Wages by Area and Occupation
Fair Labor Standards Act (FLSA)
elaws Fair Labor Standards Act (FLSA) Advisor
Overtime Pay Requirements of the Fair Labor Standards Act (FLSA)
Summary of Proposed Changes to Strengthen Overtime Protection

If You Hire New Employees Not Covered by Social Security
Employment Standards Information for New Businesses
Family and Medical Leave Act (FMLA) Advisor
Poster Advisor
Frequently Asked Questions on Federal Contract Wage Determination
Federally Financed or Assisted Construction Contracts
Wages & Work Hours Statistics

As you can see from the list above, the DOL web site provides the small business owner with a wealth of invaluable information.

In addition to the U.S. DOL, each state will have a labor department that may provide further restrictions, laws and policies. Some states for example may define a pay period as no longer than on a weekly or semi-monthly basis while other states will have a longer period. The labor division of Arizona does not have a minimum wage or an overtime law for example. However, their web site will tell you that *if* the employer is covered by the Fair Labor or Standards Act (FLSA), the federal minimum wage and overtime laws apply. The U.S. DOL defines overtime as anything over 40 hours in a workweek. So, in Arizona if an employee works more than 40 hours in a workweek they are due overtime pay. However, California goes on to further to define overtime that includes any time worked over 8 hours in a day, regardless of how many hours they work in a week. As you can see, not only must you know and comply with the U.S. DOL rules but also the laws established in the state you do business in. Each state's labor division has a direct link on the U.S. DOL web site for easy access.

Record keeping is an area where you can also get into hot water. Each state will define what records are required in terms of labor factors. Such records as times cards, work schedules, or any other document relating to wages and schedules will usually be required as a matter of record. In California an employer can be fined and charged with a misdemeanor for failing to keep required records as defined by section 1174 of their labor division. How long you must keep them is up to your state. It was our policy to never discard our records no matter how long.

As you would suspect, the U.S. DOL as well as the states labor divisions do have the responsibility to conduct investigations on complaints filed by employees. If the allegations have merit, you can bet that the labor office will begin to investigate the matter. It is interesting to note that the U.S. DOL web site has a section that displays results of some of their investigations with corresponding fines to the businesses. My best advice is that if an issue arises then contact your local labor division with your question or issue. We did so on several occasions and found them to be very helpful. They usually wont give you advice on a matter but will tell you what the laws are so you can make your decision that will hopefully keep you out of trouble down the road.

Consolidated Omnibus Budget Reconciliation Act (COBRA)

The Consolidated Omnibus Budget Reconciliation Act (COBRA) gives employees, who have lost their medical insurance the option to continue their medical insurance for a limited period of time. COBRA is administered under the Department of Labor (DOL). The program applies under certain circumstances such as voluntary or involuntary job loss, reduction in the hours worked, transition between jobs, death, divorce, and other life events. Qualified individuals may be required to pay the entire premium for coverage up to 102 percent of the cost of the plan. This means that the employee must now pay the total cost of their insurance premium. For example, Stacy either quits or you fired her and she and her family were under your medical benefits plan. Her total premium charged to you by your medical provider was $300 a month. You have been paying 50 percent of the premium. She pays the other 50 percent, which you have been deducting from her paycheck. When she no longer is your employee, she has the option to continue her coverage with the same medical provider under COBRA. The difference now is that she must pay the entire $300 to continue her coverage. Under COBRA, your medical provider will still require *you* to pay her premiums; they will not bill her for the premiums. This means that she must pay you the entire $300 to keep the coverage. If she elects not to continue the coverage or she does not send you the monthly $300, then *you* can have her coverage dropped. Some employees will try to tell you that you must pay their premiums after they leave. And, yes they are correct in that you must make the payment. But they must either pay you up front or reimburse you 100 percent of the cost. Under COBRA, you are allowed to collect 2 percent of the premiums for administrative expenses. That's how you come up with 102 percent of the premiums.

There are three main requirements that you must meet in order to extend medical coverage to your employees under COBRA.

Plan Coverage. The biggest requirement is that you have at least 20 employees in the prior year for a minimum of 50 percent of your typical business days. Both full and part-time employees are counted to determine whether a plan is subject to COBRA. Each part-time employee counts as a fraction of an employee, with the fraction equal to the number of hours that the part-time employee worked divided by the hours an employee must work to be considered full time. If you didn't have at least 20 employees the year prior, then you cannot offer the departing employee medical coverage under COBRA. You may have 100 employees currently, but if you had less than 20 the prior calendar year, then you do not fall under COBRA for the current year.

Qualified Beneficiaries. A person is qualified for COBRA if the individual is covered by a group health plan on the day before a qualifying event who is either an employee, the employee's spouse, or an employee's dependent child. In certain cases, a retired employee, the retired employee's spouse, and the retired employee's dependent children may be qualified. In addition, any child born to or placed for adoption with a covered employee during the period of COBRA coverage is considered a qualified beneficiary. Agents, independent contractors, and directors who participate in the group health plan may also be qualified beneficiaries.

Qualifying Events. The term qualifying events are certain instances that would cause an individual to *lose* health coverage. The type of qualifying event will determine who the qualified beneficiaries are and the amount of time that a plan must offer the health coverage to them under COBRA. A plan, at its discretion, may provide longer periods of continuation coverage. Listed below are the qualifying events as defined by the Department of labor.

Employees. This includes termination of an employee that was either voluntary or involuntary except for gross misconduct. It also includes employees who lost their coverage because they were reduced in hours. If you reduce an employee's hours from full-time to part-time status then they are allowed to continue coverage under COBRA if going to part-time would otherwise disqualify an employee for medical benefits.

Spouses. A spouse of an employee may be entitled for continued coverage for any of the reason of the above covered under the "Employees" section plus the following: If the covered employee becomes entitled to Medicare and thus no longer is covered under the medical coverage of the employer, divorce or legal separation from the employee, or death of the employee. These are instances where the spouse could be entitled to continue the medical coverage of the employee.

Dependent Children. Basically this covers all the circumstances mentioned above under the employee and spouse sections. In addition, it also covers the instance where the employee has lost the dependent status of the child. If the child is awarded to the spouse or someone else, then that child is entitled to maintain their medical coverage under COBRA. Also, as with the spouse, a dependent child is entitled to COBRA in the event of death of the employee.

Your Responsibilities Under COBRA

If you offer medical benefits to your employees then COBRA may apply to you. It is *your responsibility* to determine if COBRA applies to your business. Your medical provider, insurance broker or DOL are not responsible for determining or notifying you whether your business falls under COBRA. Claiming that you didn't know your responsibilities under COBRA will not fly with the DOL and certainly has the basis for a lawsuit, so be warned and know your responsibilities. The following is a brief description of employer's responsibilities, however refer to the DOL web site or contact the DOL for a more detailed discussion of COBRA.

The first order of business is to determine whether you even qualify to offer extended medical coverage under COBRA for any of the reason mentioned above or discussed in the DOL web site. If COBRA applies to your business, then you must notify your medical provider of a qualifying event as discussed above within 30 days after an employee's death, termination, reduced hours of employment or entitlement to Medicare. If the qualifying event is divorce or legal separation or a child's ceasing to be covered as a dependent under plan rules, then you must notify your provider within 60 days after the event. After the provider is notified, then they have 14 days to send an election notice to you or your employee. The individual then has 60 days to decide whether to elect COBRA continuation coverage. If the individual elects to continue coverage under COBRA, then they have 45 days after electing coverage to pay the initial premium. The individual must be notified in writing of their rights under COBRA. I have heard of some employers telling their departing employee that their payments will increase significantly up to $1000 a month for continued coverage, at which point the employees decides not to take COBRA. This is definitely misleading and calculated by the employer to discourage the employee from taking COBRA. Not only is this the wrong thing to do to an employee, it can also lead to a lawsuit! Continued medical coverage under COBRA will be at the same premiums as before the event. The only difference is that they must pay 100 percent of it. You may charge an extra 2 percent for administrative cost, but no more.

If an individual elects to continue coverage under COBRA, then you must make arrangements for payment. Your provider or plan administrator will bill your business directly for all covered individuals, which will include anyone under COBRA. It is your responsibility to collect the individual's premiums even though the individual may no longer work for you. When we had a departing employee elect to continue their coverage under COBRA, we had them sign a statement of what the monthly premiums were, the date that the premiums were due to us, the maximum time of coverage under COBRA, which was usually 18 months and the cancellation of their coverage if premiums were not received by the grace period. Under COBRA, an individual has a minimum 30-day grace period for payments after they are due. If I didn't receive payment after 5-days, then I would send a certified letter explaining that if payment was not received by a certain date then coverage would be terminated. If payment was still not received by the date specified in the letter, or the time period specified in the agreement that they signed, then I would terminate the coverage. Termination of coverage can be done by either calling the provider or writing them a letter. Both are recommended. If coverage is terminated then I would notify the individual that their coverage has been terminated.

For a full discussion of COBRA, I highly advise you to visit the Department of Labor web site at www.dol.gov. COBRA and many other topics are covered in this web site and is an invaluable tool for the business owner.

Occupational Safety and Health Administration (OSHA)

The Occupational Safety and Health Administration, known as OSHA, is the government agency responsible for assuring that the work place is safe and operates according to set standards. As one can imagine, OSHA covers a very broad area defining safety standards for nearly every occupation. Whether you have a restaurant or cleaners, OSHA most likely addresses safety and health issues related to your business. The web site for OSHA is www.osha.gov and provides specific policies for your type of business. In addition to setting work place standards, OSHA has over 2000 inspectors that perform inspections to determine compliance of set policies as well as investigate accidents and complaints. Non-compliance can and most likely will result in fines. If you want to look at previous inspection violations, you can access the data at "Inspection Data" listed under the topic "Statistics" on the OSHA home page. Remember, as an employer you are responsible for compliance with OSHA, which means educating yourself with the set standards for your business.

16   PAY AND BENEFITS

You could write volumes on this subject, however I'll cover the most essential aspects of compensation and some costly lessons learned. Your total pay package including indirect payroll costs will most likely makeup the largest expense item as compared to other expense categories. In our first 6 months of operation, our payroll costs averaged about 75% of total revenues! For every dollar that came in we paid out 75 cents in direct and indirect payroll costs. And as you can image we were definitely losing money having to barrow just to meet payroll. But when you start a new business, your payroll expenses will be very high as compared to your revenues. I don't know of any service business where this was not the case. We will exam all the categories of payroll costs and areas were you could reduce these costs without adversely affecting your operations.

Your first task as a startup business is to determine the average total pay package as related to your type of business. For example, if you are in the dry cleaning business, then see if most other dry cleaning businesses offer their employees such benefits as medical insurance, vacation pay, holiday pay, bonuses and matching 401k contributions? In addition, what is the average starting pay and what is the average pay after one, two or threes years of employment? What about starting pay for full-time versus part-time, or someone who is willing to work weekends and nights versus someone who has a more restricted availability? As you can see, compensation can be very complex and costly. As we found in our business, the spreadsheet becomes an invaluable tool when evaluating payroll costs as it relates to expected revenues in your first 6 months of operations.

Forms of Direct Compensation

Direct compensation can be in the form of wages, salaries, commissions, bonuses or any combination. In our business we used a combination of wages, bonuses and commissions. Bonuses and commissions are suitable for sales persons who are in direct contact with customers and who personally perform a service for them.

Bonuses can be established for those employees that achieve certain levels of sales or revenues as an incentive to go above and beyond what is normal or reasonable. Bonuses can be given in combination with commissions, wages or salaries. We normally would award bonuses for our stylists who achieved certain levels of service revenues from hair services. These bonuses were posted in each of our salons so that each stylist would know based on their own service revenues where they stood and how much more they needed in services to be eligible for the next bonus level. Unlike commissions, salaries and wages, bonuses should not be guaranteed but awarded based on criteria you have established. For example, you may have an employee who has had great sales and in line for a bonus based on sales alone. But what if the employee was caught steeling or walked off the job without notice? Would you give that employee a bonus on his or her final paycheck? In our operation, we would not award a "bonus" for any type of behavior that was detrimental to our operations. As covered in our employee manual, bonuses were never guaranteed and such actions as failing to show for work, stealing, lying, falsification, or any other such actions were reason enough for termination and ineligibility for any bonuses that might otherwise be awarded.

Commissions Plans

A sales commission is a great incentive pay plan for your staff provided you are busy with sales. If you are just starting out or are encountering some slow periods in sales, then a person who is strictly on commission may not hang around very long no matter how high the commission rate is. Remember 80 percent of nothing is nothing! In such cases, they may find another part-time job paying a salary in order to get them through until business picks up. The problem with that is that there will be a conflict with the work schedule. They may not be available to work when you need them since they also have a job somewhere else. The commission rate is also another factor to consider. In our business, some salons had their stylists on a commission rate ranging from 40 to 60 percent. If a commission pay plan is more appropriate for your business, then determine what the

145

norm is for your type of business. Some businesses will place their employees on salary for a few months then transition them to a commission only plan. The commission rate can also be set as a function of years with the company, sales in a given period or any combination of factors. For example, you may establish a rate of 20 percent for sales below $5,000 and 25 percent for sales above $5,000. Commissions have the advantage of simplicity in computing payroll as well as provide an incentive since their pay is a direct function of sales.

Commissions with a Guaranteed Salary Plans

We found that some businesses used a combination of both a commission pay plan with a guaranteed salary or wage. For example, you can establish a commission of 50 percent with a guaranteed wage of $6.00 an hour for any given pay period. The amount of hourly wage you establish should be lower than if you were to pay your employee with just an hourly wage and no commission. There is a distinct trade off with these two plans. In one, the employee has a guaranteed amount they will be making regardless of how much they sell. In the other plan, the employee has the potential to make more in commissions than with a straight hourly wage but must settle for a reduced guaranteed wage or salary. Lets say that the employee worked 40 hours and had commissions of $200 for a one-week period. At a guarantee wage of $6.00 an hour, his pay would be guaranteed at $240 thus he would be paid $240. However, if his commissions totaled say $300, then he would be paid $300. The disadvantage of a commission with a guaranteed wage is keeping track of hours worked, requiring the employer to compute pay based on an hourly wage. Some employers will opt for a guaranteed salary of so much a week thereby relieving the employer of having to track hours worked.

Offering benefits such as medical, dental insurance, paid vacation, holiday pay, 401K and so forth, can make a big difference in your ability to recruit and retain superior employees. One of the first things an applicant would enquire about was if we offered medical insurance or other benefits. Such benefits can be very costly to your bottom line but the bigger question is what is your competition offering? And will the cost of such benefits drive your business out of business!

There is no doubt that benefits will allow you to attract and retain a superior staff resulting in a more competitive business. We looked at it in terms of what will our cost savings be by having a lower turn over of employees alone. This type of trade off between the cost of benefits and the cost of recruiting, training and experience can be very difficult to measure without experiencing the cost of offering no benefits and then implementing such benefits. Even if the cost of benefits would have an effect of say 10% added to your expenses versus having no benefits, it would still be beneficial especially when the tax benefit is realized.

Vacation and Holiday Pay

If you are going to offer paid vacations or holidays then you will need to establish a concrete plan before you offer your first employee such benefits. Any misunderstandings will haunt you later so make sure your plan is well thought through and above all IN WRITING!

The first item on the list is establishing the eligibility period for new employees. Vacation is not as much an issue as it is for paid holidays. An employee is usually eligible to take vacation after one year of employment. But what about for holidays? If an employee starts work on Dec 15th, then will that employee be eligible for a paid holiday on Christmas? In our operation, we had Thanksgiving and Christmas as paid holidays. We were closed on those days so our employees who were eligible received holiday pay for those two days. We had an established eligibility period of 180 days from the first day of work. This meant that if an employee started work on July 15th, then they would not be eligible for holiday pay for the upcoming Thanksgiving and Christmas. You may wonder if this is fair. Its fair if the employee knows about it before they accept the job. It's probably not fair if you did not let them know about the 180-day eligibility period requirement until after they started work. If you don't tell them this before they begin work, I guarantee you the employee will tell you that this is unfair, and had they known this before their first day of work, they may have taken a job somewhere else where the eligibility period was shorter. Even when its in writing, there will be some employees who will challenge you on it for some reason such as "I have worked so hard these last 5 months and made you so much money that I think I shouldn't have to wait 180 days". So lets say you give in, how do you think your other employees will react? Those employees who just missed holiday pay from the year prior will want to be paid for those holidays. Now you will have to go back and back pay those employees. You might say, what could happen if I don't back pay them? For starters they could file a complaint to the labor board. You can avoid this mess by sticking to your policy covering eligibility for holidays.

Vacations are usually awarded after the employee has been with you for one year and can range from one week to whatever you feel is appropriate. Our employees were awarded one week after their first year and two weeks after two years of employment. We also stipulated in our employee manual that the employee was eligible for vacation pay only after each yearly anniversary. This meant that if the employee started work on January 1st of 2005 then she would be eligible for her vacation with pay after January 1st 2006. If she quit or was terminated before January 1st then she was not eligible for vacation pay. You can also award vacation pay incrementally each month so that after one year, the employee will have a full week. However with this type of plan, the employee must receive whatever amount they have accumulated if they leave before their one-year point. There are many variables to consider, and you should review the policies in your state to make sure your vacation and holiday benefits conform. Above all, your vacation and holiday plan should be described in detail in your employee manual.

Now, what about full-time versus part-time employees? Should a part-time employee receive holiday pay or vacation the same as a full time employee? You could make the argument that part-time employees are not eligible for it. But what if that part-time employee works your high volume periods such as nights and weekends and is responsible for a large part of your revenues. You see you can have part-time employees that make your business what it is and thus should be entitled to the same benefits as a full-time employee. In our operation, the part-time employee would be eligible for holiday and vacation pay if they worked a minimum of 3 days a week with no less than 20 hours a week on average. However our system for computing holiday and vacation pay was based on the employee's average pay meaning that the more one worked the more their pay would be.

There are different methods to compute holiday and vacation pay. We used a formula that took their average daily pay for holiday pay and their average weekly pay for vacation pay. We believed this was the fairest approach since it considers how much an employee works. The period we used to calculate this was the last 12 months for vacation pay and the last 6 months for holiday pay. There are other approaches that pay a set amount based on whether the employee is full or part time. But we believed that the fairest plan was the average pay approach. Now, what about if you have a commission only pay plan? The same can apply for a commission plan as with the wage or salary plan. Of course you can opt for an unpaid vacation and holiday plan for either a commission or salary pay plan. Had we gone with a commission plan, we would have eliminated all vacation and holiday pay in exchange for a higher commission percentage. We would still allow the employee to take their one or two weeks of vacation but it would be unpaid. This actually is a plus for the employee and for you. The reason is that the employee gets their pay upfront without having to wait, and you no longer have to keep track and compute their average pay amounts for vacation and holiday pay, which can be quiet involved.

A final note about holiday pay. Our two paid holidays were Thanksgiving and Christmas and of course we were closed those days. The weeks around the holidays (a week before thanksgiving through to the beginning of the year) were our busiest period. This was our most profitable time so of course it was the time of year we looked forward to. If we struggled during the year, this was the time we could pull forward as with many businesses. It also happened to be the time of year that our employees wanted to take off! It seems that whenever we were going to have a busy period, such as back to school and the holidays, that's when our staff wanted off. The reason we could afford to pay vacation pay, holiday pay, medical and so forth was because of these periods when we were very busy. Can you imagine if your favorite airline said that they were cutting back their flights during the holidays by 50% because their employees wanted off. You would find another airline. It is the same with any other business. For us, this is when our customers really depended on us servicing them and that's the bottom line. I remember our first holiday season for our 3rd salon. About October, we started getting notices from our stylists that they had plans for the holidays and we're taking off! In addition, they wanted to know when they would be getting their holiday pay! Basically, I would have to shut down for the busiest part of the year. That meant I would be in losses for the year at that location. One stylist said she had already bought plane tickets and needed off. Here is what we told them. First, we told them that they needed to ask us before making plans to take off for work. Second, we were not approving any leaves during the holidays. Third, if they decided to take off anyway, they would not receive any holiday pay or bonuses. Forth, if we hired someone to replace their absence, then they would probably not have a job when they returned. As it turned out, no one took off work. Following that occurrence we put out notices that no one could expect to takeoff work during the holidays and we never deviated from that policy. Some would say, well why don't you hire someone to fill in during the holidays as department stores do. In some business you could do that but not in ours due to the level of personal service our customers expected. Many of our customers were coming to us because they knew our staff and knew the quality we provided. The last thing they wanted was to try out someone new during the holidays. The other bigger problem was that it was nearly impossible to hire a stylist for just a few weeks especially during the holidays. Any business that requires skilled or semi-skilled employees can not just simply go out and find them on a street corner. There is cost and time involved and the result is a loss in productivity.

Medical Benefits

Offering medical benefits or health insurance is a great incentive for employees not to mention the real benefit to your employees of having medical coverage. When we started our business we offered paid vacations, two paid holidays, and birthdays off with pay but no medical. However it was our intent to offer medical once we had established our employee group. You need an established employee group to even get a quote. It wasn't until about a year after we started our business that we were able to finalize the process of medical insurance coverage. Each employee had to fill out a questioner for us to be able to get a quote. The process was quiet involved and some employees weren't sure if they wanted medical insurance if they had to pay any part of it. Some of these employees were just not going to fill out the questioner unless we were willing to pay 100 percent of the coverage. Of course we couldn't even get a quote unless all questioners were filled out and returned to the insurance broker. This is where you as the owner begin to pull your hair out. Your trying to provide a good thing to yours employees and you find that some will do anything to derail your good intentions. Like many other employers, we were willing to pay 50% of the employee rate up to a maximum of a certain amount per month. In addition, our employees who would be on the plan needed to average 30 or more hours per week or else lose their coverage. The providers usually required that at least 50% of our eligible employees participate in the plan. If our level of participation fell below 50% then we would no longer qualify for medical coverage. There are many restrictions a provider will require in order for continued coverage. Some of our employees needed the coverage or else they would seek employment somewhere else while others only wanted it if we paid 100% of the premiums. Paying 100% of the premiums was simply not going to work. The reality was that we would be in losses if we had to pay 100% of the medical insurance premiums for all our employees and then just a matter of time before we would be out of business. I found the initial process of acquiring medical insurance was quite involved, which is usually the case of most small businesses. It's not like calling a medical provider up and getting a plan to cover your employees. Once you have a plan then things go fairly smooth, but it's getting all the requirements fulfilled at the beginning that can be difficult. Offering medical insurance is a great incentive to attract employees, but the continued escalating cost of it has driven many small businesses to drop the coverage or face going out of business. Passing on part of the increased cost to the employee is one way to offset the increases and yet keep the coverage.

      As defined in our medical group plan, we had a waiting period of 90 days from the employee's start date as common with many businesses. We defined full time as 30 or more hours per week. This seems simple and straightforward. However, there were problems that challenged the eligibility for maintaining coverage. What do we mean by 30 hours per week? In other words if an employee dropped below 30 hours for only one or two weeks, does that make them ineligible for keeping their medical? What we did was to take the average hours worked per week over the previous 12 weeks. If someone's 12 week moving average fill below the 30-hour minimum then we had no choice but to drop them as per our contract with our medical provider. Although this was rare, it did occur. What turned out to be a more sticky issue was what if the employee was calling in sick several times a month thereby falling below the 30 hour average, what then? If the employee is legitimately sick then there is no problem obviously. But the problem arises when the employee is not really sick and is not seeing a doctor. We had one particular case where this indeed was the issue. This individual was just calling in sick on days she just didn't want to work such as weekends and without seeing a doctor! Finally, we confronted her and told her that if she continued to miss work and drop below the 30-hour average, then we had no choice but to drop her insurance coverage. Of course, she wanted to know how could she remain eligible if the reason she can't come to work was because she was sick. If we extend this out further, what happens if this individual works so little that she could no longer pay her share of the medical insurance? This is a great illustration of how a simple and straightforward plan can go wrong. Well, it wasn't very long afterwards that this employee just stopped showing up for work and wouldn't return any of our calls. We sent a certified letter explaining that her medical insurance was going to be dropped unless she wanted to fund 100 percent under COBRA since she no longer was an employee. Again, we herd nothing from her. We soon afterwards dropped her coverage as well as her employment status with us. This illustrates what can happen in a worse case scenario. As our insurance broker advised us, some employees will test any undefined areas of your medical coverage as we had witnessed. The best advice is to consult your medical provider with any unusual circumstances such we had. Your employee manual should also address such issues as definition of full-time status and how it is calculated.

There are many issues that that you will need to consider before you begin offering medical insurance. I have listed some of these below and certainly would recommend that you consult with both you insurance broker and provider about them:

    Open enrollment period
    Waiting period
    Coverage for part-time employees
    Minimum weekly hours for continued coverage
    Definition of weekly hours such as average of the prior 4 weeks
    What happens if an employee cant work due to an illness?
    What if an employee stops coming to work and contact cannot be established
    What if a new employee turns down medical insurance, how long must they wait before they can be eligible again

The last element of medical benefits concerns payroll deduction for employees on medical insurance. Normally, the medical provider will bill you monthly for the total premiums of all your employees who are on the plan. The employees don't send any premiums to the provider. If you have your employees paying any part of the monthly costs such as 50 percent, then you will need to deduct their share (50 percent in this case) from the paycheck. Have them sign a letter authorizing you to payroll deduct their share of the premiums. This means that you will need to compute the exact amount of their share so it is in writing when they sign the authorization. You should also spell out when these deductions will be made and for what period they will cover. For example, we would deduct the premiums for the month of June's coverage on the paychecks that came out on the 20th of May and 5th of June, which reflects the work month of May. Collecting the premiums ahead of the coverage period is highly recommended since your provider will require you, the employer, to submit the monthly premiums a month prior to the coverage period.

Games and Competition in the Workplace

Having a competition among your employee group can add some fun to the work place as well as be an incentive to higher productivity and moral. This is one of those win-win scenarios benefiting both the bottom line and employees who see the value in hard work. The type of business you have will dictate the types of programs suited for your employee group. Businesses that deal primarily in sales will benefit most from a competitive program. But service businesses as well as manufacturing type businesses can also benefit. One of our programs was a sales competition held quarterly. We had two categories: total points and total retail sales. The employee who had the most points or the most retail sales would win a certain dollar amount. On occasion the same stylist would win both the point and retail sales categories. Points were comprised of service sales, total weekends worked, number of times they would travel to one of our other salons, etc. The individual who had the most service sales would usually win the point category, however, if two people were very close in service sales, then another point category such as weekend points would make the difference. We also had an annual contest with the winners being the persons who had the most points or retail sales for the calendar year. In total we had 5 five competitions per year, one for each quarter and one annual event. In addition, each competition had two elements or two winners, one for total points and one for total retail sales. In all, there were 10 chances to win. As with any type of competition, some employees were driven to win while others just did not care. The prize was cash. The winners would be awarded a cash prize and there name announced in a letter posted at all shops with a posted certificate of accomplishment.

One might wonder if a non-cash prize would have the same incentive benefit. The answer, I am sorry to say is a big no! Cash is the greatest prize producing your best incentive. A free bottle of shampoo or a day off with pay just doesn't carry the same meaning as cash in hand. Some businesses will offer something like a free T-shirt, free movie passes or that worthless letter, but nothing says it better than cash!

Incentive programs that are based on contests are more appropriate for retail or other business that deal with personalized service. Whatever type of business you have though, you can probably develop some type of incentive plan for your employees. You will find as we did that a contest will add a bit of fun and competition between your employees and will certainly boost moral.

Bonuses

Bonus pay is a way to financially reward an employee for exceeding defined performance goals. In a sense it is also a type of incentive plan. Some employers have end of year bonuses or Christmas bonuses. Others have semi annual, quarterly or monthly bonuses. We had a bonus plan for our stylist who achieved certain level of revenues within the semi-monthly pay period. However, bonus pay was not guaranteed and other performance factors were considered such on time performance and customer satisfaction. On several occasions, an employee would achieve a bonus level but lacked other performance standards that nullified bonus pay. Bonus pay was not and should never be guaranteed or expected as part of a pay package. In addition, operating earnings becomes a factor if losses mount up too high.

Consideration should be given to addressing bonus pay in your employee manual that discusses pay and benefits if you are going to award bonuses. We defined the revenue requirements for certain bonus amounts in our pay and benefits manual. We clearly spelled out factors that could nullify a bonus award. We also clearly stated our policy that bonus pay was never guaranteed and that certain financial situations could halt our bonus program indefinitely. In a nutshell, we standardized our bonus program so that our employees would know what bonus amounts could be awarded based on their revenue performance. And we were stating up front that bonuses could stop at anytime based on the criteria we spelled out in our pay manual. This gave our employees the incentive to maximize their revenues by servicing as many customers as possible and knowing that working the busy periods would add to their revenue totals resulting in a greater bonus amount. Remember, your plan should be detailed enough so that someone from outside your business could pick up your manual and execute it without missing a beat.

Unlike a periodic bonus plan, end of year bonuses are usually not publicized and are reserved more as an option for managers and upper level personnel. In fact you can establish two bonus plans that includes a monthly bonus plan linked to productivity or performance and an end of year bonus.

In summary, a bonus plan should be just that – a plan. Just because you had a great year or half doesn't mean you should just begin handing out bonuses. If you elect to award bonuses then make sure you develop a plan that clearly establishes the criteria for bonuses, including the amounts. Whether you decide to include your bonus plan in your employee manual is up to you but at a minimum you should have some idea on how to determine who gets bonuses including the amounts.

Pay Raises

Pay raises are almost expected in every type of business whose employees are on a wage or salary. But just small increases in pay spread across all your employees will have a significant impact on the bottom line. If you pay your employees a salary or wage then you are liable for half of the FICA and HI FICA (social security and Medicare tax) plus 100 percent of Workers Compensation and State and Federal Unemployment tax, commonly referred to as SUTA and FUTA. These taxes are assessed as a percentage of gross pay. Your share of the FICA and HI FICA are about 7.5%, SUTA can vary greatly depending on the state but we will use a conservative 4 percent, FUTA will average about 1% and workers compensation also will vary greatly depending on the business and state but we will use 5 percent. All together, these add up to about 17.5 percent of gross pay. Remember, these are not payroll deducted from the employee's gross pay; these are cost incurred on you, meaning you are not allowed to make the employee pay any part of them! So you can see that even small pay increases, subject to these employer taxes, will have a major impact to your total payroll cost. Together with any planned pay increases, these additional tax amounts must be carefully considered along with your anticipated revenues. If because of strong competition, you anticipate weak pricing power, then you will have no choice but to greatly limit your single highest expense – payroll. It does not make any sense to have heavy losses and eventually go out of business because your labor cost were not in line with your revenues. Now with that said, lets look at when pay increases are justified and surrounding factors involved with pay increases.

6 Factors of Pay Raises

A pay raise to a particular employee is justified for any reason you think is justified! That's the short answer. The long answer is a bit more involved. In my book, there are 6 factors that influence pay increases. These factors are performance, longevity with your business, inflation rate, position of responsibility, unemployment rate and recruiting efforts of competitors. We are going to assume that your business is profitable with costs under control and the future looks stable for your sector. Also, no one factor should be considered by itself. Of these 6 factors, performance, longevity and position of responsibility are overriding factors. Performance is by far the most important factor and should be considered above all other factors. We will discuss each of these factors individually.

Performance. When we talk about employee performance we are referring to everything from how well they do their job to how well dress they come to work. I have had employees who had worked for us over two years yet remained at their starting salary because of their lack of performance. When looking at performance, one of the overriding factors is how productive the employee is. *Productivity* is often measured with respect to the employee's earnings or hours they work. This product is then compared to an industry average or an average of all your employees. In our business we used payroll percentage, which is the ratio of gross pay to the amount of revenues or sales for that employee. Employees who averaged a payroll percentage of greater than 50% were less productive than someone with a 45% payroll percentage. There are a number of other indices to measure productivity such as the number of widgets someone assembles per hour or the number of customers they service or calls per hour. Productivity in relation to an employee's earning is more meaning-full than compared to the number of customers they service per hour. The reason is because not all your employees will be at the same pay scale. If Julie and Jane each have average sales of $20 an hour but Julie makes $2.00 an hour more than Jane, then we can see that Jane is more productive, even though both have the same sales per hour. Productivity must include labor costs and becomes an essential element of pay raises.

Another important factor to consider deals with total sales of an employee. For example, Mike may have a payroll percentage of 40% but only brings in a total of $1000 per week. Alice may have a payroll percentage of 45% but brings in a weekly total of $2000. These types of differences can arise when some employees not only work more hours than others but work higher volume or busier periods such as nights or weekends. As you can see productivity becomes somewhat complex and certainly must be tailored to the particular business. Performance evaluation becomes more difficult to asses when the employee works in an administrative capacity or the likes of.

Listed below are the factors that relate to performance. Some are more important then others but one must consider many factors together when determining whether an employee is in line for a pay raise as it relates to performance.

               Productivity
               Appearance
               On time record
               Missed work
               Customer skills
               Cleanliness
               Flexibility to schedule
               Availability
               Resourcefulness
               Ability to work with other employees
               Attitude
               Workmanship

Longevity.   How long an employee has worked for you is certainly a consideration for pay increases. When someone comes to work for you, they will be given a starting salary or wage. But as time goes on and that person has demonstrated a commitment to your business in terms of longevity then it seems reasonable that they should share in a larger piece of the pie then when they first started with you. After all, that experience level the employee has gained does indeed contribute more to your bottom line then when they were new, at least we hope it does. My rule-of-thumb was to consider an employee for a longevity pay increase after 6 months of employment. Now, let me say that there are the other factors to consider, which I will discuss later. Just because an employee has been on the property for one year, doesn't mean they are entitled to a pay raise in itself. But we will assume everything else is in order and you have decided a longevity pay raise is warranted. This does several things, which are all in your favor. First, it puts the employee at ease about whether you will ever give them a pay raise. When an employee first starts working for you, they are very concerned of whether they will ever see a raise. Second, it opens the door as a recruiting tool by encouraging the employee to recommend your business to others they know. Third, it promotes an overall feeling of fairness about your business and it's employees.

So now the question becomes, how long does longevity become a factor in pay increases? This of course depends on you, but I would say 5 years is the max when considering longevity pay raises. After 5 years, that employee has been well rewarded for their commitment to your business, especially when you consider the compounding effect over the years. In addition, the experience level after 5 years is most likely at it maximum. This person is probably not going to gain much more experience after 5 years in terms of technical knowledge. Remember, longevity pay increases is not to be confused with performance.   A Longevity pay increase is the reward an employee earns for showing commitment and allegiance to you and your business. It is only one of several factors to considerer in pay increases.   Nothing says you have to base any pay raises on longevity. That is entirely up to you.

Inflation. Pay increases as it relates to inflation or cost of living increases is certainly justifiable but only if your revenues for the products or services your business offers reflects the inflation rate. It's not as easy as looking up the inflation rate and then increasing everyone's pay by the same percentage. From an economic standpoint, if wages and salaries keep lagging behind the inflation rate, then our buying power becomes less every year. On the other hand, in a period of deflation or very low inflation, then increases in wages and salaries based entirely on inflation would certainly not be warranted. This is why pay increases should reflect the average inflation rate over the past several years, not what the rate was last year or what is forecast for the current year.

An important consideration is whether prices of your products or services have been able to keep up with the average inflation rate or rate you expected to increase wages and salaries. Obviously, if you keep increasing your payroll to keep up with inflation but yet are not able to maintain the same rate of increase in the product or services you offer then you can expect to see less profitability and eventually substantial losses. If you are going to increase your employee's pay to account for the inflation rate then you also need to adjust your prices upward. If on average, your prices have increased only 1 percent per year over the last 5 years, then your pay increases due to inflation alone should be minimal.

Position of Responsibility. It should go without saying that an increase in pay goes with an employee's advancement to a higher position of responsibility. You should have a good idea of the pay scale for a starting manager before it comes up. This example illustrates the point more clearly. Lets say you have a set pay scale for a certain position based on years of service. Bob has been with you for 3 years and currently makes $13 an hour. A manager's position comes open and you have decided to promote Bob to this new position. You have a manager's pay scale that runs from $13 to $18 depending on how many years they have been an employee. A manager who is a new employee, such as would be the case when you opened for business, would be at $13 an hour. Bob is currently at $13 an hour because he has shown exceptional performance over the last

3 years he has been with you. Bob's pay as a manager should be at the 3 year point on the manager's scale and lets say that is $15 an hour. This may not seem a significant amount but remember it takes into account the change from one position to another with a different pay scale. Deviating away from your set pay scale for starting salaries could have adverse consequences later on. For example, if you had started Bob off at $16 an hour and then you open a new manager's position with someone who has also been with you for 3 years, then that person is going to expect a starting manager's salary of $16 an hour, even though their regular salary was at $12 per hour. Telling employees that they are not as good as another employee does not go over well. Keep it simple and fair by starting everyone at the same salary or wage for any given position. What you do in terms of a pay raise some time later is another subject. We always started everyone at the same salary but our pay raises varied depending on the individual's performance.

Responsibility also encompasses personal responsibility that is not attained through positions such as a manager. We see these types of individuals throughout our lives. These are individuals that perform tasks or other measures that are usually not asked of them. An easy example is an employee who always seems to be the person who empties the trash or who cleans out the break room or restroom without being asked to do so. It is the person who always remembers to adjust the thermostat before leaving, or the person who takes inventory and calls for re-supply when items are getting low. It is the person who will stay late if you get shorthanded or comes in to work when someone calls in sick. Having a full staff of these types of individuals can certainly add to your bottom line. These types of individuals would warrant higher pay levels then their peers who do not exhibit such personal motivation. These individuals also know who they are and are well aware that they go that extra mile for you. Don't make the mistake of not rewarding them. They may decide to move on to another job if they don't feel appreciated. Individuals like these are usually at the top of my list for supervisory or management positions. These types of individuals lead by example and sooner or later become influential among your employees.

Unemployment Rate. The unemployment rate for your area or the tightness of the labor market for your type of business becomes a very relevant factor in pay raises. This becomes especially true when you require specialized skills such as programmers, cosmetologists, auto mechanics, plumbers, electricians etc. In our business, we found that the market for licensed cosmetologist was extremely tight with stylists going from job to job, merely reacting to job offers. This type of market condition puts upward pressure on salaries while at the same time is a factor in decreased productivity. I observed new hair salons unable to open for business for some time due to the lack of hair stylists. Whether it's because of a shortage of employees requiring special skills or general tightness in the labor market, retention of employees will be a driving factor in pay increases.

As a business owner, its important for you to be aware of the economy as it pertains to the labor market. Some preventative measures can help you avoid scrambling for employees when the labor market tightens up making it difficult to attract new employees. Know what direction the unemployment rate is going and begin taking measures to ensure you don't lose employees. Check the help wanted section of your paper and determine if the number of advertisements is increasing. I used to look at the help wanted section for hair stylists not only to see what type of deals our competitors were offering but also to see if the number of ads was tracking upward or downward. If you determine that the trend will continue upward, then begin taking action. There are several steps you can take to keep your employees from getting too interested in what others have to offer. A pay raise of course is one step, but steps such as announcing an end of year bonus, providing a new benefit, or expanding a current benefit such as a dental or vision plan are such examples. The goal of these actions is to keep your employees interested in staying rather than looking for another job. Its true this will cost you but it will cost you less than if you become short handed with experienced employees walking out the door only to be replaced with inexperienced employees that may not be of the same caliber that left. The cost of recruiting and training new employees will be significant. Our average cost of recruiting a new employee was about $1500 and sometimes as high as $2000 depending on the urgency and whether we offered a sign on bonus. With other types of businesses, the recruiting costs can run into the thousands. One thing is for certain, as the labor market tightens or the recruiting efforts by your competition gets more aggressive, you will see a higher turn over of employees if nothing is done to preempt it.

Recruiting Efforts of Competitors. When the market gets tight for labor, you will find that employers will turn up the heat in their recruiting efforts of attracting new employees. This means going after employees of other businesses with offers that are simply "just too good to pass up". Incentives such as sign-on bonuses, higher salaries, triple time for holidays, paid vacations, medical insurance, guaranteed pay raises, tuition allowances, retirement plans and so forth, can certainly entice an employee to switch jobs. This places pressure on the employer to increase pay levels or offer other incentives to guard against their employees leaving for that sweat offer by your competitor. I have seen on more than one occasion, the manager of a nearby salon, enter my salon and attempt to recruit my stylists with job offers that include sign-on bonuses. Even direct mail has been used as a recruiting tool. Certain trades such as barbers and cosmetologists, who are licensed by the state, are registered with names and addresses by the state. Such a mailing list can be purchased from the state, as we had done. On many occasions, our stylists would bring in these direct mail offers from our competitors to show us that they were in demand. When the labor market is tight you may have to accelerate your pay raises to keep your employees and to attract new employees.

So other than pay rises, how does an employer counter recruiting efforts by competitors? Knowing your competition and their pay package helps. Many of these sweet offers advertised through either direct mail, newspapers or through employment guides, have offers that just seem to good to be true which is usually the case. Knowing and educating your employees with the real story behind the advertisement, can be an effective counter measure. I remember one competitor who was offering a starting wage of $2 an hour more than our starting wage. One of our new stylists confronted me about it; threatening to leave if we did not bring her pay up to at least the same level. Luckily, we had someone who had worked for this competitor and informed us that certain conditions and work rules resulted in less pay then what our starting salary was. I informed our stylist about this and referred her to the employee who had once worked for this competitor. We also pointed out some of our benefits that this other competitor did not offer. I then told her that we would certainly hate to see her go but there was nothing we could do! She stayed with us. We made it a point to know the details about our competitor's pay package so that we could better inform our employees before making the wrong decision. In some instances, stylists did leave for another higher paying job, with some returning after a few months asking for their old job back. Once they began working at these other places, they discovered those little details that were not clear in the original job offer. Sometimes it's a misunderstanding by the employee and other times it's an intentional deception by the employer. Recruiting efforts that are somewhat vague or deceitful will usually come back to haunt the employer through reputation. As mentioned before, word of mouth seems to be one of the best recruiting methods.

Considering the factors discussed above, how does one evaluate the level of a pay increase? Do we consider each factor separately or do we combine them all for an overall rating? How you weigh each of these factors is up to you and the type of business you have but in general all of the factors should be considered as a whole and not separately. Performance is by far the overriding factor under most conditions. However, in a tight labor market, pay raises, as a retention tool becomes a strong factor especially for employees who demonstrate good performance. Inflation is more of a factor in determining the degree of pay increases and is considered only when performance can justify a raise. For example, if the average inflation rate was 3 percent, then exceptional performance may justify a 5 percent raise, while average performance would justify a 3 percent raise and so forth.

We have had several employees who never received pay raises from us. Their overall pay was actually more than their performance justified so we were not going to bring their pay up until we saw an increase to their performance, which we usually did not see.

One might ask, why not just fire these individuals? We normally would let someone go if performance degraded below a certain level. However, we would not let someone go if his or her performance was above a certain level.

Suppose you decide to run a help wanted ad in the paper because one of your employees is leaving. The day the ad runs you check the paper to make sure your ad is in and discover your competition has also run an ad but with a $2000 hiring bonus and comparable starting pay that you offer. Should you be concerned about it? You bet you should. One of the first things that will come to mind is, I hope my employees don't see this! Do you think this will influence your decision to increase the pay of employees? It probably will, especially those that are your top performers. This is how competition in the labor market can greatly influence the pay package you offer as well as decisions to increase pay. It is one of the biggest issues concerning high turn over of employees. And it is certainly a factor that will influence pay offers and raises.

In our business, we would normally consider a new employee for a pay raise at the 6-month point. If the employee is exceptional and ranks as one of your top employees then I would consider a pay raise at an earlier point. On average, our employees received about a 5 to 10 percent increase in pay their first year. However, in the following years the increases averaged smaller percentages approaching about 4 percent.

The national average for pay increases is shown on the next page and includes the inflation rate (CPI-U):

Average pay increases per year with inflation rate (CPI-U)

YEAR	AVERAGE PAY INCREASE	CPI-U
1996	4.1%	3.0%
1997	4.2%	2.3%
1998	4.2%	1.6%
1999	4.2%	2.2%
2000	4.2%	3.4%
2001	4.4%	2.8%
2002	3.8%	1.6%
2003	3.3%	2.3%
2004	3.3%	2.4%
2005	3.5%	2.2% (est)

As you can see from this chart, pay raises have averaged near 4 percent per year since 1996. The chart also shows that the gap between pay raises and inflation has averaged about 2 percent above the inflation rate with the gap narrowing to about 1 percent in more recent years. As the labor market tightens up, I would anticipate the gap to increase to about the 2 to 3 percent level over the inflation rate.

One factor that is overriding when considering pay raises or expansion of benefits is of course the profitability of your business. If your business is struggling and operating in the red, then it's going to be difficult to justify increasing your labor cost. However, there are other options then straightforward pay raises. This involves offering your employees either an equity position in your business or a share of any future profits. Both of these plans involve considerable planning and protocol not to mention the cost for set up and maintenance. There are a number of web sites that provide an overview to employee ownership and profit sharing plans. Google or any other search engine can be used and will provide you with a number of sites dedicated to these subjects. One of the best sites I've have found is the National Center for Employee Ownership (NCEO) at www.nceo.org. A good article on the subject can be found on the same site at www.nceo.org/library/verysmall.html. Obviously you would need to consult a specialist for such a transaction, which may involve a restructure of your business.

17   WORK SCHEDULES FOR EMPLOYEES

For a business with employees, the work schedule will usually contribute to the highest operating cost of your business. As a business owner it is crucial that you know how to manage your highest operating cost item. The work schedule is also one of the toughest elements of a business operation. Go into any business and ask the manager or owner if scheduling is not like walking a tight rope! It seems that as soon as the schedule is posted you have employees wanting their schedule changed. Either someone can't work their shift or it has too many hours or not enough hours or they are on for to many nights or cant work a full Saturday and on and on. Too many payroll hours, especially during low volume periods will definitely impact your profitability. Too few hours, especially during high volume periods will impact your revenues. <u>If your business deals directly with the consumer public, then your schedule must be in tune with the consumer. Meeting consumer demand should be the main factor behind your schedule.</u> That's for every day of the year including holidays. Can you imagine if the airlines reduced their schedule or closed on holidays! I am sure the employees would think its great to close on the holidays, but the public would not. The bottom line is that there are certain periods of the day, and there are certain days such as weekends where your customer volume is at a peak. Failing to meet this demand with proper staffing will not only affect sales but will result in customers going somewhere else in the future. On several occasions I have seen customers walk into our salon telling me that they left the salon across the street because there was only one stylist cutting hair with many customers waiting. If your schedule is not inline with your customer then you will eventually pay a high price. There are many variables that must be factored in when building a schedule. Don't be naive to think that all you have to do is fill in a schedule and flop it on the desk. I have seen managers tear their hair out trying to build a schedule that will satisfy their owners, their customers and their staff. I have seen employees break down in tears over a schedule pleading to have it changed. And I have seen employees pick up the schedule, look at it and then gather their items and walk off the job!

If you have a manufacturing business that does not deal directly with the consumer, then meeting consumer demand is not a driving factor on your schedule, giving you more flexibility on how you schedule your employees. However, a pick up in orders for items you produce during certain times of the year, such as around Christmas will require changes to your schedule in order to meet the demand. Whether your business deals with the public or not, meeting demand on your product is the most important factor in scheduling. If you fail to meet this demand, then don't be surprised to find your business in trouble especially if a nearby competitor is doing a better job of meeting consumer demand.

There are three forces that will drive your schedule as discussed below. The first is consumer demand, which we already discussed. The second is the availability of your employees and the third is cost. Demand determines how many people you need to hire and how they will be scheduled. Cost puts limitations to your schedule in order to achieve acceptable productivity levels.

Building a Typical Schedule

What follows next is an example of the process in building a schedule for a typical business open 7 days a week. Remember this is an example and points out the process involved in building a schedule. When determining how many employees it will take, the first place to start is with your busiest periods. If your open only 5 days a week or say 40 hours a week, then the number of employees you will need will usually be fewer than if you are open 7 days a week or say 60 hours. Before you determine how many employees you will need, first determine how many *total payroll hours* you will need to meet your demand. For example, lets say from Monday to Friday you will need one employee from 8 am to 11 am, and two people from 11 am to 8 pm. Your line schedule would look something like the following:

```
8am  9   10   11   12   1   2   3   4   5   6   7   8pm
-------------------------------------------------------- 12 hrs
                 ---------------------------------------- 09 hrs
                                     Total payroll hours  21 hrs
```

The minimum number of payroll hours you will need from Monday thru Friday is 105 hours (5x21). You also estimate that you will need three people on Saturdays for 24 payroll hours and 2 people on Sundays for 14 payroll hours giving you a total of 38 payroll hours for each weekend. Thus, the total number of payroll hours each week is 143 (105 + 38). This figure represents the minimum number of payroll hours to handle your anticipated demand. Another way of saying this is that at 143 hours you will achieve your highest productivity for any given level of pay. But in reality, you will find that because of other factors that influence your schedule, you will have a higher figure than 143 hours.

The next process involves determining *how many employees* you will need to cover your schedule based on your estimated demand. The first thing to do is begin to fill your blocks beginning with the highest demand periods. The highest demand periods produces your highest productivity, therefore it should be your priority when filling in your schedule. Remember, your objective here is to determine how many employees you will need. First, you can see that you will need three people on Saturdays. On Sunday, which could easily be your second busiest day, you will need two people, which could be the same people who worked on Saturday. When you look at the week days, you can clearly see you will need at least three people each day with the following shifts: 8am to 3pm, 11am to 8pm and 3pm to 8pm, which gives you a total of 21 payroll hours. The only snag to this schedule on the weekdays is the 11am to 8 pm shift, which is a 9-hour shift. You may not find any employees who are willing to work for 9 hours straight. However, you may find some employees willing to work that shift by rotating the shift around other employees so that no one person always works the same shift.

It is clear that with three people needed for each day, except Sundays, you will need at least four employees to make this schedule work out if you are going to give each employee two days off. With four employees, the following schedule will meet this examples demand:

	MO	TU	WED	TH	FRI	SAT	SUN	TOT HRS
JAN	11 to 8	3 to 8	OFF	OFF	11 to 8	8 to 4	9 to 4	**38**
DEB	OFF	OFF	3 to 8	11 to 8	8 to 3	8 to 4	9 to 4	**36**
JILL	8 to 3	8 to 3	8 to 3	3 to 8	OFF	8 to 4	OFF	**34**
JOHN	3 to 8	11 to 8	11 to 8	8 to 3	3 to 8	OFF	OFF	**35**
HOURS>	*21*	*21*	*21*	*21*	*21*	*24*	*14*	***143***

Sample weekly schedule for four employees

From this schedule, we fulfilled three main objectives. First, we met our total hour requirement of 143 hours to meet our demand for the week. Second, we met our weekday demand with our shift coverage totaling 21 hours, which was on target of 21 hours required. Third, we did not go over our optimum payroll hours of 143 to meet our demand. So the schedule looks good, right? However, there are two potential problems with this schedule. First, notice that no one has a full 40 hours. The hours range from 35 to 38. Employee Jan has the most hours with 38. Second, at some point everyone will have to work a 9-hour shift and at some point everyone will have to work nights and weekends. If everyone is not willing to pull a 9-hour shift then the other employees will have to fill the void, which may not go over too well. This could force you to hire a fifth person, especially if you have one or more employees who are unable to work certain shifts such as a Saturday, Sunday or Friday night. Lets say everyone is willing to work the shifts on this schedule but, some or all will not work for anything less than 40 hours a week! That would be 160 hours per week instead of the more optimum 143 hours to meet your demand. Remember, anything over 143 hours per week does not increase your revenues. The revenues are the same whether you have 143 payroll hours or 160 hours. At say $10 an hour, those extra 17 hours a week will cost you $170 in direct payroll costs and if you include indirect payroll cost you end up with about $200 a week. That's $10,400 a year in added payroll costs for this shop or store. If you have multiple shops or stores, then your added costs become huge. For a business of 5 shops, this would add up to $52,000 a year. The options are; one, bring your scheduled hours up to meet your employee request, or two, keep looking for those employees that will work at the reduced hours. The right option depends on several factors. First, how tight is the labor market. If getting employees is not difficult, then set your criteria and stick to it. However, if the labor market is tight then you may have to give in and compromise on hours. Although many employees will not expect you to guarantee the hours they will want to know about how many hours they can expect. If you tell them that your schedule can support 35 hours a week and then schedule them 32 hours every week they will either look for work somewhere else or ask you to bring the hours up. The second factor concerns the quality of your employees. On occasion you may have an exceptionally outstanding employee working for you. We had some outstanding employees that if they said they needed 45 hours, we would certainly consider it or at least some additional hours. But these employees were indeed rare and came along once in a long while. The third factor and probably the most important factor are your total sales or revenues. If you estimate that the revenues generated from this location will continue to grow strong, then the added payroll cost could be justified in the long run. Remember, if your employees want 40 hours as opposed to an average of 35 hours a week, then consider meeting them half way with 2-3 more hours. Some will accept it while others will not. Also keep in mind we are talking about average hours. There will be some weeks were your employees will be in over-time while at other times they will be at your optimized hours. Such occasions as holidays or summers may require additional staffing to meet heavier than normal demand.

Another factor that seemed to be in our favor and that was particular to our type of business was customer tips as it relates to employees wanting more hours. We just seemed to have a reputation of having customers that generally tipped very well. By knowing this, many stylists were content with reduced hours since they knew that they would more than make up for it with higher tips than at a competitors business. Having multiple locations was another advantage we had. If an existing employee or an applicant told us they needed more hours, then we could offer them more time if they were willing to help us out at our other locations. If they wanted the extra hours bad enough then they would accept this proposal. This is a win-win for both parties. They get the extra hours and we are better able to meet customer demand, especially during high volume periods.

In the example schedule above, we would open with one employee and then go to two after 11am. But as your business picks up, you may have to go with two at opening and possibly three at closing with four on Saturdays or three on Sundays. What we did when we had to hire someone to cover, say 20 additional hours per week, was carry an additional person on our busiest day which was usually Saturdays. This allowed us to handle occasions of unusually higher volume. This was especially beneficial when that surge of volume was made up of new customers. I have seen on several occasions where a sudden surge of customers was because the competitor across the street had to close early or became short handed. I always looked at this type of situation as an opportunity to shine with hopes of seeing those customers back again in the near future!

Weekend Scheduling

I remember an employee told me that if we closed on Sundays, then our Mondays would be very busy since those customers who found us closed on Sundays would just wait till we were open on Monday! I suppose if you carried that logic a step further and closed every day except Wednesday, then your Wednesdays would be busy with all those customers from the rest of the days you were closed. I proceeded to tell this employee that we've been there and done that and it simply does not workout. A while back we had to unfortunately close on Sundays. Our volume on Mondays initially picked up but after time we began to lose volume. What really amazed me was that not only did our volume eventually slow on Mondays but also every other day of the week including Saturdays. Our average daily volume decreased. One of the things I would track was the number of daily customers at each of our locations. This data was entered into a spreadsheet that allowed me to monitor our average volume for any given day and compare that to the same period the years before. In this program, we had a 14-day, 50 day and 200 day moving average. After we closed our Sunday operations at this particular salon, we found that our 14 and 50 moving average began to fall below our 200 day moving average. In other words, our Tuesday average volume began to drop as well as the other days of the week. So what does all this technical stuff mean? It means that we were in trouble. We were definitely loosing our customer base. Just as interesting, when we reopened on Sundays, we found our daily moving average began to improve. This meant that our volume on Mondays began to increase as well as the other days of the week. When I explained this to this employee, she responded with, "well, I am just not going to work any more Sundays" which was the real issue. And she went on to say that she did not want her total weekly hours cut either! I quickly told her that if we close on Sundays her hours would reflect this. She responded by quitting! I go back to what I said at the beginning of this section, building a schedule is like walking a tight rope. There simply is no easy solution. If you have been lucky enough to be at the mercy of someone building a schedule at where you worked then you know how important that schedule was to you. But the fact remains that if your going to meet customer demand or at least try to improve your volume, then you will have to schedule your employees accordingly. I can't tell you how many applicants that told us they simply would not work weekends. I would tell them we could not hire them if they were firm on that.

Getting Your Manager to Build A Productive Schedule

The point of learning how to build the schedule as the owner is so that you can have your manager take over the task and build it with the same effectiveness as you expect. I think every manager should build the schedule, but they should do so in accordance with your guidelines. What we would do is provide our manager's with a shell of how many people to go into what periods for any given day of the week. For example, the shell would require 3 people on Saturdays and 2 on Sundays and so on, depending on the shop involved. It would also specify the maximum number of payroll hours per week allowed, again depending on the particular shop. The only thing left for our managers was to put names in the slots of the shell. The problem we found was that the managers would schedule themselves with the most hours and the best periods such as no Friday nights. The same people were scheduled for those least desirable hours and had the least weekly hours. Without correcting this problem, animosity and resentment would develop among these employees. Whoever you designate to build the schedule, you must set criteria for them to follow. Set a day that your manager must have the schedule complete for *your approval*. If the schedule looks good then approve it, otherwise make the changes you want and give it back to your manager with your initials and date. It's very important that you keep a copy of the final schedule for your records. If a dispute arises and makes it's way to the labor board or unemployment office, then they may want to see your original and final schedule. After the week is over make sure you attach the final or posted employee schedule to your original schedule. Keep in mind that there will be changes to the posted schedule located at your business. For example, your manager might switch Mark and Tom's shifts on Wednesday or give Karen Mike's shift because Mike wanted off for some reason. There are a variety of factors that will result in a change in your schedule almost on a daily basis. We had our managers always make any changes in red so we could identify them at a glance. At the end of the workweek, the schedule was turned in to us allowing us to compare it and attach it to the original. In our first shop, we failed to set any criteria when we handed the responsibility over to our manager of our first shop. It was a lesson learned that we did not repeat again.

18   PAYROLL

If you have employees then you must have a system to keep track of the hours worked for pay purposes. If you have a commission pay plan, then your system would be based on sales produced by your employees. Some pay packages incorporate a system of either sales produced or hours worked or a combination of both. There are a variety of systems available to keep track of employee time that simplifies payroll processing. Many point of sales (POS) systems incorporate a program module for employee sign in and out times that keeps accurate payroll records. With these computerized systems, the employee merely signs in with their pass code establishing their start time for payroll purposes. Many of these systems can be programmed so as to establish a particular workweek and payroll period. For example, you can designate your workweek as Monday thru Sunday or Sunday thru Saturday or even Tuesday thru Monday. This option allows you to synchronize your payroll workweek with your employee work schedule. Other options can be configured to allow you to set your payroll period on a semi-monthly or monthly basis. How you establish your pay period is up to you, but there are some factors to consider for each.

Payroll Workweeks and Pay Periods

Your *workweek* establishes the first day of a 7-day period and becomes significant for overtime purposes. Anything over 40 hours in a designated workweek is classified as overtime and subject to a rate of one and a half times the normal base rate of pay. Remember, your state may have additional criteria defining overtime and may provide more guidance on workweeks, but generally the employer establishes the workweek such as Monday through Sunday. If you elect to establish the workweek as Monday thru Sunday then any employee who works more than 40 hours between Monday thru Sunday is due overtime. It is not a sliding 7-day period but a fixed period you have established. On the other hand, a *pay period* is the length of time you designate as when paychecks will be based on. For example, a semi-monthly pay period means that an employee's paycheck will reflect time worked from either the 1st to the 15th and the 16th thru the end of the month with paychecks usually distributed no more than five days after the end of the pay period.

Pay periods can be on a weekly, bi-weekly, monthly or semi-monthly basis depending on your states policy on pay period lengths. We used a semi-monthly pay period with paychecks distributed on the 5th and 20th of each month. The advantage of a semi-monthly or monthly pay period is cost and time. If you have a weekly pay period for example, then your cost to process payroll is about twice that of a semi-monthly period. Also, the time involved is considerably more than a semi-monthly period. The disadvantage of a longer pay period is with employees. Some job applicants will turn down a job if the pay period is not on a weekly basis. I know we had applicants who expressed concern over the lengthy pay period. We have found that more businesses are going to a semi-monthly or monthly pay period to reduce processing costs. A pay period that coincides with your workweek is an advantage since it makes computation of overtime for pay purposes a lot easier but the disadvantage of course is the higher processing costs.

The following is an example on how to compute regular and overtime hours when the workweek is different than the pay period. Referring to the calendar below, you have a semi-monthly pay period that starts on the 1st and ends on the 15th of the month. The 1st is on a Friday and signifies the first day for pay purposes while the 15th is on Friday and marks the last day of the pay period. However, for scheduling and overtime purposes your workweek is from Monday to Sunday. From the 1st to the 3rd (Friday, Saturday and Sunday) John worked a total of 25 hours. From the 4th to the 10th (second work week in pay period), John worked 39 hours. And from the 11th to the 15th (partial third week of pay period) John worked 42 hours. In this pay period, John worked a total of 106 hours. Some might say that John worked 26 hours of overtime (106 – 80) but that is not correct. First, remember a semi-monthly pay period is not a two-week period. In this case, it involves 15 days for the period of the 1st to the 15th of the month. Second, since your workweek is defined as Monday thru Sunday, the first week includes 3 days of the current pay period and 4 days from the previous pay period. During that week John worked a total of 43 hours of which 3 hours were in overtime. So for that first week, John had 3 hours of overtime. From the 4th thru the 10th, John worked 39 hours of which he had no over time hours. On the third week of the 11th thru the 15th John so far has worked 42 hours. For this third week, John has so far accumulated two hours of overtime. Therefore, John's two hours of overtime for this week will be paid on this pay period ending on the 15th. However, anymore hours worked in this third week will be overtime and must be paid in the following pay period which starts on the 16th and ends on the last day of the month. For example, if John works 8 more hours during this third week, then he will have a total of 50 hours of which 40 has been paid in regular time and 2 have been paid in overtime. This leaves 8 hours of overtime that is due to John in his next paycheck reflecting the period of the 16th to the end of the month. In the first week that extends into the pay period of the 1st to the 15th, (the 27th thru the 3rd), John had a total of 43 hours of which 25 hours were from the 1st to the 3rd. Since no overtime was paid in the previous pay period for that week, John is owed 3 hours of overtime. Adding up the overtime hours for each week, we have 3 + 0 + 2 for a total of 5 hours of overtime. Therefore, John will have a total of 106 hours (25 + 39 + 42) in this pay period. Five of these hours (3 + 0 + 2) will be in overtime leaving 101 regular hours in this pay period. John's paycheck for the pay period of the 1st to the 15th will reflect 101 hours of regular pay and 5 hours of overtime pay. This may seem a bit confusing but its necessary for overtime calculations. Now, if your workweek coincides with your pay period, then you would avoid the extra effort involved with overtime calculations as the above example demonstrates. By now you may be asking yourself why not just contract out to a payroll processing company and avoid all these gymnastics. Most payroll processing business will require *you* to furnish them with a break down of regular and overtime hours for each employee.

M	T	W	TH	F	SAT	SUN
27 10	28 8	29	30	1 8	2 9	3 8
4 8	5 8	6 8	7	8	9 8	10 7
11 9	12 9	13 8	14 8	15 8	16	17

Calendar: Hours worked in the pay period of the 1st to the 15th.

Payroll Processing

Now that we have discussed workweeks and pay periods, the next issue deals with the actual processing of pay roll. The first step is the collection of employee time sheets or time cards. This is normally done on the first day after a pay period. Managers usually have the responsibility of finalizing each employee's time for the pay period with total and overtime hours worked. Adjustments are normally made at this time for any unusual circumstances. If your employees use a "punch machine" to record their in and out times on a time card, then the actual hours worked for each segment must be calculated manually. This is unlike computerized systems that automatically compute hours worked including overtime hours. Manual calculation can be somewhat involved and prone to mistakes, which is why we will devote sometime to this element. Even if you elect to go with a computerized system or a service that computes employee time, it is worth your time now to familiarize yourself with the process just in case you are faced with this task at some point.

The first step is to compute the hours worked for each day or segment. This can be easily done with either a hand held calculator or with a spreadsheet such as with Microsoft's Excel. One commonly overlooked element in this process is the requirement to convert the hours worked to a decimal system. Lets say John's time card shows that he clocked in at 8:03 and clocked out at 4:49 pm. Obviously, you cannot simply plug in these times in a calculator, subtract the two and come up with the hours worked, unless your calculator has a function to enter time in the format of X:XX. A mental calculation is simple and yields 8 hours and 46 minutes. However, if you have 10 employees, then a one-week period would involve about 50 such mental calculations with an increasing chance of making a mistake. An easy and more error free approach is to use a simple spreadsheet to calculate the numbers. You should also convert over to a 24-hour system instead of a 12-hour system. For example, 1 pm becomes 1300 hours, 2 pm becomes 1400 hours, and 3:30 pm becomes 1530 hours and so forth. Whether you use a calculator or spreadsheet, the times must first be converted to a decimal format. This is done as follows. Convert the minutes into hundredths by dividing the minutes by 60. 8:03 then becomes 8.05 (3 minutes divided by 60 is .05) and 4:49 becomes 4.82 (49 minutes divided by 60) or 16.82 for a 24-hour system. If you have set up your time machine to record in a 24-hour system, then we have 8.05 and 16.82 for a difference of 8.77 or 8 *point 77* hours (16.82 – 8.05). The automation of a spreadsheet will save you time and reduce the chances of errors. Once your spreadsheet is set up, then it just becomes a matter of entering the times manually or exporting them from your time sheet program. After the daily hours are computed then the sum of hours yields the total hours worked for the pay period. Adjustments can be made at this point that consider time deducted for lunches or for early sign in or late sign outs that weren't authorized.

	A	B	C	D	E
	Day of Month	START TIME	END TIME	TOT TIME (HRS:MIN)	TOT TIME (DECIMAL)
	1	9:00	14:15	5:15	5.25
	2	8:00	15:23	7:23	7.38
	3	13:05	18:27	5:22	5.37
	4	13:00	20:35	7:35	7.58
	5	11:00	20:15	9:15	9.25
	6				
	7				
	8	8:00	15:19	7:19	7.32
	9	8:05	16:10	8:05	8.08
	10	11:00	15:00	4:00	4.00
	11	11:00	20:36	9:36	9.60
	12	15:00	20:14	5:14	5.23
	13				
	14				
	15	8:00	15:45	7:45	7.75

TOTAL HOURS FOR PAY PERIOD 1st TO 15th > **76.82**

Sample spreadsheet for computation of hours worked in a semi-monthly pay period (1st to the 15th)

In the above sample, columns B & C are the start and end times that the employee worked. Make sure you are in the "time" format for these columns. Column D is C – B, which gives you total time worked in hours and minutes. Column E is column D converted to a decimal system. The formula for column E is (DX-(INT(DX))*24, where X is the row number of that cell. With your spread sheet set up in the above format, all that you need to do is enter the start and end times and the rest is automatically computed resulting in the total time worked for the pay period.

The next step is to compute overtime as discussed above. Once you have the regular and overtime hours computed then you can enter them manually or export them into your payroll software for withholding calculations and final printing of paychecks. If you use a payroll service, then you can fax, email or hand-carry these times to your payroll service. There are a number of commercial businesses that specialize in paycheck processing. You submit the employee hours to them and they process and print the paychecks. Checks are then distributed to your business location or they can be picked up for distribution. Withholdings are made for such items as Federal Income Tax (FIT), FICA, HI FICA, and any other required withholdings. Items that are the responsibility of the employer such as worker compensation insurance, state and federal unemployment taxes, FICA and HI FICA are computed and debited from the employers business account. These funds debited from the employers account, are deposited with the payroll company. The payroll company then makes payments and reports to the appropriate state or federal agency. A statement of all distributions made as well as a record of employee payroll is sent to the business owner. Direct payroll amounts are usually drawn from your business account. Remember, that the employer must compute regular and overtime hours for each employee before most payroll processing companies can process the payroll checks.

    The other method of processing paychecks is within your office. There are many inexpensive computer programs that allow the small business owner to process and print payroll checks. These programs allow you to do everything that a payroll company does. Accurate records are maintained including the amounts due to state and federal agencies. We not only processed our own employee time sheets but also printed our own paychecks using a simple accounting program. Such programs as QuickBooks or Peachtree are very versatile and provide the business owner with an in depth payroll and accounting process. There are many others that are well suited for the small business. Federal and State payments are calculated as well as required reports with these programs making it a simple task for the small business owner or manager. Some businesses hire part-time help to do the "books" and process payroll utilizing these programs. Many point-of-sale programs already have an accounting program that also processes and prints payroll checks, which is probably the best option for a small business.

The last area I present here is one of the most costly abuses I have ever seen and frankly is stealing. Its an abuse that many businesses see and involves schemes of padding "in" and "out" times recorded on an employee's time card for the purpose of increasing hours worked. After the opening of our second shop, our time recorder broke down and we were unable to accurately record employee in and out times. We elected to have our employees simply write in their times when coming in and leaving work. As you might imagine, we discovered that these "write in" times were not accurate and in many cases were grossly off from the actual times. Employees were writing times that were earlier than they actually arrived and later than they actually left thereby giving them more time then they actually worked. Of course, we bought new recorders and required all employees to use the recorders for they're in and out times. In our first month after implementing the recorders, our average weekly payroll time decreased by 400 minutes. Over a one year period that comes to 20,800 minutes or about 347 hours for 8 employees. At an average pay rate of $10 an hour, this comes to $3,470 due to inaccurate sign in/out times! Some of you might be wondering if the manager wasn't keeping an eye on these write in times? Frankly, the managers were also doing the same. When a manager or employee was confronted or caught red handed, they would usually display anger with us complaining that they made a mistake. Our mistake was allowing the employees to write in their times instead of immediately getting new machines.

Even with time recorders in all our shops, we discovered that some employees were clocking in early and clocking out later than their scheduled times. For example, if Jane was scheduled from 10 am to 5 pm, she might arrive early and clock in at 9:40, and clock out at 5:20, thereby adding an extra 40 minutes to her payroll time on this day with no additional hair services. Forty minutes might not seem excessive, but over a week that amounts to 200 minutes or 173 hours over a one-year period. Even if the average is 15 minutes a day, if you have, say 10 employees who are padding the system, then you have an overage of 433 hours over a one year period. At $10 an hours that comes to

$4,333 in direct payroll cost with no added revenues or sales from these people. Add indirect payroll cost and your up to about $5,000 over one year! We found many of our business neighbors also ran into the same problem. A few minutes here or there is not a big deal, but excessive occurrences can be very costly over time. Reminding employees to clock in or out at their scheduled times was effective only for a short time. We decided to put in place a policy into our employee manual that was effective in addressing this problem. Our policy was simply that we were not going to credit, and pay for, sign in times earlier than scheduled times unless the individual was opening the shop, which in that case was allowed to sign in ten minutes early. Late sign out times were not going to be honored unless it was clear that the employee was servicing a customer. Last minute walk in customers or a flood of customers during the final hour of business could easily push sign out times later, which is justifiable. But in cases where a late sign out could not be justified then the hours were limited to the employees scheduled time. Our employees had no authorization to start work early but they were authorized to work later if it involved servicing our customers. We have seen sign out times of over an hour after the employee's scheduled off time with no justification. The reason is simply to pad ones total hours or to go over 40 hours and into overtime. If you tell your employees that's its alright to sign in early or sign out later than scheduled than you are bound to pay them for their time. I remember an applicant I was interviewing for a job who told me that she would stay hours after her scheduled shift to "recount the cash drawer" if she was off even a penny. I asked her if it made sense to pay someone $20 to find a clerical error in the amount of a penny or even $20? I told her that if there was an error then note the error on the paper work and close out the drawer. My wife or I would find the error, as we had been accustomed to doing. She decided not to take the job with us once she knew she would not be able to get away with this scheme.

     On some occasions an employee would make the case that the late sign out time was due to customers. For example, Jane was scheduled from 9 am to 5 pm. Jane clocks out at 5:30 and claims that there were customers who came in about 5:00 although there were already two other employees on duty who could have easily serviced the customers. In examining the log sheet we discovered that Jane did indeed service the customer, but the other two employees were not doing anything. Jane could have easily left at 5:00 and the other two employees could have serviced the customers with no problems. This type of coordinated effort would be repeated with each other thereby allowing each employee to justify their later clock out times. Our policy was modified and we laid out criteria in terms of customers versus available employees that would justify late sign out times. Without a clear policy on this issue, employees can pad their time, costing you significantly. We also found that some would pad their time during the weekdays so that they could then call out sick on a weekend day without a loss in hours. If an employee came to us, or a manager and said they needed more time, we would usually offer them extra hours at one of our other locations. Or, we would ask them if they were willing to come in for someone who called in sick. So the extra time was usually there if they were willing to travel to another location, or work for someone else on a weekend! But we were not going to create hours during non-busy periods and yet be short handed during busy periods, that makes no sense. Some computerized employee time tracking systems will not allow an employee to sign in early unless approved by a supervisor. These system are linked to the schedule entered into the computer so when an employees signs in, the system knows when this employees should be signing in.

Another factor that became an issue was time off for lunch or dinner. If you give your employees an hour off for lunch, or dinner, do you think you should pay them during this time off? Most employees on hourly pay are on their own time when it comes to lunches or meal breaks meaning that they must clock off or have the time automatically subtracted from their daily hours. Now, what would you think if some of your employees said to you that they don't take off for lunches since they are on a diet, only to find them sitting in the break room having lunch! In effect, they are still on the clock while on their lunch break. If you are always at your business location then this type of action is not so common. But if you have multiple locations or don't visit you businesses often, then it's not too difficult to get away with claiming, "no lunch taken" when in reality it was taken on the clock. That's exactly what we found early on in our business. It became our policy that everyone had to take a 30-minute break if on duty for over 5 hours, with no exceptions. If they didn't want to eat then that was their option, but they were not going to be on the floor working during their break. This didn't mean we closed the shop while they were on break. The breaks were coordinated so that someone else would cover the employee while they were on a break. Without addressing this issue early in your business, your employees will think its ok to be on the clock while on their lunch break. Reversing this trend after it is deep seated will definitely create friction between you and the employees. You may only have one employee who claims they don't eat so they are not taking off for lunch. But, if this employee is taking off for lunch and getting paid for it, then your other employees will soon try the same. The other factor in all this is what federal and state labor laws say. Contact your local labor law office and speak with someone on the current law governing this issue. If you allow your employees to work 8 straight hours without taking a 30 minute lunch break, excluding 15 minute breaks, then that could be interpreted by the labor folks that you are not allowing, or discouraging your employees from taking lunch breaks. Throw in a disgruntled ex-employee, and you could have a real problem on your hands and possibly legal action taken against you! Most businesses will require their employees to "clock-out" when they leave for their lunch break and clock-in when they return from their break. Others will merely subtract the allocated time (30 minutes or 1 hour) from their daily time. Either way is fine as long as you make it policy among all your employees and they are informed of it.

19 STATE AND FEDERAL DEPOSITS AND REPORTS FOR EMPLOYERS

As you go through this section you may be telling yourself that if there was ever a time you wanted to contract out this would be it. Whether you decide to have someone do your payroll or file state and federal deposits and reports for you, you still should have a general understanding of the process. I found that the process itself was easier than it first appeared and with the many tools and programs out there, it has become almost a no brainer! Almost every small business accounting program such as Quickbooks will generate all the needed reports and amounts due.

Federal Tax Deposits (FTD)

If you have employees on payroll then you or someone on your behalf will be responsible for certain on going requirements pertaining to payroll taxes and reporting. A good web site covering your requirements can be found by first going to: www.irs.gov/businesses/index.html, then scroll down to and select "Operating a Business". On this site there are a number of useful topics covering business operations. The type of payroll taxes you will be responsible for are:

Federal Income Tax (FIT)
Federal Insurance Contributions Act (FICA)
Medicare Tax (HIFICA)
Federal Unemployment Tax (FUTA)

FIT is the amount withheld from an employee's paycheck and is a function of the number of exemptions claimed (from the W-4 statement), single or married rate, the gross pay and the payroll period (weekly, semimonthly, monthly etc). IRS publication 15 includes all the tax withholding formulas and tables for employers to determine the proper amount to be withheld. Accounting software such as

QuickBooks and Peachtree also include a complete payroll section with up to date tax tables. IRS Publication 15 is one of the most useful publications we used in our business and is mailed to the business owner by the end of the year. It can also be found by going to www.irs.gov/businesses, then scroll down and select "Employment Taxes For Small Businesses." This web site has a number of useful topics and links for small businesses. Scroll down and select "Businesses With Employees" then select **Federal Income Taxes/Social Security and Medicare Taxes"** and finally select "Employer's Tax Guide." A short cut is to go directly to www.irs.gov/publications/p15/index.html. The advantage of going through the different IRS web sites to get to Publication 15 is that it exposes you to a variety of topics and sites useful to the small business owner.

The Federal Insurance Contributions Act, also known as the Social Security Tax and the Medicare Tax (FICA and HIFICA) are shared equally by the employee and employer. The employer deducts half of the amount from the employee's paycheck. The other half is paid by the employer and cannot be deducted from the employee's gross pay. In other words, the IRS will not allow employers to make the employee pay the full amount of FICA and HIFICA. Together, the FIT, FICA and HIFICA make up the "941 Federal Deposit." The frequency of these deposits is a function of the total gross payroll averaged over four quarters and ranges from daily to monthly deposits. As a new employer, the IRS most likely will classify you as a monthly depositor. There are several ways to make these deposits. One is to make the payments, using coupon deposit slips provided by the IRS at your bank. Another way is through a system called the Electronic Federal Tax Payment System (EFTPS) which is discussed later. The other method is through a payroll company who you authorize to make 941 and 940 payments on your behalf.

The Federal Unemployment Tax (FUTA), is the complete responsibility of the employer and is called the "940 Federal Deposit." You report and pay FUTA separately form Social Security, Medicare and withheld income tax. You pay FUTA tax only from your own funds. ***Employees do not pay this tax or have it withheld from their pay.*** Report FUTA taxes on Form 940, Employer's Annual Federal Unemployment (FUTA) Tax return or if you qualify, you can use the simpler form 940-EZ instead.

The specific IRS web site that describes employment taxes for employers can be found by going to www.irs.gov/businesses/index.html, then scroll down on the left side and select "Employment Taxes". This page will bring up a number of topics on employment taxes, select the section titled, "What are FTD's and why they are important".

Who must make deposits?

Its important to keep in mind what we are going to deposit. These are the withholding taxes from your employee's paychecks as well as your matching FICA and HIFICA amounts mentioned above (941 deposits). Federal Unemployment Taxes, that are the responsibility of the employer, are 940 federal deposits. Employers may have two separate employment tax deposits:

- Employers filing Form 941, Employer's Quarterly Federal Tax Return, with $2,500 or more tax due per quarter

or

- Employers filing Form 940, Employer's Annual Federal Unemployment Tax Return (FUTA), with over $100 tax due per quarter.

When to make payments

940 Deposits

If you have a deposit requirement for Form 940, make the deposit by the last day of the first month after the quarter ends. The IRS will mail you a 940 form with instructions usually by the end of the year. However, your deposits are due quarterly. For example, for the quarter January 1st to March 31st, your 940 deposit is due by April 30th. However 941 deposits follow a different schedule depending on when the amounts are withheld from the employee's paycheck.

941 Deposits

Before going any further, lets discuss how these taxes are deducted from your employee's paycheck since this is an area of confusion. Lets say you are a monthly depositor and lets say that you distribute your paychecks to your employees on February 5th that covers the work period of January 16th to the 31st. The next paychecks are handed out on February 20th that covers the work period of February 1st to the 15th. These two paychecks cover the total amount that where *paid* to your employees for the month of February even though the paychecks on February 5th were earned in January. Five days is the normal time from the end of the pay period to when paychecks are distributed. Lets also say that the amount of withholdings plus the employer's FICA and HIFICA for both of these paydays in February amounts to $2000. To the IRS, you had a total of $2000 of 941 taxes for the month of February. This $2000 must be deposited by March 15th. Remember, the IRS is only concerned about pay dates or the day you hand out paychecks, not the period they were earned. This may sound confusing, but once you have gone through the process the first time it will make sense.

<u>The good news is that most payroll programs compute the 940 and 941 federal deposits and report for you</u>. The information is derived from the payroll checks you processed with the same software! So you do not have to manually compute these deposits. If you have a deposit requirement for Form 941, there are two options to remember:
- Make a deposit the same day you *pay* your employees.

or
- Make the deposit before the due date.

Form 941 Deposit Due Date. If you are a new employer and have never filed 941 forms, then you are a **Monthly Schedule Depositor** for the first calendar year of your business unless you are a special exception to the rule (see below). Monthly Schedule Depositors should deposit taxes from all of their paydays in a month by the 15th of the next month, even if they pay wages every week.

After your first year, employers with payroll taxes of $2,500 or more per quarter must determine if they make either Monthly Schedule Deposits, or Semiweekly Schedule Deposits. To determine if you are a monthly or semiweekly depositor, you must do a four-quarter look back. The web site mentioned above, "What are FTD's and why they are important", has a calendar to determine the look back period. <u>The IRS will usually notify you after the first year whether you are a monthly or semiweekly depositor</u>. If in doubt, call the IRS and ask them to do a review for you. If the total 941 tax deposits made during the look back period are $50,000 or less then you are a monthly depositor. If they are more than $50,000 during this period then you are a semiweekly depositor.

Monthly Schedule Depositors

- Deposit each month's taxes by the 15th day of the following month.

Semiweekly Schedule Depositors

- For wages paid Saturday, Sunday, Monday, or Tuesday, deposits must be made by the following Friday.
- For wages paid Wednesday, Thursday, or Friday, deposits must be made by the following Wednesday.

The Exception!

If you accumulate a tax liability of $100,000 or more on any day during a deposit period, you must deposit the tax by the next banking day after payday, whether you are a monthly or semiweekly schedule depositor. For more information about the $100,000 One-Day Rule and the applicable deposit period, refer to Publication 15, Circular E, Employer's Tax Guide, Depositing Taxes.

Remember!

- **Deposit rules are based on when wages are paid, not earned**. For example, Monthly Schedule Depositors with wages earned in June, but paid in July, deposit August 15.
- If the due date for a deposit falls on a federal or state bank holiday, or on a Saturday or Sunday, the deposit is considered timely if it is made by the close of the next banking day.

How to make deposits

If you have a deposit requirement, you may be able to choose one of two deposit methods:

- You may be required, or prefer, to use the Electronic Federal Tax Payment System (EFTPS). The web site covering EFTPS can be found from the "What are FTD's and why they are important" site or at https://www.eftps.gov/eftps/. EFTPS is not mandatory for most small business employers but may be used voluntarily as a convenient alternative to depositing with FTD coupons. Check out the most frequently asked questions about EFTPS: Publication 966, "Choices for Paying ALL Your Federal Taxes" (PDF) which can also be found on "What are FTD's and why they are important" site. We used the EFTPS and found it very simple and reliable allowing us to make our payment from our office computer instead of having to make our payment at the bank.
- If you are not using, or required to use, the EFTPS, mail or deliver Form 8109, Federal Tax Deposit Coupon, with your payment to an authorized financial institution or if you prefer, you may mail your coupon and payment to: Financial Agent, Federal Tax Deposit Processing, P.O. Box 97-0030, St. Louis, MO 63197. Make your check or money order payable to Financial Agent. As always, check with the IRS for the most up to date procedures and addresses.

Making Electronic Deposits using EFTPS

- All taxpayers can use EFTPS.
- You must enroll with EFTPS before making deposits.

Making Deposits with FTD Coupons

- Verify your name and Employer Identification Number (EIN) on the coupon.
- Use a separate coupon for each type of tax deposited, for example, one for Form 941, Employer's Quarterly Federal Tax Return, and another for Form 940, Employer's Annual Federal Unemployment (FUTA) Tax Return.
- Darken only one box for the correct type of tax and only one box for the correct tax period.
- Use FTD coupons only for current taxes, not for delinquent taxes.
- New employers are automatically pre-enrolled in the Electronic Federal Tax Payment System (EFTPS), giving them the opportunity to choose the government's free electronic payment program, rather than using coupons. New employer's have the option to order FTD coupons if they want to make additional payments by check, but will need to allow 5-6 weeks for coupons to arrive by mail. The number to call for ordering coupons is 1-800-829-4933.
- The IRS tracks the number of coupons used and sends more automatically. If you are a new employer you will not automatically receive subsequent coupons until after you place your initial order.
- Use Form 8109-B if you are unable to obtain preprinted forms. You can call 1-800-829-4933, or visit your local IRS office to get Form 8109-B.
Note: If you choose to visit your local IRS office, the IRS personnel are required to complete the Form 8109-B information identifying the depositor before issuing the coupon.

193

Additionally, you must be a responsible official of the business OR have a signed Power-of-Attorney or Tax Information Authorization (or have one on file with the IRS) to receive the completed Form 8109-B.

Caution

If you have a deposit requirement, do not send tax payments with your tax return directly to the IRS. If you use the FTD coupon method, your deposit must go to your authorized bank. Contact your local bank to obtain information concerning check clearance and daily cutoff schedules. For more information, refer to "Depositing Taxes" in Publication 15, Circular E, Employer's Tax Guide.

Whether payroll is processed in house or contracted out, the business owner should have an understanding of the federal reporting and deposit requirements commonly known as the 941 and 940 reports. Each state will have their own system of reporting for state withholding tax and state unemployment tax. Most states have the employer mail in the payments along with the quarterly reports. In addition, there is an annual federal (IRS) consolidated report along with the federal IRS copy of the W-2's for each employee who worked at the business anytime during the year. The state also has a separate report covering the year along with the state's copy of the W-2's for each employee. Obviously, the annual federal and state consolidated reports should match each other with the same gross payroll amounts.

There is a lot of information we have discussed above for the new business owner. It's advisable that instead of trying to memorize when and what deposits to make, simply mark on a calendar the day what deposits are due for the coming year. Write down every report and deposit required including the end of year reports, even if you don't do your own payroll processing. If a deposit or report is missed, the IRS will notify the folks who do your payroll then you. The employer is ultimately responsible for all federal deposits.

20 LEADERSHIP MANAGERS AND OWNERS

Leadership

As an owner or manager, leadership will be a critical element of your business. A company without effective leadership is like a ship without a rudder, it just wonders aimlessly until it sinks. Those of you who served in the military, especially as officers probably understand how vital leadership is to the mission. The military and many large companies understand its importance so well that they spend a great deal if time, money and training to ensure its officers and managers become effective leaders. Your ability to make decisions, to motivate, communicate, to instill confidence, or generate enthusiasm are but a few of the elements of leadership. Is there any one element that is more important than the others? If I had to choose the most single important element it would be the ability to inspire and motivate others. However, let me add that the situation will dictate the most important element of leadership. Leadership is so important to your business that I believe it can mean the difference between a successful or failed business.

Communication skills deserve special mention when we talk about leadership. I am sure most of you have heard that it's not what you say but how you say it that makes the difference. Always barking out orders to your employees is not going to help your rapport with your employees on a long-term basis. On the other hand, a soft spoken, middle of the road approach will probably not give you the desired results. Throughout the years, I have learned that the appropriate style of communication depends on the situation, the urgency and the person or persons involved. Learning how to communicate, as an effective leader is not something you can learn in a few days. It may take some people years of learning and practice. My best recommendation is to visit your local library and pick out a few books on leadership and communication. Also look for books on some of our past corporate and national leaders that demonstrated a distinguishable but effective leadership style.

As an owner, you will be able to identify employees who are leaders and those who prefer to follow. It was interesting to me to see that in some cases the most influential person was not the manager. However the manager was still the best person to be in charge simply due to other factors such as knowledge, experience and dependability. The managers, who were the most influential as well as possessing the essential factors mentioned above, usually had the best overall performing shops.

There are two main roles that leaders will find themselves in. The first role involves the performance and effectiveness of employees in established day-to-day operations. This means the ability to motivate employees in their normal everyday functions of their job such as, on time performance, attendance, proper dress and grooming, following procedures, being respectful and courteous to customers, and other elements vital to the success of any business. Individuals vary and it's not enough to assume that everyone will perform up to acceptable standards without some motivating. If you have 10 employees with 8 performing well, then getting each of the other two to conform with the other 8 will be easier on an individual basis than if you had 8 employees that are performing in a substandard fashion. As an owner or manager, you should be well aware of who and how many are performing to your acceptable standards. If you see a trend developing of more employees performing in a substandard fashion, then action must be taken before the erosion continues to develop and becomes irreversible. This is why it is so important for a leader to recognize trends early and to take action before it becomes nearly impossible to recover and turn things around. <u>Its essential that a leader be aggressive in recognizing a problem and doing something about it before the problem takes control</u>. Eventually, the last few remaining motivated employees will leave for another job if things don't change. If you walked into a restaurant and found the employees dressed sloppy, the floors dirty and the hostess unfriendly, then you would probably ask yourself if the owner was aware of what was going on. If the owner is aware, then you have to question the owner's ability to get things done correctly. If the owner is not aware of the problems, then we simply have a case where the manager doesn't care and the owner is not minding the business. Either case, you have a poorly led and managed operation that if left to continue will most likely fail. We have all seen the difference between a well-run business and one that wasn't.

The other role of a leader has more of a strategic significance that deals with the direction and change of the business. Most workers feel more comfortable and secure when there is little or no change in the work place. I think most of us can identify with that. For example, lets say your business hours are from 8am to 7pm. You have determined that you could improve your business significantly by staying open another hour, so you decide to change your weekday hours from 8am to 8pm. How receptive do you think your employees will be in staying open another hour? If they didn't like working till 7, they are certainly not going to like 8pm. Simply telling them that you are going to stay open till 8pm may not go over well. In fact, you may see some employees finding work elsewhere. Getting your employees to accept changes will be challenging and certainly could result in a turn over of employees. Informing your staff of unpopular changes you have decided to take must be combined with the positive aspects of such changes. Every change will have a positive aspect and it must be up to you to get your employees to see and believe in your decisions. The objective is to get the employees to see the benefits of any change and how it affects them in a positive manner. One of the biggest challenges for today's owners and managers is to recognize necessary changes to their business and getting the employees to see the value of such changes. This ability to motivate employees and others involved in the new direction is what separates good from poor leadership.

Whether the task is motivating individuals on day-to-day performances or setting a new direction, leadership skills will play a major role in your business. Without question, the effectiveness of a leader depends on the relationship between the leader and those that are lead. This relationship cannot happen over night. It is a relationship that takes time to develop and is built on trust and credibility and where "lead by example" has meaning. Leaders shape peoples opinions and win their enthusiasm, using every available opportunity to send out their message and win supporters. In many ways, it is very similar to someone who is campaigning to win the support of voters. In order to get the support of the people, a leader must get them to believe in what the leader is trying to accomplish. There is a big difference in forcing someone to do something and having that person do it because they believe in it. Imagine having to go to your employees to tell them they need to take a pay cut. Getting them to see that pay cuts are essential to the survivability of the business is critical. Snap back measures of pay or bonuses, based on business performance, is one way to make the sacrifice more tolerable as well as other incentives. Too many times a person in a leadership position will not convince the individuals of the need or benefit of the new change or sacrifice.

Visibility is another vital element of leadership. You simply cant be a good leader if your not visible to your employees. If you're going to have a meeting or conference with your staff, what do you think would be more effective, an in person meeting, or a conference call? Obviously, an in person meeting would be more effective. Visiting your place of business and conversing with your employees is also very beneficial. We never went more than a few days without visiting our shops and helping out our employees or on occasion, bringing them lunch or snacks. We personally knew each of our employees and always inquired about their personal life. Your ability to personalize and interact with you're employees is part of building that relationship between a leader and those that are lead.

Management

In most small owner operator businesses, the owner is usually the manager, which makes sense. But some businesses, especially those with multiple locations require a manager other than the owner. In our business, the state cosmetology board required each hair salon to have a licensed cosmetologist as a designated manager. Since my wife and I were not licensed cosmetologist, we were not allowed to be shop managers! How about that for state regulation. However, we could and were managers over all our individual shop managers. The law does make sense when you consider the unique sanitation and operating requirements of a salon when dealing with chemicals. As part of a certified cosmetology course, students are required to receive a number of hours in sanitation and safety, which are then tested by the state when a cosmetologist applies for a state license. However, owners are not required to attend cosmetology school, thus the requirement for a licensed cosmetologist as a salon manager. This didn't mean that the owner couldn't be fined or have their salon owner license revoked; they certainly could for repeated violations. As with this business, there are probably other examples where the owner might not be able to act as manager. Which means the owner must hire or designate a manager and be in that delicate position of having to supervise their manager on an overall performance level.

We found it best to designate a manager from within the employee group as opposed to hiring someone off the street as a manager. Someone who has been working for you has many advantages over someone from outside your business. First, this individual is already familiar with your business and its operations. They know you and how you like things done. Second, you have had an opportunity to observe them and evaluate their ability as a manager. Fourth, they are very familiar with your employees who in turn are more likely to support your manager than someone they have never worked with before. Finally, you have demonstrated to all your employees that the reward for doing a good job is advancement along with higher pay. Once you have designated a manager then you must clearly spell out their responsibilities and make sure they are on the same page as you.

At our first salon, we hired a stylists who was very competent and who was motivated to be a manager. Having just opened, our business volume was very slow as expected. After only four weeks our new manager had decided to quit because it was too slow and she wasn't making the tips or the productivity pay she was accustomed to before. Loyalty is a very important factor in your employees and especially for a manager. Determining the loyalty of a future manager is difficult if you have never observed this person. After this individual quit we found another stylist who was eager to jump in as a manager. The two other stylists we had working were simply out of the question as managers. Betty was experienced, fast, good with customers and had great quality in her work. But as a leader she was not very effective and her motive for wanting the manager's position became obvious after some time. At first, we routinely worked at the shop helping out where we could and making out the schedule. One day Betty confronted us with the schedule and wanted us to give her the responsibility of making out the schedule. As she pointed out, she was in a better position to work out everyone's individual needs and yet ensure coverage of the schedule. We agreed and handed over the responsibility of making out the weekly schedule. After all, the manager should be able to make out the schedule and ensure coverage. But after some time it became clear why she wanted to make out the schedule. It was her aim to take the best shifts without working the weekends or Friday nights. She gave herself the best hours to work while the other stylists were given much less desirable hours. After some time the other stylists were getting fed up with Betty and her complete monopolization of the schedule. However, when we intervened, they felt it was an intrusion, putting us in an awkward position. One stylist ended up quitting which made the scheduling problem even worse. Betty then told me one day that we made things worse by coming to the salon and that we should avoid coming down! They didn't want the owners watching them was the message. Well, we still made our visits; I was not going to stay away from my business just because it made them uncomfortable. Eventually, we were able to bring some people in to cover the schedule. Betty was replaced as manager after we had failed our first state inspection and eventually the salon returned to a more normal operation. This was our first salon and it was a good lesson to us on how bad things could get when the tail begins to wag the dog!

Responsibilities and Owner-Manager Relationship

Ok, so you have selected a manager, what now. Before you sit down with your new manager and discuss their responsibilities you must first have a firm operating policy in place. Our managers were responsible for ensuring that the policies outlined in our operating manual were followed. They were not responsible for making policy but only to carry them out. I can not stress how important this is so I will say it again. <u>The manager's job is to make sure your policies are followed. They are not there to make policy!</u> The owners are responsible for making policy and it is the owners who authorize the manager to enforce policies, plain and simple. These policies are very similar from business to business and have more to do with such things as hours of operation, policies covering refunds, appointments, check and credit card acceptance, tardiness of employees, attendance and etc. This concept is fundamental to your organization, especially when it is a new business. I recall an interesting incident to this matter. We were having problems with a stylist who had decided that it should be OK to service her family and friends in our salon without charging them, at least at the salon. In addition, she was on the clock getting paid while performing these "free" services. When we found out about this, we confronted her and warned her that we would deduct the price of these services from her paycheck. This stylist wrote us a letter to tell us how unfair this was and how much she didn't like how we ran our business. She went on to tell us that managers are in charge to run the business and that we were breaking the law by interfering with a manager's duties! I let her know that it is the owners who make policy, not the managers. I further explained that it is the manager's responsibility to ensure the owner's policies are followed. It is important to establish the role and responsibility of your manager from the very beginning. What may seem obvious to you concerning management's responsibilities may not be entirely obvious to your new manager. Many new managers have the impression that they are now in a position to call the shots. I remember that in one of our salons I discovered they had closed 5 hours early because the manager had felt it was her call to decide when to close! It was not unusual for a manager to call us with request to close early, which we had never granted, but to have a manager close early without consulting us was unheard of.

You should have a manager's manual that describes their responsibilities in detail. Don't be vague. For example, don't tell your manager that she should have periodical meetings. Instead, you should spell out that meetings will be conducted once a month or held the first Wednesday of every month. You should also determine whether such meetings if conducted after store hours are paid. If paid, then you need to establish the amount such as $10 per meeting. If not, you might find that your managers meetings could be excessively long if they are on the clock. Hiring an employee from within has the advantage that this person is already familiar with the operating manual and the things important to you as the owner. They know the basics of your operations and now only need to know their specific responsibilities. This list of responsibilities should be clearly spelled out in your manager's manual and reviewed during your manager's training session.

Initial Manager Training

At a minimum, you need to set aside a few hours devoted to initial manager's training. You should have a lesson plan that closely mirrors your manager's manual. You should also devote some time to discuss your priorities in running your business. One of our top priorities of our manager's was to ensure that our salons complied with state cosmetology rules and regulatory policies. If you're in the restaurant or food business, then your state will have rules and policies governing the food industry. If you are a franchise, then your business must comply with your franchise's rules, policies and codes of conduct. Our second priority for our manager's was to ensure the salon was open during the posted business hours. You are telling your manager that they are responsible for keeping the doors open to the public. This means that if Mike calls in sick on Saturday morning, then it's your manager who must find someone to replace him, not you as the owner. You would be surprised to see how many managers who do not think it should be their responsibility to find a replacement if someone does not show for work for whatever reason. If you let them, they will try to convince you that its you're responsibility to handle such matters. There are many subjects you will want to cover with your manager. Listed below are some of the main subjects that you should consider. Another purpose for training is for you to gage your manager's attitude towards how you want your business to operate. If during your discussion you find your manager opposing some of your policies or is trying to push their own procedures then this might be a red flag of what to expect later on. It should be understood from the beginning that you as the owner establishes policy and your manager carries out those policies. This isn't to say that you don't welcome suggestions; on the contrary, your manager and employees should be encouraged to make suggestions. But ultimately it's the owner who must approve and implement those suggestions. This should be very clear to your manager. We found that managers and employees certainly had no end to suggestions, but many of those suggestions were counter productive or just not feasible. For example, in the first year we were open, many of our stylists wanted to be closed the day after Thanksgiving, claiming that people would be out shopping and thus it would be a slow day for the salon business. By doing this, we could save on payroll, they claimed. Well, we decided against this and remained open. It turned out to be our second busiest day to that point in our business!

Recurrent Training for Managers

Many businesses incorporate an on going or recurrent training review for their managers. It's important to bring your managers in and refocus on things that have deviated in one way or another. People simply get lacks and complacent and before you know it things have deviated from the established procedure. For example, our check acceptance procedure required our cashier to write the driver's license number and current phone on every check. But after some time we noticed that some employees were not asking for driver licenses or a current phone number from our customers. Soon, we found fewer and fewer driver license numbers on checks from our salons. Then, we got clobbered on a bad check for retail product purchased, a hair service and for cash back. The name and address printed on the check were fake. Further more, the customer or thief, actually wrote down their drivers license number on the check before handing it to the stylist. The stylist who took the check failed to visually verify the license number on the check, which was a bogus license number. Because we had gone so long without asking for a driver's license, our stylists were very reluctant to ask for it. This is just one example of how complacency and deviating from established procedures overtime can eventually get you in trouble. As a side note to this example, would you take the amount of the bad check from the cashier who took the check? Is it legal to do so? If you don't have it spelled out in your operating or employee manual then you may not be able to withhold the amount from their pay even though it was due to their neglect of established procedures. In this case, the stylist was clearly at fault for not asking to see the driver's license and for allowing the customer to get cash back, which was not our policy. Having a recurrent training program for your managers is one step towards relearning and reemphasizing procedures that you as an owner want followed. Many large companies have recurrent training programs for their managers and employees. The concept is simple, policies and rules are more likely to be followed the more often you train for them. When I was a young fighter pilot we trained routinely and had a saying, "you fight like you trained".

When you have more than one manager such as when you have multiple locations, then its best to have all your managers attend a single meeting or training session than to have individual meetings with each manager. There are several reasons for this. First, it saves you time and time is a resource you simply don't have enough of. Second, your managers begin to build a rapport with each other that leads to a more cooperative atmosphere. Lets say for example, the manager of one of your stores needs someone to fill in for another employee. The manager calls the manager from one of your other locations to request if they have anyone available to work a few hours until someone else comes in. Managers are more likely to help each other out when they know each other and have developed a rapport. This type of rapport and cooperative atmosphere is not going to happen automatically. Having manager meetings in conjunction with recurrent training is one way to establish this rapport. We had many occasions where one salon became short handed at a very busy period while another salon was not busy and could spare one of their stylists. If you can establish this level of cooperation between your managers than your business will function more smoothly and efficiently. Third, experiences can be more easily shared between managers in a group setting. Good and bad experiences can be shared and learned from one manager to the next. Fourth, special recognition for exceptional performance means more when it is before a group of your peers. In our military units, we would have a monthly officers meeting comprised of all the officers of the wing. As part of this large meeting, awards and medals would be presented to officers by the Wing Commander along with the citation (explanation of why the officer was receiving the award) to accompany the award. This lets everyone know the award the person was receiving and more importantly the circumstances for the award.

It's also nice to conduct your meeting at a location where interruptions are at a minimum and where food can be served. Avoid having your meeting at night. Most likely, your managers have already put in a full day and are more interested in getting home then listening to you. Above all, don't single out a manager and attack them in front of your other managers. If you need to, do it privately, but not in front of a group. Nothing will turn off your manager or employee than scolding or criticizing them in front of others. For example, lets say store A has had more missing retail product then the other stores over the same period. In the meeting, you say to your manager of store A, "Bill, you have had 20% more missing product then the other stores, what's going on?" Immediately you put Bill in a position of having to defend himself when you identified the problem with him. A more effective way of describing the problem is to say, "we need to reduce our missing product, especially at store A where its missing 20% more product than the other stores." The difference between the two is that instead of attacking Bill directly in front of the group, we have identified a problem at store A. I would still discuss the problem with Bill but on a one on one basis. Remember, Bill is not the cause of the problem but can certainly be part of the solution. As a fighter pilot we learned how to debrief air-to-air engagements that de-emphasized criticizing individuals for mistakes in the training environment. Instead, we would identify the aircraft or fighter such as "Bandit 11, was too slow to gain an offensive position." It may seem like we are dealing with semantics, but the effect of personalizing problems could be damaging in the long run. Now, if the problem keeps re-occurring in a particular store then clearly the time has come to try a different strategy with your manager. This is where knowing your staff is vital because what may work with one person may not work with another. You as the owner and leader must be able to determine what works with whom.

Discharging Your Manager

Here is a situation for you to think about. Your manager is one of your top producers who has a small army of loyal and dedicated customers who would follow her or him wherever they go. However, your manager's skills are poor and your employees are threatening to quit unless you relieve your manager. You've discussed the problems with your manager and made recommendations but still there is no improvement. You haven't yet asked her to step down but you are confident that if you do, your manager will walk and most likely attempt to take many customers with her. This is probably one of the toughest decisions that you will have to make and there are no easy solutions. Some would say you could have it both ways by substituting her loss of manager's pay with a pay raise or bonus just to keep her on the property and not risk her leaving with your customers. But I don't recommend that approach for the simple reason that you will be rewarding her lack of performance as a manager. The result is that she no longer has the burden of the manager's duties but gets to keep her same pay level. Worse yet, your employees will eventually find out and that will really cause animosity and reflect poorly on you. My approach is to keep it simple, reduce the blast pattern and do what is right which means replace her as manager. But be ready for her to quit. If you can, gather the names of your customers that you think will follow and be prepared to direct mail these customers with sweet deals. Some customers will bite on the deals while others will follow her. Some of those who will follow her will return for one reason or another eventually, as we have found. Every time an employee left with customers, most of those customers returned back to us. Almost every time we relieved a manager that person quit within a short time, so expect it.

Another option that deals with the problem in a more procedural way is to hire your manager under a trial basis similar to a probation period. Let your new manager know that the position is good for a specific time period at which time you will determine whether to maintain them or replace them as manager. This lets them know up front that they could lose their manager's position.

Management by Walking Around

One of the most effective management styles I found is what many call management by walking around. It's vital that managers must be visible in all facets of their area of responsibility. They must know their employees, their operations, issues and related activities. For example, how would a manager know the problems that occur during the evening shift if they never are around during that period? Managers must get out and personally be involved with each aspect of their area of responsibility. It's easy for a manager to fall into the same routine of supervision overtime. We saw this as a common routine of our managers who would attempt to entirely eliminate themselves from any night or Sunday shifts. When you asked them why they weren't working any night or Sunday shifts, they would reply that managers shouldn't have to work those undesirable shifts. My wife and I made it a habit to visit our businesses any time on any day especially the so called "undesirable shifts." People who are in a supervisory or management position need to personally observe their staff, customers and operations. This also includes the owners. Not only does this allow you to observe your operations first hand but it also allows you and your managers to build a better rapport with the employees. If your business operates till late hours or all night, then you and certainly your top manager need to occasionally "visit" during these hours. Announcing these visits are not necessary and in fact should be unannounced. We never announced when we would come by our shops and I would sometimes visit the same location twice in one day, including closing time. I had some employees tell me they had never met or seen the owner from their previous job. If you have multiple locations and have an area manager or supervisor, then you should expect them to be making visits during all phases of your business, no matter how late. Observing your operations first hand should be a top priority.

21 DELEGATING RESPONSIBILITIES AND DUTIES

Many so called authorities on small businesses will tell you that business owners should delegate duties and responsibilities to their employees. Some will go as far as to tell you that you should not intervene, even if they are headed down the wrong road. How else are they supposed to learn, right? Bull! Every mistake they make will cost you money and time. I am not saying don't delegate. Just make sure that close supervision comes along with the deal. I found that the smaller the business, the less that delegation is justified. Delegation is really for large businesses where you have layers of management and organizational structures and where the top boss is removed from the labor floor. But when you have just a few employees, especially with a high employee turn over rate, then delegating for the sake of delegating is senseless. Furthermore, when you delegate, your employees will *expect* to be compensated or given a pay raise for that extra work that was not originally spelled out when they were first hired!

If the decision is made to delegate responsibilities and duties then you must make sure you accurately define the details of what you're delegating. To tell your manager that she is responsible to do the weekly schedule is not going to hack it. When we made our managers responsible for the weekly schedules, we established criteria they had to follow. We defined the number of people on duty as a function of the day and hours as well as the maximum number of daily and weekly hours. Otherwise, we would find too many people working the day shift with too few to work weekends or nights when we were busier. When we delegated the supervision of 3 of our business locations to one of our managers, we came very close to a full disaster. Over a period of 1 month, we failed a state inspection by the board of cosmetology, two of our managers quit and one of the salons called us one day and warned us that they were all going to walk off the job if we didn't intervene. This was all due to the mishandling of our area manager. Our area manager warned me that if I did intervene, then she would lose all credibility making things worse. My wife and I did intervene, resolved the issues and readjusted our area manager's responsibilities. My biggest mistake was not intervening sooner. The root cause was that we did not define precise requirements and objectives for the job of our area manager. You just can't say your job is to supervise the managers and shops, make out the schedule, keep the books, recruit and hire.

Another factor with delegating responsibilities and duties is the cost involved. If you tell one of your employees that they are now responsible for such and such, I guarantee you that they will expect to be compensated for it. The question is can you afford the extra cost in payroll. For example, a business owner I know, made it the responsibility of the manager to make the evening deposits after work. The manager, cried foul, claiming that this was extra from her normal duties and wanted to be compensated for it. The owner didn't see it that way claiming that it was part of their responsibilities even though it was not written anywhere. If the job is not specified under the original terms of employment, then your employees expect to be compensated for the extra duties. The same is true if you take a certain responsibility or duty away. If you are compensating someone extra then that compensation should go away when they are no longer responsible for the job. Just be aware of these little details when you start thinking about delegating. You may or may not agree with paying an employee extra for accepting an added responsibility but the reality is that many employees will expect to be compensated in some way.

22   COMMUNICATIONS AND SUPERVISION

Communications

If you run a small business with just a few employees then communicating with them is as simple as just talking with them. But if you have several locations with different shifts then communicating with everyone becomes a little more involved. Some things just can't wait until you can have an employee meeting. I found a simple note or letter posted at each location works best for those more urgent matters that can not wait for a more formal group meeting. For example, let's say you're changing the way your employees accepts checks. You want your employees now to write down the driver's license number with a current home phone number on all checks. A hand written or typed letter describing the change and posted in a place that all employees can see it such as at the checkout desk works well. Of course verbal communication is the most effective form and should be used whenever possible. Some owners with many employees will feel that all communications to their employees should be done through their managers. This makes sense when it comes to management directives and lessens the impression of micromanaging by the owner or president of the business. But there are times where the urgency warrants a more direct approach.

The best formal method of communicating with your employees is with a meeting. Our managers were instructed to have meetings at least once a month. Other occasions would require us to call for a meeting involving all our employees from all our shops. Whatever the forum make sure you have an agenda with points you need to cover. Don't rely on memory since it's easy to skip over something important that needs to be discussed. Don't make your meeting too one sided with negative issues. This may turn off your staff and form an "us against them" attitude. Highlight the good with the bad and solicit ideas from the group. Don't be indecisive but at the same time don't commit to something without proper planning and research. If something needs to be researched or accomplished then solicit a volunteer who would welcome the opportunity. Keep your meeting limited to no more than an hour. If issues are unresolved, then schedule another meeting or let your staff know when you they can expect a decision from you.

Occasionally, your manager or another employee will come to you and tell you that your employees want to have a group meeting with you. Your initial reply should be "about what". The last thing you need is to walk into a meeting and be broadsided with an issue before having some knowledge of it before hand. We have had on occasion a manager or employee tell us that *their* shop wanted to have a meeting with us. When I would ask them "what about" I would get a "well just some things some people have on their mind." I would tell them that I needed to know the issues first before I would decide on a meeting; otherwise it could wait till our next scheduled meeting. I remember a specific case early in our business when a manager asked if we could have a meeting. I said sure, lets have it before we open on Saturday. No sooner than the meeting started did our manager say, "I want more pay and if not I don't think I can continue as your manager." I was totally caught off guard. Well, this individual was being paid more than she would get anywhere else so a pay raise was out of the question, especially since she had been at the job for less than a month. When I told her "not at this time" she informed me that she could continue as manager until we found someone else. I told her that I had someone already picked out and that her last day as manager was today! As you can imagine, calling a meeting to ask for a pay raise would not be something justifying the meeting, not to mention the extra pay for everyone to attend the meeting. Remember unless you make it clear otherwise, employees expect to be paid for attending a meeting. You can give everyone the option to attend an unpaid meeting but don't be surprised if no one shows up.

As a small business owner, keep in mind the following 6 rules concerning communications with your employees:

- Urgent matters require the most direct and quickest form of communication
- Verbal communications is always the best form
- Informal one on one communications helps to build strong relationships

- Directives and policy changes should be in writing, dated and signed
- Staff meetings should be held at least every 3 months
- Listen to your staff as if you were listening to your business partner

Supervision

Supervision is one of the most important responsibilities of a business owner and manager. It allows the business owner to see first hand how the day-to-day operations are conducted. Everything from how your customers are handled to the cleanliness of your business is observed. Proper supervision isn't conducted from just an occasional visit to your business. If you are actively involved in the operations of your business then you are continuously supervising your business. As an owner, I did not have a working position at any of our businesses, but we would be actively engaged through various activities to include working the reception and checkout desk, delivering supplies, opening or closing, cleaning, taking inventory or just visiting. This goes hand in hand with management by walking around. As part of their responsibilities, managers must also take on the role of supervising their area of operations just as the owner must supervise their business. The following list is a sample of what activities can and should be supervised by you and your manager:

Proper sanitation and safety procedures followed
Quality of work by employees
Signs of theft by employees or customers
Excessive breaks or use of the phone by employees
Dress and appearance of employees
Cleaning responsibilities
Tardiness
Inappropriate behavior of employees or customers
Excessive waste or abuse by employees

These activities are by no means all inclusive. There are many other areas that deserve careful supervision depending on the type of business. As the owner, I know you would certainly take an active role in supervision. But your manager may not feel it is their job to actively supervise. I've had managers tell me that they did not think that it should be their job to watch for anyone stealing or to intervene if someone was not following the dress code! Our first state inspection by the cosmetology board was unsatisfactory due to a sanitation violation by some of our stylist. Our manager felt that she should not have to conduct inspections of employees for proper compliance. I obviously fired her. Managers must be made responsible for proper supervision as well as enforcement of rules and policies. I had one manager call me to me that there was a problem with one of our stylist who was not dressed appropriately and wanted me to say something to her. I told her that as the manager she must find the way to tell her. She did and she found it was a lot easier than she thought. Proper supervision means that the manager or person supervising not only has the authority to enforce the rules but also must enforce the rules. It is not an option. Taking it one level higher, it is your responsibility to make sure your managers and supervisors are doing their job. And that is not an option either. This all goes back to your training program for managers. It is essential that you make this a major part of your manager's checkout phase. Let me add that just because you make someone a manager, that doesn't mean they are instantly qualified. Learning the ropes in becoming a good manager will usually take six months depending on the business and will definitely require help from you.

As an owner supervision can certainly be accomplished in a more subtle fashion. Many times I would collect our previous days deposits in the morning and make out the bank deposits while checking over the numbers. This was an effective way to observe the operations. The point is that supervising your business does not have to be from an official supervisory role. My attitude was that when I was at one of our locations, I would help out any way I could. I would run the desk, sweep the floors, take phone calls, clean the windows, wash and fold the towels, dust the shelves, get change, and any other job I saw fit. You might be asking what on earth are your employees doing during this time? Simply said, they were performing the services I was paying them to do, as they should! Even when we had a receptionist we would still come in and help out any way we could. One of the things I was very interested in was how our employees greeted our customers. No one is going to appreciate the customers as much as the owner. And that shows in the way you greet your customers to the way you thank them when they leave. In our business, probably the most important function of supervision was to see the quality of hair services our stylists provided. You could always tell by the expression on the customers face on how pleased the customer was about the service. One area I found by visiting our shops that proved to be a problem was our sound system. All our shops were wired to play music through a sound system in the backroom. The music was for the listening enjoyment of our customers. However, some of our stylists believed the music was for there benefit. In one of our salons, some stylists would set the radio to a hard rock station, which after ten minutes would give you a headache. Of course every time I would change the station to a more middle of the road music, the stylists would complain. The older customers never complained to me when I was in the salon about the music so I was not sure how much they liked or disliked the hard rock music. One day after changing the station, a young male customer looked up at me and said in the most sincere manner, "oh thank you". These are types of things that you could not possibly know without observing them first hand.

    Looking for trends was more important to me than one-time occurrences. An example in our business would be if the stylists were following the correct sign in and receipt procedures we had in place. It was very important that all customers be signed in with a properly filled out receipt with the customers name along with an entry in the appointment logbook covering the type of service and amount charged for that customer. Occasionally we would walk in to a salon and see that some customers were not signed in or the stylists had not made out any receipts or entered their service in the log. A one-time occurrence is not so bad and can be dealt without too much heartburn. However, when the problem is widespread or reoccurring then it becomes a serious problem. The problem in this case is that it becomes very difficult to verify your day's sales, which may be the objective! Again, without observing such practices first hand you probably would not know that was occurring. In a more fully automated system, the problem is not as likely but there are ways to circumvent such point-of-sales systems. Observing a trend such as in this example leads one to ask, why isn't the manager doing something? Good question and one that should be asked of the manager. Sometimes they are not at the shop when its happening, but they should make sure it doesn't continue once you point it out to your manager. This is why it's important for your manager to work all periods of your operation. Now there will be times when the problem is with your manager! You must ask yourself, who is supervising the managers? Ultimately, you are the supervisor either for lower level managers or for higher managers of larger businesses. If you demonstrate a lack of concern or action for things that should be otherwise, then its guaranteed that so will your managers. Just remember, you also must wear the hat of a supervisor as the owner.

23 POLICIES, RULES AND OPERATING MANUAL

As a business owner one of your primary responsibilities is to establish company policy. What is a policy? Policies are predetermined decisions that effect your operation. It is the structure within your business that determines what your business position is under certain circumstances. Well-established policies bring consistency and standardization to your organization. It means that a given situation will be handled in the same manner each time. The policies you have established determines the rules that you want followed in the best interest of your business, your employees and your customers. Developing these policies is not easy and involves considerable thought and knowledge. When we opened our first shop, we had a few unwritten policies, which was sufficient especially since my wife or I were there to oversee the day-to-day operations. However, as we grew to 3 salons it became apparent that our managers needed to have established written policies.

It's important to keep in mind the relationship between your managers, policies and the ownership. Simply stated, the ownership determines policy while it is the responsibility of your managers to ensure your policies are followed. Managers do not make policy. This may seem obvious but you may be surprised how many managers think that their job includes making policy. I had a manager who on one occasion bought lunch for the entire staff and paid for it with money out of the register. When I asked her about it, she became insulted that I would even question her authority about it. She believed that a manager should not have to get approval for such an expense! She was trying to make a policy that the manager has the authority to treat every one to lunch with money out of the cash drawer. It was our policy that only the owner could authorize such expenses. As your business grows and you become more mindful of your particular business, then it will be clear what policies need to be established. But for beginning businesses use a basic format as outlined in the example below.

Essential Policies

Your policies should be divided into three main categories: policies on employees, customers and operations. The following should serve as a basic outline of subjects when considering policies.

EMPLOYEES
- Dress code
- Work schedule
- Clocking In/Out
- Termination of Employment
- Reporting of Tips
- Personal Grooming
- Personal Items not allowed at work
- Parking
- Tardiness
- Calling in Sick
- Vacation
- Required Additional Duties
- Sexual Harassment
- Employees with a Permanent or Temporary Disability
- Disciplinary Action
- Personal Phone or Cell Calls
- Injury While on Duty
- Lost or suspected Stolen Personal Items
- Breaks
- Discounts to employees
- Arriving or Departing from Work other than Scheduled

OPERATIONS
- Hours and Days of Operations
- Opening Duties and Responsibilities
- Closing Duties and Responsibilities
- Posted Closing Time and what it means
- Phone
- Appointments
- Price Menu

        Schedule
        Evacuations
        Fire
        Suspected break-in
        Burglary
        Inventory
        Customer Service Priority
        Cash Register
        Job Applicants
        Smoking
        Cleanliness and Sanitation Requirements
        Discounts and Coupons
        Payouts from cash drawer
        Supply Request

CUSTOMERS

        Refunds and Exchanges
        Acceptance of Checks and Credit Cards
        Unacceptable Behavior
        Customers Dress Requirements
        Customer Complaints
        Damage or Loss of Customer Personal Items
        Injury of Customer
        Customers with Disabilities
        Priority Of Service

    Your particular business my warrant a different set of policy items than the above list. But almost any type of business will have a variant of these subjects. I believe you will find that as your business grows and matures within that first year, you will have a deeper understanding of the above items along with a refinement to your policies. I would suggest that your initial policies should be brief until you have adequate experience to establish your policies in detail appropriate for your organization. For example, what would your actions be if an employee came up to you and said she is missing her $300 cell phone (or any other personal items) and they believe some other employee stole it. Then, this employee wants to know how your insurance is going to cover it? This happened to us. I explained that it was our policy that we were not responsible for personal items at work, whether they are for personal use or used in their job. Furthermore, our insurance didn't cover such matters. I think everyone can understand excluding coverage of personal items but what about those items used for work such as sheers for cutting hair? I had an employee who came up to me one day and said she was missing her $500 sheers from her station and wanted to be reimbursed! I told her sorry, but we are not responsible for lost personal items and neither was our insurance policy. As our insurance agent explained, personal items used in the course of their job can be insured but at an additional cost the employee usually pays that for. The bottom line is that your staff must assume responsibility for their own belongings. This is an example of why it's so important to think through each policy item and to have a clear understanding of its implications. Another example has to do with employees that arrive or depart work other than their schedule time. We had several employees that would arrive to work early (20 to 30 minutes) and then clock in. Others would clock out as late as an hour after their scheduled shift. Our policy was that no one would be paid for an early sign in if it was not busy enough to clock in early. It was also the same for departing or clocking out later than scheduled. Staying late because it was busy was one thing but staying late on the clock while waiting for their ride was quite another thing. Now, if you tell your employees that they must arrive to work early then, they are certainly justified in signing in when they arrive. But as in our case, some employees were arriving early, signing in and then sat around or went to the store until their normal scheduled shift started.

      Your policies should also conform to state and federal regulatory directives. State and federal regulations affecting your business will depend on the type of business. For example, restaurants have different state regulation than hair salons. Even barbershops have different regulations than beauty salons. Other regulatory agencies will affect your business such as OSHA (Occupational Safety and Health Administration) requirements and child labor laws. Make sure you have a current list of regulations that pertains to your business.

Employees Driving While On Duty

It's important to remember that you are responsible for your employees when they are on duty. If you have an employee who gets injured while performing their job, then you are liable for that injury. And in most cases, your workers compensation will pay the related costs. What about if you send an employee out to get some supplies and while they are out driving they get into an accident and it happens to be their fault. You could be liable for not only your employee but for the losses and injuries suffered by the other parties involved. The best advise, is to consult with your business insurance company and ask them about this type of coverage. The last thing you want is to find out that such an incident is not covered by your insurance policy. If it is not covered by your basic plan then you have two options. One is to not allow your employees to be on duty while on the roads and the other is to have an insurance policy that indeed covers such occurrences. We had an incident where our manager claimed she was in route to get some supplies when she got into an accident, which was her fault. We had not even thought about the liability for such an occurrence until this time. Luckily, her insurance covered the damages. Days later of the accident, we discovered after some investigating, that she was no where near the supply store and was really running personal errands on our time! She was later relieved of her manager's position.

The Operating and Employee Manual

An operating manual fulfills several functions in your operations but most importantly it is a written document that serves to standardize the way you conduct your business. Simply stated, it is how *you* want the business to operate and run. Our operating manual also served as an employee manual, which included rules and policies we wanted our employees to follow. It contained all the items listed above under Policies and Rules and to a degree also projected our values and codes of conduct as a business. After we opened our first business, we began to learn more and more about the small details of day-to-day operations. We learned from our mistakes and we learned how to run our business in a more efficient manner. This is why it's so essential to be involved with your business and learn every aspect of its operations. We learned nearly every aspect to include opening, closing, running the reception desk, setting up appointments, doing the schedule, the book keeping, processing and distribution of payroll, recruiting, advertising, customer complaints, inventory, retail acquisition and cataloging, discipline, firing and any thing else that came up. When you feel that there is absolutely nothing in your business that you cannot perform, then you are in the best position to determine the rules and policies of your business. This in turn will allow you to develop your operating manual.

After we had opened our third business, we were finding that our employees were doing things differently between our shops. In other words, we lacked standardization. This would especially be evident when we would have an employee work at another location due to understaffing. Comments such as, "well, this is the way we do it at my other shop" was common when we would temporarily assign an employee to another one of our locations. By standardizing your operation, you will avoid for the most part, some unpleasant surprises. After I completed our operating manual, I briefed our employees that although they didn't have to memorize the manual, I did want them to refer to it. It was especially useful for new employees. On several occasions, I would get a call from a stylists asking what the policy was on something such as what is the cost of performing a color service on another stylist at work. My response would be, "lets grab the manual at your shop and see what it says." Even when I knew what the policy was I asked them to check the manual. I wanted them to get in the habit of picking up the manual and referring to it. One of my favorite questions from a new stylist would be "what is the dress code here." My reply would be, "lets grab a manual and see what it says about it."

Your operating manual can also serve as a protective net between you and your employees for any given circumstance. For example, a policy in your manual covering sexual harassment, employees with disabilities or policies towards stealing and falsification can keep you out of trouble at some point. We had an employee who worked evenings with a starting shift at 2 pm. After she became pregnant, she advised us that she could no longer work evenings. She told us that she wanted to come in "around" 10 or 11 am and maybe work till 5 pm with no weekends. Well, we didn't have a 10 "or" 11 to 5 shift nor could we justify such hours. She told us that if we did not give her that shift, she would file a disability discrimination suit against us. I called the labor board and told them the details. Their policy was that the granting of a special shift is never warranted but they went on to tell me that her pregnancy was to be treated as a disability and as such should conform to our policies for employees with disabilities. Luckily we had such a policy in place covering employees with disabilities. As it turned out, we did accommodate her with her request anyway. However, during one week, we did not have anyone to cover a particular Friday evening so we schedule this employee to cover that evening shift. That Friday morning, our manager called her to confirm if she was coming in and she replied she would be there. At 2 pm she came and told our manager she was quitting on the spot because we scheduled her for an evening. Two weeks later we received notice from the unemployment office that she had filed for unemployment against us for our actions. We contested it on the grounds that we had a policy on such matters and that for the most part we went out of our way to accommodate her request. Her request for unemployment was denied but she was able to apply and did receive state assistance for low-income individuals who were unable to work! This is why it is important to know the federal and state labor policies to make sure your policies conform to them.

The amount of detail you include in your manual is up to you but it should be sufficient for a worst-case scenario. What is the worst-case scenario? For a small business owner, it should be complete enough to cover your operation if you become incapacitated or unable to participate in the business. I call this the cement truck scenario. If my wife and I are driving down the road and we get hit by a cement truck, then will the business be able to continue to operate without us? Will someone be able to come in and run the business without our help? To illustrate this even more, lets say you die and you were also the manager! Lets assume that this was a profitable business and it will be the main support for your spouse and kids. Will your operating manual be complete enough for your spouse or someone else to come in and continue to run the business just like you would until they are comfortable enough to make their own decisions? When I was on active duty as a fighter pilot, our squadrons had many branches or areas of responsibility other than our flying duties. We had the training branch, safety, scheduling, standardization, evaluation, weapons, tactics and so on. And each of these branches was run by one of the squadron pilots. Each of us who were in charge of a section had to maintain an operations manual with enough detail so that someone else would be able to take over our section without disruption to the operation. I took this same concept and applied it to our business. It may seem like a lot of work but once its complete and in place it will be a great benefit to you and your employees. The subjects covered in your manual should contain those listed under the Policies and Rules section. Other areas you may want to cover should be specific to your business and you. The question is how specific do you want to be. Leaving you policies too vague and open to interpretation can result in confusion and friction down the road with you and your manager or staff if things are not run the way you want them. Be specific enough to leave out interpretation.

24   WORKERS COMPENSATION AND UNEMPLOYMENT BENEFITS

Workers Compensation

If you have employees then workers compensation insurance is not an option, you must have it. Not only must you have it but you also need to post a notice so that your employees are well aware of it and their rights. The big question is how much does it cost and who pays for it. You or your business pays the premium costs. It is not a cost that your employees must bear. In fact it is illegal to make your employees pay any part of workers compensation insurance. However, you are allowed to expense it as an operating cost. The premiums will usually be a percentage of your gross payroll on an annual basis. The administrator will send you forms to complete asking for gross payroll amounts for the previous year. Once they receive these forms back then they will determine the amount for the year with any adjustments and then send you or your payroll company a statement for the amount due. Accuracy of gross payroll is important when consolidating the year-end statement. If you get audited and your numbers fall short of what they should be, you could be in some trouble! In our second year, the workers compensation agency audited us, which for Arizona is a privately owned business. My numbers were off by a small amount and the error was caught. The auditor identified the mistake as an issue with our payroll period versus when our employees actually got paid. The problem was corrected so the same mistake would not be repeated and no action was taken. If you contract out to a payroll service then they will assume responsibility for the proper computation and payments relieving you of the paper work.

Just like any other insurance, your premiums will be based on several factors to include the state your business is in, the type of business, the number of years you have been in business, and the amount of claims your employees have had against your business. Obviously, the more the claims you have, the higher your premiums will be so its important to make sure your work environment is safe not only for the sake of your employees but also to keep your costs down. In today's worker environment, the employer must make sure everything has been done to minimize short or long-term injuries and disabilities. For example, if your employees deal with dyes such as in hair color, and protective gloves are not available, then your employees may overtime develop certain long-term illnesses.

Unemployment Benefits

Similar to workers compensation insurance, state unemployment insurance is a tax levied on the employer. States, by law, must provide unemployment benefits to workers who become unemployed. The amount of the benefits depends on the individual's earnings and how long they have worked over the past year. There is also a minimum amount of time between unemployment awards. For example, if an individual collected unemployment for 4 weeks and then went back to work, that person may not be illegible to apply for unemployment benefits until a year later. To pay for the program including administrative costs, states impose a tax or an assessment on employers. This tax is a function of the total payroll of the employer, the particular state, the type of business, the experience level or how many years the employer has been in business and the amount of previous unemployment awards to their employees. The more the awards the higher the state unemployment tax rate will be on the business owner. Unlike workers compensation, the tax rate is applied only to a certain maximum amount of each employee's gross pay. For example, in Arizona, the unemployment tax rate is applied only to the first $7,000 of your payroll for each of your employees per year. If after 3months, all your employee's have earned at least $7,000 under you, then you would owe no more to the state until the next year. However if you have a large turn over of employees then your payroll subject to the tax will be far greater than with a low turn over. This, along with other reasons is why it is so important to keep your employee turn over low.

The process of applying for unemployment benefits for employees is dependant on the state but all are very similar. Basically, the process involves a visit to the local unemployment office where the ex-employee fills out an application for unemployment benefits. Typically, the application will ask the length of employment, the employer, the reason for unemployment (fired, quit, closure, etc) along with other details. After the application is processed, the employer will receive a letter from the unemployment office alerting the employer that the employee has filed a claim for unemployment benefits with the reason for unemployment. In Arizona, the form letter contains a section for the employer to respond and mail back to the unemployment office allowing the employer to dispute the claim. It is very important that the employer respond before the deadline because failing to do so will most likely result in an award even if you could show that the application has false or misleading information – don't be late! Remember, if the unemployment office grants unemployment benefits to the employee, then it will most likely increase your unemployment tax rate. If you have a large number of employees, then even a small tax rate increase can have a significant impact.

From experience, most of the unemployment applications from our ex-employees had false or misleading information. On one occasion, we had an employee who had worked for us for a total of 3 days. One day she did not show for work and after several phones calls our manager discovered she was out sick. Well, this individual never called us back to let us know when she could return for work. Many attempts to contact her were made and after several weeks of no contact, we dropped her from our employment assuming she had found work somewhere else. About two months later I received a letter from the unemployment office alerting me that this individual was applying for unemployment benefits against us. The dates of employment she listed showed we had employed her for several months. I quickly responded on the form contesting any unemployment award on the basis that she had actually only worked for us for 3 days and annotated her total payroll amount. Since this individual could not support her claim with pay stubs, the unemployment office denied her claim. As I quickly found out from the unemployment office, the burden of proof lays with the employer, not the employee! We could prove she only worked 3 days, but she could not prove otherwise.

On another instance, we had an employee who quit after a year of employment to go work for another employer closer to her home. After about 3 months, her new employer let her go for unknown reasons. This ex-employee then applied for unemployment benefits even though there were plenty of jobs available. To my amazement, we received a letter from the unemployment office alerting me of her unemployment claim and that any award would be fully charged against our account. Apparently she realized that if she listed her last employer then she might not be eligible for unemployment benefits. Her best bet was to list us as her last employer and not mention that she actually went to work for someone else after us. She even listed on the claim that she quit working for us with no reason given. I responded by letting the office know that she had quit working for us to work somewhere else and to contact the salon she was fired from! After several weeks, I resent a copy of the reply form since we had not heard from the unemployment office on the status of this matter. Again, we did not hear from the unemployment office. I then left several phone messages but still no reply or acknowledgement. I assumed at this point that her unemployment benefits were denied and that would be the end of it. About two months later I received a letter informing me that she was awarded unemployment benefits and that the award would go against our business. It also informed us that the deadline to appeal this case had expired. After unsuccessful attempts to contact the unemployment office, we made a formal appeal to the state governor's office to look into this matter. The governor's office ordered the unemployment office to review the case and after several months, we were notified by the unemployment office that our account would not be charged. By law, the unemployment office must notify the employer of a determination of any award with sufficient time to appeal the case. Not allowing the employer to appeal a decision is a violation of the employer's rights. We were never sure why the unemployment office did notify us of the award decision but we suspect that this practice was being employed routinely with many unsuspecting employers being unfairly charged for unemployment benefits.

    Another example highlights our experiences with the unemployment office even more dramatically. One day we had a customer who wanted her money back for a hair color and haircut that one of our stylists had performed a few days earlier. I had just returned

227

home from a trip and my wife had informed me about the refund. I looked at the receipt and saw that the service performed was a color process called a weave, which had a minimum fee of $45. However, the receipt showed a charge of only $35. I asked Deb to call the shop and ask the stylist why she only charged $35 and not the regular $45. I assumed that maybe the customer didn't like something about the service or something didn't go well so our stylist discounted the service by $10. When Deb asked the question of what happened, Kelly became annoyed and replied, "I have a problem working for you guys" and then hung up on Deb. Well, I decided to pay a visit to the shop. When I got to the shop I asked Kelly to join me in the break room where I asked her if she told Deb that she had a problem working for us. In a display of rage, she threw back her chair and said, "Yes I have real problem working for you guys". To which I replied, "you know you don't have to work here if you don't want to". She replied, "I quit" then proceeded to clean out her station. Her friend Joyce also began to clean out her station and told me that we should not question what they charged for a service. Well, as long as I pay their salary regardless of how much business we do then we had every right to inquire how much they charged our customers!

    About 3 weeks later I received a letter from the unemployment office informing me that Kelly had applied for unemployment benefits. In the application, Kelly had stated the reason for leaving was termination (fired) by the employer. Of course I contested any award on the grounds that the employee voluntarily quit and that she had lied on the application. I also stated in the letter, that since I did not fire her and she claims that she did not quit, then technically she is still employed. How can she be unemployed if I did not terminate her employment and she did not quit? To my disbelief, the unemployment office sent me back a letter explaining to me that since this was a he said, she said issue, then the burden of proof that she quit was on me. If I couldn't offer proof then Kelly would receive unemployment benefits, which would go against out business. When my wife and I went to the local unemployment office to argue our case, we were told we had no chance of changing their decision and we would just have to live with it. I couldn't believe what we were hearing. In addition, the representative told us we were at fault, that we were lying, and we just "had it in" for this employee! I quickly discovered that the other individuals in the office were of the same anti-business owner mentality. I was now determined to fight this case even if I needed to hire an attorney. It no longer was a case of cost but of principle and what is right.

I contacted our local US Representative to see what could be done. We gathered character references from other stylists that worked with Kelly and got letters from the merchants next to our salon. We even had a letter from a customer testifying to Kelly's volatile nature. We talked to employees working at the shops next to us who were working at the time of the incident to see if they herd any yelling from our salon during the time of the incident. Kelly had claimed that they became frightened when I walked in the salon and began yelling at them. I had quite a sizable folder of evidence to support our position. It showed that Kelly was, at times, rude to customers and rude to other stylists. It showed that at times she easily lost control with outright rage. Next, I sent a copy to the unemployment office and to our US Representative. The office of our representative told us that they could not intervene in this case but that they would forward the folder over to their liaison at the unemployment office. The unemployment office replied to our request for review of the case with a statement saying that they were not going to review the case nor change their decision.

A few weeks later I received official notification that Kelly had been awarded unemployment benefits charged to my employer account and that I had the right to appeal the ruling under Arizona state law. Of course I replied that I was requesting a hearing to appeal the decision. A date was set to appear in front of a judge to hear our case along with our ex-employee. During the hearing we presented our case and actually presented material that showed Kelly had lied in her testimony concerning factors supporting her case. The hearing went on for about an hour with the judge witnessing the explosive character of Kelly when it became quite clear that Kelly had lied in front of the Judge. A few days later I received a letter from the Judge on the ruling. The judge reversed the decision of the unemployment office in our favor and a judgment was made against Kelly to repay the unemployment she had already received. In her letter to me, to Kelly and the unemployment office, the judge cited the evidence but more importantly, cited our demeanor as compared to Kelly and the consistency of our evidence compared to Kelly's. I really had no doubt of the outcome once we had a chance to present our case to someone who was not biased and willing to listen to the evidence.

If this instance sounds like a lot of work, you're right. It's a lot of work and its time consuming. I suppose if you have a large business then its probably not worth the effort or time in fighting every unemployment claim even if you know they are wrongfully filed. But if you're a small business with a small group of employees, then it takes just a few unemployment awards to have an impact on your state unemployment insurance rates. In addition, it sends a message to your other employees that you will fight any claims that are false or misleading.

Even more frustrating is the fact that while some of our ex-employees tried to falsely get unemployment benefits, our labor market was extremely tight during this period with many employers unable to get adequate help. This was especially true in the service businesses where anyone could walk in and get a job on the spot. With few exceptions, a qualified stylist who applied for work with us and was able to work without restrictions to the schedule was hired. Knowing this, it was frustrating that many individuals were getting unemployment benefits not because they could not find work but because they did not want to work until forced to. This leads to lost revenues and an overall loss in productivity for the business.

So what are the lessons learned? First, build a rapport with your unemployment office. Eventually you will find someone at the office who is employer friendly. Once you find this individual, ask for this person by name if and when you need help with an unemployment claim against you. Second, keep good records on each employee, especially if the employee starts showing signs of problems. Third, never have a consultation in private with an employee. Either have another individual such as a supervisor or have the session taped. One of the things that the unemployment office would look at when there was employee – employer problems, was whether the employer notified the employee of the problem and at what point would termination be exercised. Last, know the policies and laws of your unemployment office. Call your local unemployment office and request the pamphlet describing local unemployment laws and policies. As an employer, they can't deny this request, you are entitled to one.

Remember, any of your ex-employees can file for unemployment benefits and the unemployment office will process the application. As an employer, it is up to you to make your case with supporting data of why that individual should not be entitled to unemployment benefits. Unemployment benefits are intended to help those who have been laid off while they find work elsewhere. Unfornutely, some exploit the system as a paid vacation from work. Reducing your unemployment claims can certainly reduce your operating costs and improve your profits.

25 OUTSOURCING AND CONSULTANTS

Outsourcing

First let us define what we mean by outsourcing as it applies here. When you contract with a bookkeeper to maintain your books or a human resource company to handle your employee's pay and benefits, then you have outsourced these activities. Listed below are common activities that could be outsourced:

Bookkeeping
Payroll processing
Janitorial
Maintenance
Advertising
Human Resources
Customer feedback or surveys

The benefit of outsourcing is that it relieves you of the time to maintain these tasks. Without having to be directly involved with say bookkeeping, you are able to focus more on other urgent needs of your business. The question becomes one of affordability. Can you afford to pay another business to do these tasks? You might be asking why don't you just hire an employee to perform some or all these tasks. The problem becomes one of expertise and resources. Remember, if you hire an individual as an employee to be responsible for certain tasks then you must also furnish them the tools to do the job. That can be quite expensive and probably unaffordable for a new startup business. When you outsource to a company or individual to perform a task then you are no longer responsible to acquire and maintain specialized equipment. Nor will you have to worry about all those indirect payroll cost that go along with employees such as medical insurance, state and federal unemployment insurance, workers compensation insurance, payroll processing, vacation, retirement benefits and so forth. And you also don't have to worry about that individual calling in sick or just not showing up for work. While outsourcing may be suited for one business another may find it more beneficial to not outsource.

In our business my approach was to personally do as much of the administrative functions as we could. This accomplished two things. First, it forced me to know every aspect of my business. For example, we processed our employee's payroll. Processing your own payroll may be an eye opener, as it will uncover things you may not be aware of. Second, the cost savings of doing our own payroll was enormous. Your goal as owner of a start up business is to learn as much as you can about the administrative elements of your business. Only by knowing your business at the lowest level are you able to make better and more effective decisions. The net result is a more efficient running business and better profitability. As your business matures and you have a good handle on the day-to-day operations then outsourcing some of your administrative functions would be a viable option. This is especially the case when you are ready to expand and grow your business. In this case your time is more productively spent on growing your business than on administrative functions. However, there are other areas where outsourcing is a more viable and least expensive alternative than doing the work in house.

In our business, we had intended to outsource some of our administrative functions such as bookkeeping and payroll after our business had increased in size. I remember on one occasion when I was consulting with the owner and president of a company that owned over 50 stores. As we were reviewing his profit and loss statements it became apparent that some of their shops had excessive payroll costs. Payroll and accounting tasks were outsourced, as I would suspect. As we went through his payroll summary sheets it became apparent to him that some of his employees had been racking up quiet a bit of overtime and apparently for unknown reasons. It was also apparent that he had not noticed this before our meeting and was obviously concerned. And this was just one element of the business. The point is that when you hand over some elements of your business to someone else, you as the business owner still need to keep an eye on the details of your business. Whether a business owner decides to outsource common tasks will depend on the type of business, affordability and time available for such tasks. If your willing to learn and tackle some of the more administrative functions of your business then I would certainly consider performing these tasks in house.

Consultants

I always found it mystifying that an owner will hire someone as a business consultant who never owned or operated that type of business. Or worse, never owned a business at all, other than the consulting business itself! How would someone who never owned your type of business know how to run your business better than you? I can see a consultant who actually owned and operated a business especially the type of business your in. I can even see the justification when your just starting out in the planning phase. But I have a hard time with it for an established owner of a small business who says they need a consultant. Who else should know more about your business than you, the owner and operator? If you are so out of tune with your business that you must resort to a consultant then I am sorry to say you have not been doing your job. Some will say that a consultant brings experiences from all kinds of businesses and represents a different look or perspective. Believe me, you are your best consultant, not someone else. Each and every business is different with its own set of peculiar problems. Just as there are no two people exactly alike the same is true of businesses, no two are the same. To know the solutions you have to know the problems and that means knowing your business and the environment it operates in. Why not just hire yourself as your businesses full time consultant. I assure you that a business consultant is not going to guarantee results and this will become very evident after you sign all their disclaimers!

Now, what about if you need the services of a consultant for more specific issues such as the marketing of a new product or service? Areas that are outside of your expertise or operating boundary of your business can certainly justify a consultant. For example, you be planning to expand your business into an area were there are environmental issues present. Use of an environmental consultant would be warranted before plans are made for your expansion into this area. This type of consulting provides research of data and current laws that allows you to make a better-informed decision from a host of options. Or, lets say that you have a product or service for a particular population type. You want to know a bit more about this group such as what music they usually like, what radio station they normally listen to, what their leisure activities are, what web sites do they normally visit and so forth. From this type of information you can then develop you marketing and sales plan. Although you might be able to do the research yourself, you may not have immediate access to the type data needed or access to the data may come at a high monetary cost. There are a variety of consultants that are need specific. Choosing a consultant should be made with emphasis on the area of expertise, location of firm, years of experience and cost. In the end, the price of the consultant must be weighed with the long-term outcome.

26   IDENTITY AND SENSITIVE INFORMATION THEFT

It has often been said that if you own a business, eventually you will experience a break in or some other type of theft. The same can also be said for personal information theft, your customers, vendors, employees or yourself. It's just a matter of time before it happens. Listed below are examples of the types of information that might be useful to identity thieves:

Types of Sensitive Information

- Social Security Numbers
- Phones numbers
- Bank Accounts
- Birth dates
- Drivers License numbers
- Home addresses
- Credit Card Numbers
- Passwords of any type
- Account numbers such as for vendors, utilities, or other services
- Email addresses
- Mothers maiden name

To this list you could include any type of information that is particular to an individual. And the other thing to consider is that any item by itself may not be damaging but together with other types of personal information, could be quite damaging. For example, the address alone may not be damaging but together with bank accounts, social security or credit card numbers, then there is the potential for serious damage. A thief may have the intentions of using the information for themselves or selling it to larger and more organized entities.

Potential Thieves

Most of us visualize a thief as someone unlocking the secret department of your computer files or rummaging through your trash dumpster. But a thief could be one of your employees, a customer, a representative of one of your vendors, the cleaning person, or anyone that could have access to sensitive information either directly or indirectly. You might have your customer records being transported to another office either via the Internet, mail service or commercial transportation. If you have a wireless network or have Internet access, then your exposure is limitless. Access to your sensitive information can also be gathered through spyware intent on recording every key stroke or entry and then passing it through the internet, of course all without a hint that this is being done. And who knows what types of methods will be exploited in the near future.

Protection of Sensitive Information

It's safe to say that you would not leave the front door to your business open at night. Locking your door is the first line of defense followed by an alarm system, a motion detection system and so on. The more layers of defense you have the harder you make it for a thief. And although you'll never be able to achieve a 100 percent anti-theft defense, you will definitely reduce the chances of someone robbing your business. Securing your business against the most sophisticated thief may not be always achievable, but you can protect yourself from most thieves. The same is true for sensitive information. You may not be able to make it full proof but every level you increase your protection, the more you reduce your risk. Just simple precautions can significantly reduce the risk. And don't forget the potential of litigation against you from a victim if it can be shown that you were careless with customer personal information. Listed below are precautions that can reduce your risk of comprising sensitive information:

Shredding. Purchase a large shredder capable of shredding large amounts of material from your business and home. Don't allow anything to be discarded without it going through the shredder.

The Mail Box. Don't leave outgoing mail in a non-secure area waiting for pickup. Stealing mail from a mailbox is not uncommon and can sometimes occur without you knowing it. Drop your mail off at a post office drop box. Mail coming in should also be protected. If you have your employees get the mail, then make sure they put it in a secure area. Leaving it out on a desk could be trouble if you haven't been by the business for a few days.

Credit Card and other Receipts. Any credit card receipt that is the merchant's copy should have the card number partially truncated. I have seen a credit card receipt not only with the credit card number on it but also the expiration date printed on it! These receipts are usually printed from older style credit card merchant terminals. Newer versions do not imprint this information. Make sure yours is up to date. Cash register receipts that print credit card information should also be updated to make sure this information is not printed on them.

Storage of Sensitive Information. Any type of electronic storage of customer information, employee records or business data should be protected. Computer security measures encompass a wide range. First, your sensitive information should be accessible through passwords only. At no time should this information be accessible without a password. Fingerprint authentication systems are an alternative to passwords and may provide you with greater security than common password measures. If you use a password, then make sure you change your password. The more often you change your password, the less likely someone will be able to determine your password. If you keep records in a file than make sure the file cabinet is secured to the floor and locked. The same for your hard drive where your electronic files are kept. You may have the best electronic protection but if someone can pick up your hard drive and take it with them, then your sensitive information could be compromised. In addition, that may be the only copy of records you have. Many point-of-sale systems have the hard drive in close vicinity of the terminal, making then vulnerable to theft. Consideration should be made to having the hard drive located in a more hidden and secure area of your business and securely attached to the foundation.

Access. Limit the access of your information to only your most trusted individuals. Just remember the more people who have access, the greater the risk. You may completely trust your manager, but your manager may be careless with the password. For example, lets say your manager has a live-in friend. Your manager has your password written down at home in a drawer accessible by the live-in. From there any possible scenario can develop. This is why it's important to limit access and to change passwords. Also, anytime an employee leaves or is terminated, your passwords should be changed.

Distribution. When information is passed from the customer to your business, either electronically or through employees, how secure and protected is this process. How many times have you heard a customer say the phone number out load at a store with other customers waiting in line? You may not be able to conceal every bit of information 100 percent of the time but reducing the exposure as much as possible will go a long way in reducing your risks. The more other people can hear or read other peoples information the more likely some information will be comprised into the wrong hands. Any statements or correspondence mailed to customers should be carefully reviewed for sensitive information such as SSN or account numbers. Account numbers or other information should be truncated so that only part of the numbers is displayed.

Disposal or loss of Computers and Credit Card Terminals. If you dispose of your old computer, then your hard drive should be removed and destroyed. Simply deleting or erasing your records is not good enough. There are many programs that will allow you to recover deleted data from your hard drive. When you delete something from your hard drive, it is not really deleted until it has been over written. I guarantee you that if you bought a computer from one of those donation centers such as a thrift store, you could access information on the hard drive even if it was deleted by the previous owner! The best bet is to remove the hard drive and have it destroyed. Credit card terminals can also be a treasure chest of information. We had credit card terminals that would store all the day's transactions until they were batched released at the end of the business day. This meant that prior to a batch release, you could bring up a particular transaction with all the information on the credit card including expiration dates or you could bring up the entire day's transactions. If our employees forgot to batch release the transactions and someone broke in and stole the terminals, they would then have access to the day's credit card transactions. Or, let's say that your terminal stops working mid-day for example and an employee of your credit card company picks up your terminal leaving you a replacement. Chances are that your business transactions are secure and will be released as soon as they can get it working again. But I would certainly be cautious about releasing your credit card machine to someone I didn't know.

Keep your eyes open. Keep your eyes open for any type of suspicious behavior by anyone who has access to information. You may have a trusted employee but who knows down the road what will motivate them. They may be selling sensitive information to someone outside. Or, they may be preparing to leave but have not yet informed you of it. Prior to notifying you or leaving, they steal sensitive information. We had an employee, who on their last day at work went through our customer's information on their hair services, addresses and phone numbers. We didn't identify it until we reviewed the shop camera tapes and saw the individual removing some of the cards of our customers. Not only were the cards gone containing customer information, but also the types of information needed by a stylist for their next service.

Back up your files. If you don't back up your computer files, then you are living dangerously. If your customer files get stolen with sensitive information, then you will not know who's information got stolen and not be able to let them know. Keep a back up copy of your files in a secure area outside of your business or office.

There are other measures available to the business owner for protecting sensitive information. Consideration should be given to using a company specializing in data security since most new business owners will not know what measures are available to them. Cost is certainly a consideration in how secure you want to make it. But as with insurance, your paying for something you may never need. However, sure as the sun rising, when you don't have it is when you'll need it. I would pay the money and sleep better!

27   RUMORS AND CRISIS CONTROL

Small businesses can be very susceptible to rumors and misinformation. Sometimes, the misinformation is intentionally rumored while other times it is just a matter of conversation with no intended objective. I'll never forget the phone call from one of my employees asking me if it was true that we were closing and going out of business! Her and the rest of the employees wanted to know so they could begin looking for another job. I asked her if it made sense that I would be opening another shop if I were out of money and really going out of business? I immediately put out a letter explaining how damaging an untrue rumor could be, and that if they didn't hear it from me then it wasn't true. Who knows what the outcome would have been if I wasn't told about this rumor or if I delayed in my actions. Another source of a potentially damaging rumor is the business owner. For example, in a discussion with an employee, you may have said something that they have misunderstood and before you know it, your harmless conversation has mushroomed into something totally different among your employees. I have seen on several occasions where a conversation with an employee had grown into a rumor that was totally out of context of what I had originally said. Regardless of where a rumor originates, rumors can hurt your business and even lead to a disruption of operations. Sometimes a simple letter to your staff or customers is sufficient while other times more drastic measures are needed. Even when you attempt to dispel a rumor, your employees, customers or vendors will still have some doubt about whether your telling the truth or not.

The following example shows the damage a rumor can have on your business. One day my wife and I walked into one of our shops and discovered a distinct difference in our employees including the manager. Instead of the usual pleasant and friendly character, we found our employees quiet, and almost hostile to us. I asked our manager, Lisa if there was anything wrong. She simply said no and that was it. I told her that we know something is going on and if it concerns the shop then we should know about it. She still refused that anything was wrong. A couple of days later I came in and found Lisa packing her equipment getting ready to quit. Lisa was so upset that she finally told me what was going on. Apparently our area manager, Sharon invited Lisa and another stylist out to breakfast one morning. Sharon supervised two other shops other than the one she managed. At the breakfast, Sharon had told them that I was providing her shop with medical insurance. Lisa was quiet upset that we were only providing insurance coverage to Sharon's shop and not the other shops. I know this sounds too ridicules to be true. Of course, I explained that this was totally false, no one had insurance as of yet and we were in the process of looking at different providers through an insurance broker. Whether intentional or not, Lisa was lead to believe that we were partial to certain employees. I told her that when we did decide on a provider, medical insurance would be offered to all our employees. Although I had tried to assure Lisa of the facts, the damage had been done and a certain amount of mistrust lingered. We suspected there where other things said but were never able to find out from Lisa. Lisa never regained her trust in us and subsequently quit a short time later. When questioned about this, Sharon denied any such conversation, which we knew was not true. We soon relieved Sharon of her duties as the area manager. A business acquaintance told me he had been told by someone in the office that their company would be filing for bankruptcy on a certain date. He immediately sold his stock in the company fearing the rumor might be true since the company had been losing money for some time. The date came and went without the company filing for bankruptcy. In addition, the company got a positive outlook for the following quarter and the stock nearly doubled in price. The point in this case is not what was actually said, but the fact that a false rumor can be taken at face value among your employees with little or no supporting evidence. It only takes one minute for a bad rumor to undo what months of trust and good work can accomplish.

    Sometimes the source of a rumor or disinformation is from a competitor. For example, a competitor can maliciously send someone into your place of business, acting as a customer, and convincingly spread a rumor to your employees that your business is filing for bankruptcy and may soon close the doors. By the time you hear about it, the rumor has become the hot topic at work and your employees are looking for any evidence that it may be true. I know on more than one occasion this happened to us from a nearby competitor whose purpose was to get a few of our employees to quit and go work for them. We contacted their office letting them know that we were aware of their tactics and kindly asked them to stop.

Time is of often a critical factor when taking action against an unwarranted rumor. The sooner you know about a rumor, the better chance you have to dispel or at least clarify a rumor. However, more than likely, the owner will be the last person to hear of a damaging rumor. You can preclude this by interacting with your employees on a regular basis to build better communications. The more of a personal relationship you have with your employees the more likely someone will tell you about the newest rumor. We found that in each of our shops, there were one or two individuals who would ask us about a rumor they heard. Getting an employee on your side to help dispel a rumor is invaluable and can save your hide. If the employees feel that the owner will be straight with them when asked about a rumor, then the employees will be more likely to communicate with the owner about the latest rumor.

Help, We Have a Crisis

There are going to be times when a situation has developed to a level where your operations or the very survival of your business is at stake. A situation that is damaging your business must be met head on with actions focused on immediate control. There are a number of instances that could damage your business and risk it's very survival. Each one will require a different approach to limit the damage. Your reaction is an important factor and is time critical. The longer you wait to act the greater you risk of having the situation escalate to the point where regaining control will be very difficult at best.

For example, getting a poor or unsatisfactory rating on a state or federal inspection of your business could gain you a damaging reputation with your customers and community. A surprise visit by the local police to arrest one of your employees suspected of dealing drugs could also paint an unpleasant picture of your business to the public, to your employees and the property management who may have grounds to revoke your lease and ask you to leave! You may have an instance where someone develops a severe case of food poison from your restaurant. Or, someone has gotten access to your customer records including credit card numbers, bank accounts or other sensitive information. There are many other examples of such instances that could affect the operations of business.

There are steps you need to take when a damaging situation occurs. First and most important, evaluate the situation making sure you have all the facts straight. This means interviewing people whether employees, customers, law authorities or other businesses at your location. Going to the next step requires you to have the "real picture" or else you could make the situation worse. Next, implement the actions necessary to stop or reverse the adverse situation including consulting with an attorney. Use whatever you can to boost the confidence of your employees and customer. And finally, learn from the situation and put in place the changes needed so that a similar occurrence is not repeated.

A situation that is a crisis to a small business owner may be an insignificant event to a larger business and so on. You will find that as your business grows, things that were major problems are now small manageable events. Learning how to manage or handle significant problems is an important element of your business operation. Being prepared for rare occurrences is the first step in your ability to handle a crisis and return to normal operations. Of course the best line of action is prevention. Guarding against most major potential problems will keep things from getting out of control and into a crisis situation. But in order to have the ability to prevent you first must have an idea of what to prevent. Only by knowing the areas of potential devastating problems can you formulate your defenses and help prevent them in the future.

The first thing a small business owner should do is to list all the problems that you would consider as a major event that will have a major impact on your business operations. Such problems as credit card fraud where someone has obtained your customer's credit card numbers, food infected with a harmful bacteria, a robbery, a broken water line that has flooded your business, an employee that has claimed sexual harassment, or a sudden work stoppage by your employees are but a few of the potential problems you might encounter and that would require immediate attention. If you have all your customers and their transactions with credit card numbers on computer file then you have to ask yourself, how accessible are those files to a hacker. Even if there are no internet connections with your hardware, if you have a wireless network between your computers, then you are vulnerable to attack. Or, you may have an employee with access to your computer intent on stealing your records. The next step after you have listed these potential problem areas is to list the actions you think would be appropriate in handling each problem. Have a list of contacts and their phone numbers that you would need for each problem. For example, if the front door window was smashed in the middle of the night, then you should have the phone number of a window and door repair company that would be available 24 hours a day, near your location. You may not be able to construct a complete action checklist for each problem, but having at least the first few steps will save you much aggravation and time. Next, include your action plan in a binder with contact phone numbers you may need and keep a copy at your business for reference by your employees. Don't forget to update your plan with current information. As your business grows, there will be additions and modifications. By having a thorough plan of action, not only can you help prevent a crisis situation, but also you can better manage a crisis when it does occur before it gets out of control. Remember, the purpose is to get back to normal operations as soon as possible minimizing the impact on revenues and earnings.

28 GROWING YOUR BUSINESS

Growing your business can be in the form of acquiring more floor space or opening another new location. Growing your business obviously provides the opportunity to increase your revenues and of course your net earnings. But expanding your business has other benefits that deal with productivity and efficiency that add indirectly to the bottom line. When we expanded our business, we enjoyed certain benefits that were not achievable with fewer locations. For example, one of the benefits we enjoyed was the ability to have employees work at different locations when faced with a shortage at one of the other locations. Or, you may have two locations that instead of needing a full time employee would require a part time employee. By having one individual working both locations, you then avoid having to hire two part-time or full-time employees. The other advantage deals with advertising. For the same advertising rate we could list all our locations giving the consumer a better choice of locations. Having multiple locations also has the added benefit of improving consumer confidence in your business. When the consumer sees that you have 10 locations then they become more confident in your product than if you have just one. More locations also contribute to brand name recognition by the consumer. The other thing it does is it gives your employees greater confidence. The bigger your business, the more likely it can survive hard times. Your employees will more likely to have greater confidence in your business surviving if times get tough.

The biggest advantage of expanding your business to other locations is that you have diversified your business over a larger geographical area. This reduces your risk from exposure to an area that at some point may decline, or in the case of a shopping center, the closure of its main anchor. We have seen a number of shopping centers significantly decline in business after the anchor moved out of the center. As we found, you will have some locations that due very well while others may do poorly. Being well diversified allows you to close the poorer performing locations and move to better areas.

The decision to expand your business should be based on several factors. First, is there the opportunity to acquire more floor space or another space in a well-suited area? For those that deal directly to the public, nothing says it better than location, location, and location. It's not as easy as just picking a location in a busy shopping center and moving in. We found that many of the shopping centers with great traffic had clauses in their leases with other salons that gave them an exclusive in that shopping center, preventing anyone else from coming in. Even many of the proposed shopping centers that had not yet begun construction already had merchants lined up with signed leases giving the operators exclusive rights. If a particular location becomes available that meets your requirements than you should give serious consideration of acquiring it. Contact property management companies in your area and let them know your desires and requirements. Getting on their list at least gives you an option in case a location becomes available that meets your requirements.

Another factor to carefully consider is the cost of expanding. Higher rents, constructions cost and supplies and equipment costs are the primary cost components of expansion. But as with most leases, built in rent increases and common area maintenance costs can significantly reduce operating profitability making expansion less cost effective. We found that rents, common area maintenance, equipment and construction costs significantly increased as we expanded to new locations. Many would say that in order to offset higher expansion cost, prices of your product would also need to be increased. That works well when you have no competition, but when your competitor across the street can offer the same product or service at a lesser price then it would be suicide to maintain higher prices. In addition, you want to maintain the same price structure for your products or services among all your stores. Your customers should know that your prices are the same among all your location, not a different price for each location.

A final note to your decision to expand concerns the tightness of the labor market. In a tight labor market it's going to be difficult to find adequate help without offering greater starting salaries than your competitors. Offering a higher salary may seem reasonable but one problem will be with your current employees who might be working for less money then your new hires at a new location. This seems to be a common problem concerning expansion and wages. When you have a new location ready for business but are not staffed to open due to a tight labor market then you will feel the pressure to succumb to higher starting salaries. This becomes even more apparent when the meter is running on your rent. If you can't open due to a lack of employees then you will feel the pressure to offer higher salaries to job applicants! The problem is that your current employees will eventually find out which could likely result in some leaving. One solution that we used successfully was to ask current employees from our other locations if they would be willing to travel to the new location temporarily. You may have to offer them some type of incentive travel pay but at least you can get the doors open. The other remedy other than giving in to a higher salary demand is to offer a sign on bonus. We had good luck with this but some of our employees demanded the same sign on bonus, even though they had been employees for some time. Expanding your business can certainly add to your success but the decision must be made carefully with consideration to a number of factors.

  Financing your business expansion can certainly be the biggest issue of whether to grow or not. If you're looking at borrowing the money then the prevailing interest rate is going to be the leading factor. Interest rates over 10 percent means your going to have to be generating good business to service your debt depending on the amount you need to barrow. If the economy is at the tail end of a strong growth phase, and your going barrow at say 15 percent interest then you are definitely taking a big risk. The last thing you want is a slowing economy with a heavy debt load. That could not only jeopardize your new expansion but also put the entire business on shaky ground. As always, careful planning is a must and don't hesitate to drop your expansion plans if things start to get sour.

29 TURNING YOUR BUSINESS AROUND

At some point you may find that your business is not going in the right direction and its time to turn your business around. For many, recognizing that there is a problem has come too late, making it nearly impossible to salvage their business. **The most likely signs that your business is in trouble are:**

Slowing sales or revenues
Fewer customers
Declining profit margins
Fewer orders
Poor moral
Decreasing cash flow
Having to barrow to pay bills on time
Greater customer complaints

These warning signs usually develop slowly making it difficult to recognize especially when you are caught up with the day-to-day regiment of running your business. There are a number of reason your business is running into trouble which include, poor customer service, rising competition, declining economy, declining productivity, higher business cost and so on. Many small business owners will not have a clear set of established parameters to indicate when its time to change the direction of their business. Even when the warning lights have come on, many owners will not react quick enough or not with the right solution. Being able to turn your business around before its too late requires planning during the early stages of your business.

The Signs of Turbulence Ahead

The first step in any turn around plan requires you to be able to identify the red flags that spell trouble up ahead. This means collecting and analyzing performance data about your business from the beginning. Keeping track of such indicators as average daily and weekly customer volume, sales, orders, customer complaints and profit margins is a must if you want to avoid trouble. In our business, we kept track of daily customer volume averaged over a moving 14 and 50-day period. This allowed us to maintain a record of average daily volume for any particular day of the week. This in turn provided us with a base line to compare future numbers and determine whether our volume was steadily increasing or declining. For example, if our daily volume for the month of June was 5 percent less than the prior year, then this would be a red flag. One might say that comparing revenues for the same period would serve the same function. This might be true provided there were no price increases. But if you had raised prices by say 5 percent then your revenues might not show a decline from the year prior even with a decline in customers. In fact, there are a number of other factors that can skew your revenue picture such as deep discounting or changes to your product or services. This is why we used <u>customer volume as a more reliable indicator of the health of the business</u>. But even customer volume can be affected by factors from one year to the next. For example, you may have extended or reduced your daily operating hours or had to close for several days due to remodeling. Remember, when you compare one year or month to another, you must make sure that they are similar. If, for example you were open 2 more days last June than the current June for some reason, then you would need to look at your customer volume on a different basis such as on an hourly basis or average daily basis. When computing customer volume on an hourly basis then comparisons are on an equal basis and tend to be more of a reliable indicator. Other trend indicators such as the number of customer complaints can be a prelude to declining customer volume. This indicator however must be compared with total customer volume and analyzed as a percentage. For example, lets say that for the month of June you had 3 customer complaints for every 100 customers giving you a 3 percent complaint rate. This year you had fewer total complaints for the month of June, but since you had fewer customers, the percentage as a total of customers increased from 3 percent to 5 percent. We see this same type of analysis almost on a daily basis such in our national economic or labor figures. For example, you may hear the news say we had a total of 3 million unemployed for a certain month which is 5 percent higher than last year. But when compared to the total number of eligible workers, the percent unemployed may be lower than last year. As we can see, when comparing data, its important to make sure that we view it in relation to other data in order to get a more accurate historical status.

We found that keeping track of such performance indicators was easily accomplished using a spreadsheet. Such data might also be available from a point-of-sale system allowing you to analyze directly from your point-of-sale system or downloaded onto a spreadsheet. We found using a spreadsheet was more versatile allowing us to refine our product to our specific needs. Once your system is in place and giving you the information you need, then the next step involves setting the levels that indicate significant trends. As a minimum, consider keeping track of these performance factors of your business: Customer volume, sales, profit margin, operating profit and customer complaints. In our business, I relied primarily on customer volume. Total volume for each month would be compared with the previous years volume for that particular month. Three consecutive months of lower volume than in the previous year would be evidence that trouble was mounting. In addition, we would also look at volume on a semi and annual basis. Of course, any of these would be signs of trouble but if all three were in the red than there is no doubt that action would be required. Let me point out that you may still be profitable, but not for long if the trend continues. At this point you need to admit to yourself that your business is declining and if continued your business will fail. This is probably one of the most difficult realities that a business owner will have to face. But its vital that the business owner accepts the grim reality and takes steps to turn things around before it is too late. Remember, businesses don't get into financial difficulty overnight, it usually occurs over a long period with subtle signs at the beginning. Businesses that recognize the problems early and take action are more likely to avoid a financial crisis.

Getting Out of Trouble

The first step in the action phases is investigating the probable causes of your business decline. For example, lets say that March, April and May show lower volume than last year for the same months. We will assume that there were no other factors to account for the decrease in volume such as a reduction in hours or days. Ask yourself, what, if any changes occurred in February or March of this year. Also look at last year's activity during those three months. You may have had a special or sale that temporally pumped up the customer volume or a nearby competitor had to close temporally. Next, if you don't already have a customer feedback program than I would certainly develop one. It's important to try and find out from your customers how they rate your service. If you had a customer feedback program in place since last year, then look at how many negative responses (as a percentage of total customers for the month) you had versus the same period for the current year. Many times this will reveal a problem that you were not aware of until now. If you had been looking at each of the customer responses then you probably would have identified any problem area by now. Of course the key word is "if" which means you had been minding your business all along. Also look at any new employees you may have had working since February or early March. In one of our shops, we saw a decrease in customer volume and sales, shortly after we hired a new stylist. Customer volume was unusually slow when this person worked alone. Sure enough, we discovered, through our video camera, that this employee was pocketing money and not having our customers sign in for a service. She was quiet good at it and had all bases covered except the monitoring camera. We had her arrested using the recorded tapes of her activities. If you cannot find any significant factors to explain the decrease of customer volume, then the next step is to look outside of your business. You may have had a new competitor open for business nearby or a super sale by a local competitor. The road or a lane in front of the shopping center or place of business may have been closed for construction. The parking lot may have been closed for modifications or resurfacing. Or the major anchor of your shopping center has closed. The point is that there may be a number of external factors that could affect your business. Some of these factors are temporary while others such as a new competitor are long term. The problem could also be attributed to a combination of factors such as a new competitor and poor service from one of your employees.

Once you have identified the problem, then the next step involves implementing changes to get your business turned around. This may involve a short-term solution or a very long and costly remedy. If you have been paying attention and keeping a pulse of your business as part of your normal routine then you will have more time and more options then if you waited until there is a financial crisis. In the fighter business, we termed this "out of energy, out of ammo and out of fuel" situation! The first item of action should be to reduce your operating cost until you have halted the erosion. You should sort through all of your monthly expenses beginning with the miscellaneous category first. Evaluate each item and try to rank order them in terms of contribution to sales. For example, if you are paying for bottled water, then look to see if you even should provide it and if so could you replace it with a cheaper alternative. Magazine subscriptions, long distance and cell phone service, internet, paper or other supply products, cleaning services, travel expenses, insurance and so on, are all areas that should be examined for alternatives or elimination. The more of a cash crunch you are in, the deeper the cuts must be. Be careful not to cut areas that directly impact your sales. For example, marketing and advertising is an area that I would not eliminate and in fact you may even need to increase your advertising efforts to attract new business. But I would certainly look at the types of advertising and focus on the more effective and less costly forms of advertising. For example you might want to eliminate radio advertising and go with coupon mailers or door hangers that offer a coupon worth so much off on their next visit. Items such as rent, mortgage, loans or other long-term obligations should be examined to determine if there is room to renegotiate and reduce your monthly payments.

Payroll is most likely one of your biggest expenses and certainly deserves consideration. Elimination of overtime will definitely save you considerably. For starters, look at your total payroll to include indirect payroll costs such as workers compensation and employment tax. Now compare your total payroll with total expenses and revenues. For example, if your total payroll is $10,000 for the month of June and your revenues is $15,000 then that works out to be 67 percent of your revenues, which is very high. If your payroll to revenue ratio is greater than 50 percent, then you will need to look at cutting back your payroll. Look at your schedule, which is one area to reduce payroll hours. Don't cut back in your busiest periods. Instead, look at you slowest periods and see if you could cut back there. Solicit recommendations from your staff especially your managers; however don't be swayed into something that doesn't make business sense. When we got short handed at one of our locations, my manager suggested we close on Sundays. It did not make sense to close on the second busiest day of the week so I told her that if we do close it would be on Wednesday, our slowest day of the week. Cutting back during your busiest periods is guaranteed to drive your customers away, which is the last thing you want. Reducing your expenses allows you to improve your cash flow and reprioritize to make better use of every dollar spent.

Reducing costs should also be a part of your plan when business is good. Don't wait until you absolutely need to reduce cost. When times are good, many businesses will go out and spend their profits as fast as the money comes in. Be frugal and watch where the money is going. Businesses that watch every penny on overhead and equipment will be able to survive when times get tough. Plan on building a cash reserve that can get your business through at least 6 months of un-profitability. Remember, the lower the expenses the longer you can go before business improves.

The other essential area of a turn around strategy focuses on increasing your revenues. You can cut costs all day long but if your revenues are lacking then eventually you must close your doors. The real problem concerning insufficient revenues is usually poor customer volume. <u>Declining or stagnant customer volume is the most serious problem for any business</u>. The reasons are many and include greater competition, poor marketing or advertising, failing to change with the times, change in your store hours, customer dissatisfaction, a declining economy, or a lack of employees or sales staff. Customer dissatisfaction is a big area and can be the result of anything from poor customer service to unreliable products. But whatever the reasons, customer volume must improve for an effective turn around.

Your first order of business should be with your present customers. Your customers can be your greatest source of information on how to better your business. Know your customers by building a rapport with them. Ask them what they think and solicit their ideas on how you could better service them. As mentioned earlier, customer feedback and surveys is a good way for you to gage how your customers think of your business. You might be surprised with what they come up with. Your customers can also be a great source to find out what your competition offers that they particularly like. Sometimes, you need to take a step back and look at your business from a different point. Look at everything from the appearance of your business to how you display your products. When that customer comes in or your sales person visits with a client, you want them to come away with a healthy positive impression and who will recommend your business to someone else. We found that <u>customer recommendation was the most effective form of advertising in our business</u>.

Bringing in new customers is the other side of the solution for an effective turn around strategy. This may mean offering new products or services, expanding your business hours and days, offering customer loyalty incentives for repeat business, changing your marketing plan and increasing your advertising. Education in new products and markets also plays a big role for the business owner. The business owner must learn everything they can about a new market and not rely on what they knew before. Take Apple Computer for example. Here was a company with a great product that saw its market share decreasing from stiff competition. Apple began offering a new product called the ipod, which was a big hit with music lovers. Apple has thrust forward with dynamite sales on its line of pods and has seen its stock triple in price while its main competitors continue at the same levels. This was no accident; Apple just didn't stumble on a new market. Their success was built on knowledge of the market and how they promoted their new products. In the early 80's, Chrysler Corporation made a successful turn around after nearly being left for dead on the road. Sure, U.S. government help allowed them to make the come back, but it was their new line of cars that made the difference. The minivan proved to be a big hit with young families needing lots of room and an economical and versatile car. The loans guaranteed by the U.S. government were repaid and Chrysler went on to be a highly profitable company. Dell computer began offering a new line of products to pump up revenues after a steady decline of personal computers sales. Desktop computers now account for about 40 percent of sales compared to nearly 100 percent of sales years earlier.

Underestimating you competition can be deadly for your business. In fact, I would say that failing to compete effectively with the competition is the main cause of business failures. As an example, Chrysler and the other automakers were continuously losing market share to the Japanese automakers that made smaller and more economical cars. U.S. auto companies failed to deliver cars that could compete with Japanese automakers and continued to lose market share. The fast food business is continuously offering new items on their menu's competing for each other's customers. If your competitor begins offering a new product or service then this would be a good time keep a close watch on customer volume and sales.

The last leg of your turn around plan involves continuously monitoring the progress. It's almost guaranteed that your turn around plan will need to be adjusted as time goes on. Failing to make these adjustment can put your business back on that slippery slope again. The other pit fall is to abandon the turn around plan altogether after your business shows a strong rebound. Just like not finishing the antibiotics that a doctor prescribes can allow the illness to resurface stronger than ever, so it is true for a business to no longer stay with the plan just because the patient feels much better. Of course, the best advice is to not allow your business to get into a position where a critical turn around plan is needed. Hopefully by minding your business and following the recommendations covered in this book, you wont need drastic actions to get your business back on track.

30   EXIT STRATEGIES

There will come a time when most business owners will need to consider a transfer of ownership of all or part of their business. As with so many other types of investments such as real estate, stocks or bonds, the problem is not so much knowing when to get in but knowing when to exit. Getting out could mean a sale or non-sale transfer, liquidation or simply closing a poor location and moving to another location. Of course, the best option is to sell your business before things deteriorate to the point where a sale is unlikely. When we opened our salon business I knew the reality of business ownership and that someday we may have to let go of this business for some unforeseen reason. In our case, my wife became affected with Parkinsons disease and we could no longer cope with this business and the illness. With my wife's illness getting worse, and performance of our business strong I decided it was possibly a good time to sell our salon business and move to something else less intense. One year later we closed on the sale of our salon business at a substantial profit, reinvesting in a real estate business. There are many reasons why a business owner may need to transfer the ownership of the business. Divorce, illness, age, money, relocation, burnout, declining revenues and profits or simply cashing out of a successful business are a few of the more common reasons affecting the decision to leave your business. My best advice is to have an exit strategy early and modify it over time. Whether your plan is to transfer it to a relative or list it with a broker for sale, you should be mindful of the things needed for a smooth transfer.

Proper records and documentation is essential to any transfer, especially in the sale of your business. Remember, the time to think about a transfer is from day one, not months or years down the road. We kept meticulous records of nearly every aspect of our business such as the number of women versus men customers on any particular day for any of our salons. With good software or point of sales program this type of detail in your sales is easy to achieve. Your records should also include all servicing, maintenance and replacement of business equipment over your ownership period. If you are selling your business and the buyer is attempting to finance it, the lender is going to require records for up to five years or possibly as long as you owned the business. The buyer will probably require you to provide any records or data you have on your customers. The last essential area is your employees. You should have a folder on each employee with performance information that includes a history of any problems. However, customer and employee records should only be disclosed after the sale. You don't want to hand over personal information before the sale. The more information on the performance of your business that you can provide, the easier it will be to affect a sale. Not having a complete set of records may appear that you are hiding something.

If you decide to sell your business then consider listing your business with a reputable broker who specializes in your type of business. A broker who knows the particulars of your type of business can very likely save you a great deal of frustration later on. And that broker will have a better idea of the price to ask for your business. They will also be more suited to negotiate with the buyer or buyer's agent. Also the broker will be more up to speed on the legal issues of the sale as it applies your type of business. Remember, your broker will be there to find the right buyer, negotiate the right terms and close the deal with no loose ends to haunt you later on! It's well worth the commission.

A business that is not profitable or that is struggling will make it that much more difficult to sell or unload. Some businesses do well for some time and then begin to run into problems either because of competition or other factors affecting sales. There are a variety of reasons why a business may be struggling but we'll assume for now that you have tried to salvage the business but nothing has worked and it is time to move on. The question is at what point should you decide to sell your business. If your intention is to sell a highly unprofitable business then it may be too late. A business that shows a steady decline of profits or decline in revenues may be impossible to sell. If you've been keeping good records with good trend analysis and have at least two years of data then you can at least determine if your business is performing in line with similar businesses in your area. If sales, profits, customer volume or what ever other index you use to gage performance, shows a steady decline for at least one year, then it may be time to consider selling your business. Here is where the expertise of a consultant might be worth the expense. But whether it's the location, the economy or the way your running it, at some point you need to make a decision to get out. A big factor that enters the picture on whether to sell your business concerns the lease of your building or space. Most lease terms are for five years, making the decision to sign off on another 5 year term lease questionable for a struggling business. In the case where your lease is about to expire and you have not been able to affect a transfer, then your only option may be to sell whatever equipment you can and walk away. This may seem as a harsh option but if you are not able to consider such a reality today then you might want to reconsider business ownership for you.

Another option other than a sale to an outside party is a transfer to an individual or group of employees. This may be in the form of a transfer of all or a majority of the business involving periodic payments over a certain length. Instead of receiving a lump sum amount, the new ownership agrees on monthly or quarterly payments over so many years. A business owner I consulted for had a restaurant he wanted to sell. We found that best approach would be to transfer 50 percent of the ownership to the manager in exchange for a flat monthly payment plus a percentage of the revenues over 10 years. This way he avoided the 10 percent brokerage fees and the hassles of records plus there were certain tax advantages he enjoyed. He receives a nice monthly check without the hassles of owning and running a business. The new owners have done well with the business and the previous owner gets a nice check every month without getting involved with the operation. Another option is to settle for a certain percentage of the revenues or annual profits. I would avoid using a percentage of profits since operating expenses and end of year deductions can drastically affect profits. And there are different definitions of profit. There are profits (earnings) calculated before taxes, after taxes, before or after amortization and depreciation or any combination of the above. So if you are going to use a percentage of profits then make sure you have a well-defined meaning of profit. Also, a greedy new owner may pump up the expense sheet by giving themselves a hefty pay increase as manager or for "consulting services". You can see that a creative mind can truly affect the bottom line.

Aside from knowing when to sell your business, the other important factor is having an idea of what price to ask for. One of the important factors in business valuation is annual profits and the trend of profits over the years. Some types of businesses, especially those that lease their space and equipment, would have a tough time finding a buyer at any price if the business can not show profitability. In other words, for these types of businesses, the worth of the business is a direct function of its profits. Also, the longer you can show sustained profits, the more impact the profitability factor become. Businesses that own their equipment and especially the building and land, have a value even if the business is not profitable. The business may not be worth more than the value of the land and building, but at least its worth something to someone.

31   SUMMARY

I commend all those who are willing to take on the challenges of owning and running a business. Owning your business can be quite rewarding financially and psychologically. But it can also be quite unforgiving financially and psychologically. It can take a toll on your health, pocket book and family. It can put you in a position where you can never recover. By now, you may be questioning whether business ownership is for you. There is no question that owning and operating your own business carries a heavy burden especially when employees are involved. How successful your business becomes depends on how well you run and operate your business. Factors such as temperament, communication skills, organization, discipline and knowledge play a big part in ones ability to take a start up business and turn it into a successful profit machine. As a new business owner, learning the basics of operating a business is a fundamental requirement in creating a successful business. This book covers many of the essential elements of running a business from real life experiences. Many of these "there I was" examples were drawn from our businesses but are representative of many businesses. Knowing the basics of marketing, hiring, employee management, setting goals, payroll processing, scheduling, and competition give the business owner a solid foundation to run a successful business and a definite edge over their competition. From experience, I've seen two competing businesses across the street from each where one prospered while the other failed and closed its doors. I know from experience because we were the business that prospered. And it's no accident that it happened that way. The story is the same for many businesses that fail or succeed. Being able to compete effectively is probably the biggest element in a businesses success. But as I have found, the same elements that make a business a strong competitor are the same elements that make it a strong and successful business even if there were no competition.

There is a great deal of information presented in this book. Some would liken it to drinking out of a fire hose. The same can be said of many books written on small business ownership. But then again, what profession doesn't require a great deal of learning and preparation. You wouldn't expect to be able to fly a plane or practice law without learning volumes of material. The same is true of owning and running a business. As a business owner, you should read this book as well as others that deal with running a business but more importantly this book should be used as a guide. I think you will find that this book will serve you better as a reference guide in the day-to-day operations of your business. As your business matures you will develop your own techniques tailored for your type of business, personality and personal needs. As any business owner will tell you, the learning process never stops. New technologies and ways of doing business are always brought about reshaping the way you run a business. Keeping abreast of these changes is as an essential of business ownership.

Best wishes.

Web Sites for Business Owners

www.irs.gov

www.socialsecurity.gov/employer/critical.htm

www.uscis.gov/graphics/formsfee/forms/I-9.htm

www.irs.gov/pub/irs-pdf/fwr.pdf

www.acf.hhs.gov/programs/cse/newhire/employer/private/nh/newhire.htm

www.americanpayroll.org

www.irs.gov/businesses/index.html

www.irs.gov/businesses/

www.irs.gov/publications/p15/index.html

www.nolo.com

www.nceo.org

www.nceo.org/library/verysmall.html

www.dol.gov

www.osha.gov

www.sba.gov/starting_business/planning/basic.html

www.eftps.gov/eftps/

INDEX

A

Accounting
 software 42, 95, 182, 187
 method, 15
 tasks, 233
Advertising
 general 55-58
 layout, 57-58
 radio, 58
 TV, 58
 door hangers, 58
 direct mail, 57-58, 66, 85, 163, 206
 flyers, 58, 60-69
 effectiveness, 59
American Payroll Association, 134
Anchor
 shopping center, 22, 26, 86, 246
Automation, 96

B

Bar coding
 inventory products, 101
Bonuses, 71, 82, 106, 124, 144-145, 155-156
Bookkeeping, 8, 13, 232-233
Brand name recognition, 246
Build-out
 allowance, 29-31
 lease or building improvement, 28-29, 38, 48
Business bank account, 12-13, 19, 22
Business cards, 12, 18, 66
Business name, 12, 18-19, 22, 59, 66-67, 78
Business plan, 7, 12-14
Business Structure, 14-16

C

Certificate of Occupancy, 29
Checks
 accepting checks, 203, 210, 218
 payroll checks, 182-183, 190
Commissions
 Agent, 25
 Sales, 62, 71, 82, 104, 115, 144-146, 149, 176, 258
Common Area Maintenance, 26, 247
Communications, 210-212, 243

Compensation, 134, 144-156, 209-210
Competition, 2, 6-9, 14, 23, 26, 32, 56, 62, 64, 69-70, 79-90, 247, 249, 254-256, 258, 261
Consolidated Omnibus Budget-Reconciliation Act (COBRA), 136-142
Consultants, 232-239
Contractors, 29-30
Cost of expanding, 247
Credit Cards, 218
Cross promoting, 67
Customers
 general, 10, 14, 18-19, 24, 34, 72
 feedback, 74-75
 complaints, 76-77

D

Demand
 consumer, 2, 6, 8, 24, 64, 69, 98, 168-175
Department of Labor (DOL), 136-143
Disabilities
 customers, 218
 employees, 221
Discounts, 55-56, 66-70, 85, 87
Diversified, 246

E

Electronic Federal Tax Payment System (EFTPS), 188, 192-193
Employee
 interview, 5, 37, 52, 105-108, 110-115
 hiring, 110, 112, 117, 130
 recognition, 123-125
 recruiting, 2, 106, 108-109, 147, 157, 159, 162-163
 supervision, 123, 207-208, 210, 212-214
 termination, 119-121, 126-129
 theft, 9, 46, 100-103, 126, 212
 training, 121
Employer Identification Number (EIN), 15-16, 193
Employer's Quarterly Federal Tax Return (Form 941), 133, 189, 193
Employment Eligibility Verification, 130

Ethicalness, 113-114

Expenses
    capital, 13, 38, 42-45, 96
    operating, 13, 38, 42-47, 88, 259
    start-up, 22, 48

F
Fair Labor or Standards Act (FLSA), 136-137
Federal Deposits
    940 Tax, 188-189
    941 Tax, 189-194
Federal Income Tax (FIT), 131, 182, 187-188
Federal Insurance Contributions Act (FICA), 152, 156, 158, 177-187, 191
Federal Unemployment Tax (FUTA), 156, 187, 188, 189, 193

Form 941, 133, 189-190, 193
Form I-9, 130-132
Form W-4, 130-131, 133
Fraud, 133-134, 244

G
Goals, 9-10, 15, 91, 94, 155, 261

H
Health Insurance, 150
HIFICA, 187-190
Holidays, 10, 33, 56, 63, 68, 96, 98, 107, 147
    Pay, 116, 122, 144, 146-150
Hours of operation, 31, 50-51, 53, 80, 85, 90
    Cost analysis of, 51-52

I
Incentives
    customers, 255
    employees, 92, 107, 115, 163, 198
Inflation, 28, 160, 164-166
Internal Revenue Service (IRS), 5, 14-16, 19-20, 22, 38, 133, 187-194
Inventory, 2, 5, 69, 72-73, 95-96, 101-102, 221
Investment, 9, 42-43, 47-48, 53, 64-65, 257

J
Job
    application questioner, 111-112, 151
    resumes, 106, 110, 112

L
Labor, 8

costs, 45, 63, 158
    market, 10, 54, 114, 116, 162-166, 172, 230, 247-248
Leadership, 94, 195-198
Lease, 12, 23, 44
    agreement, 13, 24-30, 50
    improvements, 29, 38, 44
Location, 6, 12, 22-27, 36, 39, 44-47, 50, 79-80, 86-87, 89, 90-91, 246

M
Managers, 195-205
    Initial training, 202
    recurrent, 203-204
Manual
    employee, 145, 148, 152, 155, 184, 203, 220
    manager, 201-202
    operating, 36, 74, 121, 156, 200, 202, 220-223
Marketing, 55-56, 234-235, 253-255, 261
Medical Insurance, 122, 138, 144, 151-153, 163, 232
Medicare Tax, 135, 156, 187-188
Microsoft Publisher, 85

O
Occupational Safety and Health Administration (OSHA), 142-143
Outsourcing, 232-233
Overtime, 105, 110, 136-137, 176-179, 182

P
Partnerships, 16, 37-38
Pay period, 137, 146, 155, 176-181, 190
Payroll
    processing, 1, 8, 133, 176, 178-182, 194, 232, 261
    taxes, 96, 187, 191
    workweek, 137, 175-179
Peachtree software program, 43, 95, 101, 133, 182, 187
Point-of-Sale (POS), 101, 183, 238, 251
Policies, 121, 136-137, 142, 148, 200-203, 213, 216-217, 219-223, 230-231
Prices, establishing
    manufacturing, 63-64
    retail and services, 62-65
Probation, 119-121, 206
Productivity, 39, 43, 53, 63, 95, 98, 115, 150, 154, 156-158, 162, 169-170

265

Property Manager, 23-30, 37
Publishing programs, 85
Q
Quality of Service, 72, 80, 83-84, 90
Quickbooks, 43, 95, 101, 133
R
Rent
    base, 27-29
    percentage, 27-28
Retail spaces, 24
Rumors, 241
S
Sales,
    discounts, 69-71
    retail, 91-93, 154
Schedule,
    Employee, 8, 168-172, 174, 183
Sensitive Information, 236-238
Sexual harassment, 217, 221, 224
Shrinkage, 91, 100
Small Business Administration (SBA), 5, 13, 16, 50
Social Security Department, 5, 133
Social Security Tax, 188
Spreadsheets, 40, 98
    microsoft Excel, 95, 180
State Unemployment Tax (SUTA), 120, 194, 225
Storefront, 31, 33
Surveillance
    cameras, 102
    system, 102-103
T
Tenants, 20
Theft
    customers, 206,
    personal information and identity, 236-240
Time-lapse recorder, 103-104
Trend analysis, 95, 196, 214, 251
U
Unemployment rate, 120, 157, 162-163
Unemployment tax, 120, 135, 156, 182, 187-189, 194, 225-226
V
Vacations
    employees, 63, 107, 147-150, 163
Val Pac, 57
W
W-4 Withholding Allowance Certificate, 130-131

Wages, 38, 43-44, 62, 71, 107, 136-137, 144-145, 160, 190-192, 247
Work Period, 190-191
Workers compensation, 134, 156, 220, 224-225, 232, 253
Y
Yellow Pages, 18, 57